ALSO BY RONNI LUNDY

Shuck Beans, Stack Cakes and Honest Fried Chicken:

The Heart and Soul of Southern Country Kitchens

The Festive Table

The Festive Table

Recipes and Stories for Creating Your Own Holiday Traditions

Ronni Lundy

North Point Press
A division of Farrar, Straus and Giroux · New York

Published simultaneously in Canada by HarperCollinsCanadaLtd
Printed in the United States of America
Designed by Liney Li
First edition, 1995

Library of Congress Cataloging-in-Publication Data
Lundy, Ronni.
The festive table : recipes and stories for creating your
own holiday traditions / Ronni Lundy. — 1st ed.
p.   cm.
Includes index.
1. Holiday cookery.   2. Holidays.   I. Title.
TX739.L77   1995   641.5´68—dc20   95–6751 CIP

Permissions for quoted material are on pages 365–66.

Acknowledgments

AS WE COME TO ANY FESTIVE TABLE, OUR FIRST ACT IS TO acknowledge those who made the blessings of it possible. This one has been created not only by the grace of the spirit but also by the good graces of the many people who have so willingly shared with me their stories and recipes, ideas and energy. To all whose names appear in the text, my deepest thanks for your generosity.

Heartfelt thanks to my husband, Ken, and daughter, Meghan, for patience, tenderness, and good appetite throughout, and to my mother, Jerry, for teaching me well and loving me lots.

To my editor, Elisabeth Kallick Dyssegaard, for intelligence, patience, encouragement, and humor well above and beyond the call of duty. To my agent, Beth Vesel, who opened all the doors and nudged me through them.

To all those intrepid tasters who have eaten trial-and-error as well as triumphs, but most especially to the mouths of the South, the Horvaths: Mary, David, Michelle, Jason, and Michael Huggins. And to Amy Attaway, Sara Hedges, Dan Lehocky, Antonia Lindauer, Julia Schagene, and the fabulous, famished Keel boys, Eli and Jonah, many thanks for dedicated scarfing and reasoned commentary.

For good leads and wonderful follow-ups, thanks to Sandra Kalio of the *Wisconsin State Journal* in Madison and Barb Durbin and Merle Alexander at the Portland *Oregonian;* and to Ann Crowder, John Knight Doe, Ann Wall Frank, Alexandra Hart, Jessica Harris, Kelly Hammers, Helen Lang, Steve Lee, Barbara Levinson, Bonnie Lucas, Dorothy Ormes, David Ruggiero, and Alice Friedman.

For food, lodging, and/or necessary moral support, thanks to Mary Anderson; Kathy Carpenter; Dan Dewayne and Christine Myers; Diane Koosed; Jane and Gene, Liz and Mac Lorendo; Will and Brett Mustard; and Niya Standish.

For books whose pages I've dog-eared countless times, always gratefully, thanks to Janet Bailey for *Keeping Food Fresh,* Joan and John Digby for *Food for Thought,* Harold McGee for *On Food and Cooking* and *The Curious Cook,* Elizabeth Schneider for *Uncommon Fruits and Vegetables,* and John Egerton both for *Southern Food* and for March Egerton, editor of *Since Eve Ate Apples.*

For the unselfish support of colleagues, thanks to Elaine Corn, John Egerton, Sarah Fritschner, Camille Glenn, Maggie Oster, David SooHoo, Vince Staten, and the irrepressible Lynn Winter.

And for the many friends and colleagues whose names are not here, but whose support most certainly is, my very deepest gratitude.

Contents

❖❖❖ Contents ❖❖❖

❖❖❖ Contents ❖❖❖

Introduction

IT WAS MORE THAN TWO DECADES AND AT LEAST A COUPLE OF lifestyles ago that I cooked my first full Thanksgiving dinner on my own. A Kentucky girl living in New Mexico, I was fifteen hundred miles from "home," staying in a geodesic dome with a woodstove and surrounded by a cast of friends who were literally a cast (committed to four performances of Dickens's *Christmas Carol* at a nearby dinner theater that day). Since I was the only one of our group not actually needed for the play, I volunteered to make turkey with all the trimmings and have it ready to serve when the cast came home.

We had come from all parts of the country. Despite the obstacles I faced in preparing such a feast alone, it seemed to me that what we really needed to make us feel like a community was to gather around a table filled with an all-stops-out traditional American Thanksgiving dinner.

But what was that tradition?

"I'll make turkey with cornbread dressing on the side, fluffy mashed potatoes like my mom's, fresh cranberries cooked until they pop, pumpkin pie, and for something green, a can of peas with one of mushrooms," I said.

"I hope you'll leave the skins on those mashed potatoes because that's where all the nutrients are," said health-conscious Rosalie.

"And what about the chestnut stuffing? It's not Thanksgiving without chestnut stuffing," my friend from Wisconsin, Cecy, said.

"And you have to put it in the turkey, not on the side," said Rachel from New York.

"And I want canned cranberry sauce," someone else whined. "The kind that is jellied and still has those ridges from the tin on it so you know exactly where to slice."

"And it's not Thanksgiving without mincemeat pie . . ."

". . . no, chocolate pie with meringue on top . . ."

". . . and canned sweet potatoes . . ."

". . . no, mashed sweet potatoes . . ."

". . . no, sweet potato casserole . . ."

". . . and green bean casserole . . ."

". . . and corn like the Indians gave us . . ."

". . . and sauerkraut . . ."

That's right. Sauerkraut. It turned out that my Baltimore-born husband-to-be had had sauerkraut with turkey every Thanksgiving of his life and knew it just wouldn't taste like the holiday without it.

So, combing every pantry within walking distance and spending every hour from dawn until 9 p.m., when cast and crew finally got back from the theater, I cooked and stuffed, sliced, diced, mashed, and baked everybody's favorite Thanksgiving dish. And late that night a dozen or so of us sat around a feast of such proportions and peculiar pairings as I've never seen before. But we ate and laughed and drank.

And it was good.

And from that first Thanksgiving I learned two very important things.

One: Sauerkraut is really tasty with turkey.

Two: Tradition is what you make of it.

SOME TWENTY YEARS LATER, I FOUND MYSELF REEXAMINING CELEBRATION and tradition again. This time it wasn't the demands of a particular holiday that sparked my interest. Instead it was a curiosity born of the realization that for many of us the concepts of family and community have dramatically changed. The nuclear nugget has been split apart and reconfigured with single parents, stepparents, step-siblings, ex-spouses, friends who feel like relatives, and relatives who are more like friends. Our mobile society has moved many of us far from the religious, social, or ethnic communities we were born into, and so have our own choices.

As the contexts of our lives have changed, so must our celebrations, it seemed. And I wondered how that change had affected the celebrations themselves. Had old traditions become meaningless in new contexts, or had they become even more precious for the tenuous link they gave us to our past? Could new rituals resonate with the same depth and complexity as the old ones?

To discover what contemporary celebrations were really about, I asked everyone I knew or met to tell me of anyone who celebrated in a particularly meaningful or memorable way.

The leads I got led me across the continent and sent me to my own backyard.

I found people like Anoosh and Sharron Shariat, who are trying to keep alive the Persian New Year traditions of thousands of years. And I found Pat and Dean Murakami, who invented a summertime pig roast party a few years ago that has become the social event of the year for their Sacramento friends.

I learned that the most important element of a New Year tamale party as it's practiced in El Paso is the involvement of everyone in the food's preparation; but I also discovered that for Madison, Wisconsin's Shelley Hamel, the best part of her annual Valentine dessert party is doing all the work herself.

I learned about the Cajun Thanksgiving of the Lege family of Abbeville, Louisiana—a feast with no turkey but a history of ritual and a respect for the harvest that is in tune with the most fundamental concepts of the holiday.

I learned about the Passover seder of Jackie and Leon Olenick of St. Paul,

Minnesota, a meatless meal in keeping with their philosophy of Eco-Kosher.

But the most important thing I discovered is that there are no rules about real celebrations. Tradition is still what you make of it.

· · · · · ❦ · · · · ·

THERE IS ONE THING THAT ALL THESE CELEBRATIONS HAVE IN COMMON, however. At the center of each is a festive table.

Just as it is natural to celebrate the triumphs of our lives, share the passages, mark the changing of the seasons, so it is natural that we want to share these celebrations with the people who make up our community. And it seems to be equally natural that when we come together to celebrate, we do so around a well-laid and inviting table.

The people you will meet on these pages have breathed fresh life into their rituals and have brought fresh interpretations to the table as well. This new approach to festive foods may be as exotic as saffron-scented rice or Vietnamese salad, or as quirky as a potluck of nothing but comfort food in casseroles.

The recipes here move across cultures and rummage through the pantry with delightful results. They range from a "traditional" Jewish chicken soup with tangerine-zest wontons to a spice-and-pepper-stuffed Cajun pork roast. They include Jamaican Easter bun, honey-kissed Polish vodka, and a Native American–style wild-rice and cranberry casserole. They are as traditional as potato latkes and Chesapeake Bay steamed crabs or as original as chocolate–yam cake or empanadas made with grill-smoked turkey.

What these recipes share is that each is delectable and in its own way contributes to the jubilant spirit of the gathering. Each has also been tested and adapted for the home cook, and any can become a part of your own repertoire. The recipes are presented in each chapter as suggestions and inspirations. These new dishes can be mixed and matched with one another or added to your traditional bill of fare. Although the recipes in some sections do form a complete meal, they are not necessarily meant to be used that way.

In *The Festive Table* you will find stories of people who have created celebrations that are marked by a spirit of community and feelings of joy. And it's my hope that they will inspire you to create such celebrations of your own.

The Festive Table

The New Year

Ring out the old, ring in the new,
Ring, happy bells, across the snow:
The year is going, let him go;
Ring out the false, ring in the true.

—ALFRED, LORD TENNYSON, "In Memoriam"

We begin the New Year with earnest resolutions to shake off old, harmful habits and to embrace new rituals that will give more meaning to our lives. Too bad, then, that we frequently precede the New Year with the habit of the New Year's Eve debauch—a party that often has too much drink, too much confusion, and too much forced hilarity to have much meaning.

A New Year's Eve revel followed by a day of penance and good resolutions is deeply rooted in many cultures, but the rituals of older times seem to have been smaller and more community-rooted and perhaps to have had more meaning than those of today.

The tradition of sharing food with friends at the New Year

is as old as the celebration itself and full of deep symbolism. Breaking bread with one another—no matter how meager the bread or raucous the occasion—has long been held as a ceremony that binds the sharers to one another, and to whatever spirits guide them. As such, it is an especially potent ritual at the beginning of a new year.

Some histories credit the early Dutch settlers of Manhattan Island with introducing the tradition of visiting and eating with friends to the New World, but many Native American tribes already celebrated their New Year in this way. By Victorian times in America, New Year's open houses with an attendant progressive feast were well entrenched.

In modern times, however, we seem to have moved away from simple observances with family and friends toward more public spectacles. New Year's celebrations in bars and ballrooms often find us with strangers who have little common bond other than a willingness to drink too much and pretend to have a grand time. Such a night is most often followed by a day of hangover and reluctant remorse spent slack-jawed in front of the television, connected to our "community" only by the electronic impulses that make us all simultaneously passive spectators at a football game.

· · · · · ❦ · · · · ·

SOMETIME IN THE EARLY 1980S, MY HUSBAND, KEN, AND I MADE A NEW Year's resolution to give up the old ritual of public partying. He had worked for several years as a bartender and so had experienced more than his share of drunken New Year's celebrations. On his first New Year's Eve off, while our daughter, Meghan, was still a toddler, just staying at home with the family was celebration enough for the three of us.

She and her dad went to the store and stocked up on the bright-colored cellophane bags of junk food that she got little of during the rest of the year. We combed the house for good noisemakers, Meghan inventing one herself— a plastic yogurt cup filled with beans. And we dressed up—Ken in a blue velvet jacket found in a secondhand store, I in a black strapless gown, and Meghan in a white furry evening jacket that had been in our family for years. Through the night we played games nonstop, watched the Times Square party on TV, and ran out on the porch at midnight to scare the demons and neighbors alike. Then we toasted ourselves and our future with crystal flutes filled with champagne for us and fizzy soda for her.

The year she was four, Meghan, surrounded by a bounty of Cheez Curls, Oreos, corn chips, and pretzels, looked up and pronounced, "Oh, I get it. Candy, Cokes, cookies, chips—New Year's Eve means anything goes."

But while junk food and watching the Times Square ball drop on television seemed party enough in her early years, as Meghan got older she and we began to think about having a greater—and more meaningful—celebration.

So we returned to the idea of an annual New Year's Eve party—not a bash, however, but a gathering of a few close friends and their children. Over the years the details of the party have gradually changed and its significance has very gradually intensified. It has taken a New Year's evolution—one that is still in progress.

The party moves from house to house each year. Board games, charades, and decks of cards provide entertainment, and we push back the table, turn up the stereo, and dance to zydeco, Texas blues, and old rock and roll—music that both the adults and youth share an appreciation for. At midnight we rush to the porch and make a glorious din with the loudest homemade noisemakers we can devise. Once our friends Phil and Deane filled a sheet with balloons and loads of confetti, releasing it from their second-story loft just as midnight chimed. It was an event our kids have never forgotten (nor have Phil and Deane, as they continue to sweep out piles of confetti from behind the stove, refrigerator, and couch). Another year Mary and David blew up dozens of small balloons, which we scattered on the porch, then jumped on to pop.

Amazingly, as our children have grown older, entered their teen years, and established their own friendships and social lives, with invitations to New Year's parties with their peers, they have often opted for ours instead, inviting a close friend or two of their own.

For them, perhaps, and certainly for us, this annual party, complete with an off-key but heartfelt rendition of "Auld Lang Syne," has become a yearly renewal of the vows of friendship and community.

The food aspect of the party has also evolved. The first year we got together at our house, and I made cooking a typical holiday performance. I turned down offers of help from our friends and instead made several dishes—posole from New Mexico, black-eyed peas—that had ritual significance. It was tasty, but too much: too much food, leaving us all feeling more than sated and slightly sluggish; and too much of a production. I had so much invested in how the meal came out that I felt slightly out of step and harried through much of the night. My friends and family, on the other hand, were cast in the roles of audience for the evening—not quite the community spirit we had hoped to share.

Over the years, though, the food preparation has gradually turned into more of a community event. It's not a potluck, with everyone preparing a dish at home and bringing it. And it's not formal group cooking, with everyone assigned a role in the kitchen to produce a gourmet dinner. Instead, it's evolved into a casual collaboration. Whoever is hosting starts loosely planning a meal a week or two before, and in the course of conversation with the other guests, a full menu takes shape. Sometimes the guests bring full dishes or sometimes just ingredients. The early hours of the party are usually spent in the kitchen, with everyone cooking and kibitzing.

The process of planning and preparation has become as much a part of the celebration as sitting around the table, relishing the finished product. And when we lift our glasses to the magnificent food we all now bring to the table each year, we are really toasting the love, cooperation, and spirit of sharing that created it.

January is named after the two-headed Roman god Janus—one countenance looking back to the past, the other facing the future. In many cultures, New Year's customs acknowledge this turning from one aspect to another. To be rid of the old year, debts were paid off before the new one began and old grudges and slights were apologized for and forgiven. Cleaning the house, top to bottom, is part of the preparation for the Chinese New Year and shows up in several European cultures as well. Running outside and slapping pots, pans, and other noisemakers together is supposed to scare the old demons away from the house.

As for the new start, this is where the tradition of making resolutions began. And numerous rituals and foods became associated with the New Year celebration because of their believed power to transmit good luck.

Eating traditional foods thought to bring luck occurs in virtually every culture, although the foods themselves vary from the posole of northern New Mexico to the black-eyed peas of the Deep South. Cabbage—especially sauerkraut—is thought lucky by many people of German and Dutch descent, while pastries in the shape of a ring (ranging from the simple doughnut to an ornate cake filled with lucky charms) are prized for their symbolism of wholeness. In ancient Rome, the wealthy exchanged baskets of figs and dates decorated with gold leaf; and in parts of Britain, neighbors go out at midnight and trade triangular mince pies, called "God" cakes, with their friends.

READY, SET, NEW YEAR!

Health-conscious revelers in Portland, Oregon, who want to get the New Year off to a running start often celebrate by taking part in the First Run, a 5K race at midnight on New Year's Eve. About three thousand folks annually line up in the city's Waterfront Park. It's an equal-opportunity event, so tortoise types may choose to walk instead of race. Everyone gets fed breakfast—usually something high-carb like pizza and fruit—after the race is over, courtesy of Northwest Natural Gas.

THE TAMALE PARTY

Tamales look like a party. Fragrant packages no longer than your palm, wrapped in textured corn husks folded in at each end and tied in the middle with a piece of string, they are tiny gifts. Or tied off at either end with perky strips of corn husk, they resemble a homespun version of the English party cracker. But when you open a tamale, you won't find some silly toy but a subtle edible delight.

A delicate corn mush seasoned with broth and spices surrounds the filling—either savory or sweet, but always tantalizing. First comes the unfolding of the wrapper, then the unfolding of flavors on your tongue, a leisurely experience of discovery and surprise—perfect for ringing in the New Year.

The making of tamales is a little complicated and very labor-intensive; but they are a surprisingly forgiving food. Fat ones, long ones, rough ones, smooth ones—all have their singular pleasures, and none have to be perfect to be delicious. This makes tamales the ultimate party food—for a party in which you revel in the making as well as in the eating.

Such parties are among the most significant traditions Leo Fernandez recalls from his growing-up years in El Paso, Texas.

Leo was born in 1938, the second child of the three sons and two daughters of Salvador and Mary Fernandez.

"My family was not very big on tradition simply for tradition's sake," he says. "We didn't do a lot of the celebrations or rituals that are normally associated with Hispanic or Catholic cultures. But traditions that brought a bunch of us together, particularly those centered on food—now, that was another story."

The annual tamale parties of New Year's and Christmas Eves were his favorites.

"Everybody gathered for the tamale making—aunts and uncles and cousins. And everybody worked putting together the tamales—even the kids had jobs. I guess you could be very precise in how you made them, but that's not the way we did it, and I don't think anyone ever had better tamales than we did.

"My mother was a rough-and-tumble cook with quick hands, and she kind of slapped things together. You can ruin a tortilla by being too slow and careful in the making of it. My mother was fast and almost furious in the way she made hers, but they tasted quite wonderful. It might not look pretty, but sometimes it's a better way to make foods."

And sometimes a party that brings everyone into the kitchen, no matter what their level of expertise, is the best way to make a celebration. It underscores the value of community, transforming what may be a tedious and time-consuming chore for one person into a delightful dance for a crowd. It allows everyone—old or young, skilled or clumsy—to make an important contribution. It reminds us viscerally that the process, the act of getting somewhere, can be as rewarding as the result. And it's just plain fun.

"While we were putting together the tamales, there would be so much talking and laughter," Leo says. "Then, after we'd eaten as much as we could, we'd push back the tables and there would be dancing. When I was young, it was often live music—a mariachi band or some kind of border band. Any music that was danceable.

"When I got older, it was records. There was one uncle who sort of did that thing where he would bring all the records and play them on New Year's Eve. And we'd dance right in the kitchen—because it was warm and bright and such a good place.

"Nothing would be exactly the same every year, depending on who had the energy and who wanted to host it. Some years, instead of someone making all the tamales at one house, different people would make their tamales at home and bring them over—and one sister would be known for one kind of taste and another for something a little different.

"But I liked the times when we all prepared them together the best. On Christmas Eve we'd get all the different tamales wrapped and ready to steam, then put them on in several pots and go to Midnight Mass. When we got home, they were ready and we'd eat and eat. And then it would be nearly dawn, so we'd open presents and eat some more and stay up all night.

"But what I really enjoyed was the tamale parties to greet the New Year. We'd make the tamales a batch at a time, eating a little from each as they finished, but never really filling up. Then, when it was midnight and the New Year, we'd begin eating seriously. Everybody would feast. And we'd drink cold beer and dance until we were hungry again, and it would be a very fine time that lasted all night and into the morning."

A NEW YEAR'S EVE TAMALE PARTY SHOULD START IN THE EARLY EVENING. Because it takes a few hours before the tamales are ready to eat, and all that time the scents of the steaming tamales fill the air, it's a good idea to have a pot full of a savory soup on the stove and plenty of chips and guacamole on hand. You'll find recipes for a Native American–style winter squash soup, spicy cornbread, and the classic avocado dip, along with instructions for a variety of tamales, including sweet ones for dessert. You don't have to make all the varieties of tamale at your party, of course. But Leo says it's a shame to let that good manpower go to waste when you've got it. And the tamales freeze nicely and reheat tastily.

Perhaps you don't have an uncle with a stack of mariachi records as long as your arm, and there's not an accordion or bajo sexto *player among your friends. Don't despair. There's excellent music to be found at most any good record store. The discs recommended here are packed with pulsating rhythms just right for dancing or cooking to.*

Easiest to find and absolutely wonderful is anything by Los Lobos, the popular Mexican rock band out of East L.A. and on the Slash/Warner Bros. label. I have everything they've recorded and love it all, but think that Kiko *is perhaps the finest, and certainly the most diverse and danceable, of all their records.* La Pistola y El Corazon *is the band's exquisite tribute to its Latino roots, a good traditional choice.*

The Iguanas' eponymous debut on MCA records offers a Gulf Coast brio with Big Easy charm, samba rhythms, and a touch of bowling-alley élan.

For a blend of Tex-Mex rock and south-of-the-border rhythms with attitude, try Joe King Carrasco's Bandido Rock *on the Rounder label. Joe King once made his entrance into a club by riding his motorcycle through the front door, down the hall, and up onto the stage. His album can similarly rev up your party.*

If you are looking for something more traditional, your best choice is the brothers Jimenez: Flaco and Santiago, Jr. Sons of Santiago Jimenez, Sr., one of the finest performers of the Tex-Mex conjunto style blending polkas with rancheras, these San Antonio natives have recorded dozens of albums between them. Most have been on small regional labels, but you should have little trouble tracking down their more recent CDs for Rounder Records: Santiago's Familia y Tradicion *and Flaco's* Arriba El Norte. *Santiago is an eccentric, charismatic live performer, but Flaco's album is better—perhaps because he's recorded with pop stars from Dylan to Dwight Yoakam.*

For more mellow moods, try any of the albums by Panama's Rubén Blades, but most especially Escenas *on the Elektra label. It's my favorite for the magical pulse of its rhythms and the beauty of the real-life escenas its lyrics evoke.*

New Year Squash Soup

This soup, though hearty in effect, has a very delicate flavor. It uses ingredients—squash, beans, and peppers—associated with the New World. Powdered achiote (small red bricks of processed achiote/annatto seeds) is a staple in south-of-the-border kitchens and readily available in almost any specialty food store. If you cannot find it, substitute paprika and use only half a tablespoon.

This is a sustaining appetizer while you wait for the tamales.

¼ pound (1 cup) dried
   small red beans
½-inch-thick piece of salt
   pork
1 tablespoon powdered
   achiote (annatto)

2 medium-sized acorn
   squash (3½ pounds)

2 tablespoons canola oil
1 large onion (½ pound),
   coarsely chopped
1 large red bell pepper,
   coarsely chopped
1 tablespoon coriander
   seed, crushed
1 quart chicken broth
1 tablespoon brown sugar
Salt to taste

Rinse and sort the beans. Put in a heavy saucepan and add 3 cups water. Bring to a boil over high heat and let boil for 10 minutes. Remove from the heat and let sit for an hour. Then add the salt pork and return to medium heat for 1 to 2 hours, until the beans are soft, adding more heated water if needed. When the beans are tender, you will have about 2½ cups. Add the powdered achiote to the beans and mix well.

While the beans are cooking, bake the squash. Preheat the oven to 400° F. Rinse the squash well and pierce a few times all around with a fork. Place on a cookie sheet in the preheated oven and bake for 1 hour, or until the squash are very soft. The skin may be a little charred in spots, but that is okay.

Let the squash cool. When you can handle them comfortably, split them open, remove the seeds, and then remove the peel from the pulp. Mash the pulp with a potato masher or a wooden spoon until it's a uniform puree with no lumps.

When the beans and squash are ready, heat a 4-quart pot over medium heat. Add the canola oil, and when it is heated, toss in the onion, cover, and cook for 8 minutes, until the onion is soft and transparent. (Shake the pan or stir several times during cooking to keep the onion from sticking.) Add the bell pepper and sauté about 5 minutes. Sprinkle the coriander over it all and stir for a minute or so, then add the chicken broth and slowly bring to a gentle boil.

Stir in the brown sugar, then add the squash, a large spoonful at a time, stirring after each addition to blend it in. When the soup begins to boil again, add the beans and turn down to a simmer. Taste and add salt—but don't be hasty about adding too much. This soup has very delicate, subtle flavors. Cover and let simmer for at least another 20 minutes.

This soup may be made a day ahead, refrigerated, and reheated gently just before serving. It is good with warmed flour tortillas, a dark, earthy bread, or the green-chile cornbread (recipe follows). This recipe may be doubled.

Feeds 6 to 8.

In Mayan hieroglyphics, "wherever the Kan sign appears in conjunction with a god, it refers to crops and the powers for good and evil that affect them. Kan is also the symbol wah, which denotes bread, tortilla, tamale."

—BETTY FUSSELL, *THE STORY OF CORN*

Green-Chile Cornbread

There are several versions of "Mexican cornbread" that use *jalapeño* peppers for their spicy kick, but for my money those peppers are just too plain pushy—too much heat and not enough flavor. New Mexico green chile (see page 15) can be quite hot, too, but it has a more complex flavor and makes a far superior bread. Also, most other recipes have you add sugar to their cornbread—a flat-out sin. This bread has none and has a tangy flavor that can't be beat. Using buttermilk instead of plain milk will enhance that, though it's not necessary.

As for drippings, use bacon grease if you have it. Or butter. Or a couple of spoons of butter with a couple of spoons of canola oil heated together. And, yes, you can bake this in a conventional baking pan—but I strongly urge you to use a large (10-to-12-inch) cast-iron skillet that has been well seasoned. You can get the proper crust only with such a skillet, and no kitchen should be without one.

4 tablespoons drippings
2 cups finely ground white
  cornmeal
1 teaspoon salt
½ teaspoon baking soda
½ teaspoon baking powder
1 large egg
1½ cups milk
1 cup chopped green chiles
1 cup shredded Monterrey
  Jack cheese

Turn the oven on to 450° F. Place the drippings in a 10-inch cast-iron skillet and put it in the oven to melt the drippings and heat the pan while you mix the batter.

Put the cornmeal in a large mixing bowl, add the salt, baking soda, and baking powder, and mix together well. Add the egg and milk and stir until all is blended. Stir in the green chiles, then the shredded cheese. Remove the skillet from the oven and carefully swirl the very hot drippings around the pan to coat it, then pour the drippings into the batter. Stir just enough to mix the drippings in, then pour the batter into the skillet. Bake in the oven for 25 minutes or so, until the bread is firm in the middle, browned around the sides, and golden on top. Serve right from the skillet.

Makes enough for 8 to 10.

The ancient Cora Indians of Mexico's west coast believed that the first man, Narama, brought the world chile in a most provocative way. It was in the middle of a banquet for some friends, the story goes, and Narama, feeling a little feisty, jumped up on the middle of the banquet table and began a rather risqué dance. At that instant, his genitals were changed into a ripe chile pod, which he began to shake over the foods, covering them with spice. Not wishing to insult the host, but nervous nevertheless, his guests tried some of the food—and the rest is chile lovers' history.

Aficionados would hardly argue with a tale of such potent and magical origins. Chiles inspire fierce passions, but while habaneros and jalapeños are the favorites of fire-and-brimstone fundamentalists, the chile that provokes the most serious devotion would seem to be the New Mexico green.

Not so hot (though able to pack a wallop that kicks in seductively at the very back of the mouth), New Mexico green chiles have a distinctive crisp, ever-so-subtly sweet flavor as well. If you drive through the Hatch-Mesilla valley outside Las Cruces, New Mexico, at harvesttime, the scent will permeate the air and make you drunk with the anticipation of eating.

Anaheim is the proper name given to these slightly twisted, plump peppers, 4 to 7 inches long and the color of pole beans. But Anaheim refers to all such chiles no matter where they are grown. Anaheims developed independently in California (and were named after an early-twentieth-century pepper cannery in Anaheim) and in New Mexico. Anyone worth their salsa will tell you that the ones grown in New Mexico are far superior in flavor and fire to their more laid-back California cousins.

Until recently it was almost always California Anaheims that could be found fresh in groceries outside New Mexico. But in the last few years some enterprising chile processors in Santa Fe and Albuquerque began shipping frozen green chiles to specialty food shops around the United States. The chiles freeze beautifully and are far superior in flavor and texture not only to the canned ones available in most groceries but also to fresh California Anaheims, which tend to be stringy and watery. If you have a specialty food store in the neighborhood, check to see if it stocks frozen green. If not, see ordering information on page 17.

Fiery Guacamole

With the advent of frozen avocado puree, guacamole has fallen on hard times in American restaurants. The bland, processed-tasting dip you are likely to encounter when eating out these days bears little resemblance to the fresh, flavorful condiment that once graced the tables of the best restaurants of the Southwest. But you can make a fabulously flavorful guacamole at home using California avocados (smaller, with a nubby skin and more buttery taste than the Florida "alligator pear"). Pick three that are exceedingly ripe—tender to your touch, but with no super-soft or hollow spots, which indicate that the flesh inside is too ripe, already turning brown.

Many traditional guacamole recipes emphasize the smoothness and buttery flavor of the avocado alone; but I like to set if off with the bite of green chiles and other spices. Roasting the cumin and coriander seeds is easy and essential for the rich complement their flavor gives this dish.

Tomato or not tomato? That is the question when the chill of winter is in the air and the tomatoes in stores are as hard as frozen snowballs and about as tasty. Nevertheless, the tiny tomato chunks in this dip add textural interest and tang. Sometimes you can find good Italian plum tomatoes around the New Year, or even hothouse tomatoes that have some character. If you can find a fresh tomato with some fragrance and tender but not mushy flesh, use it. If not, omit the tomato and chop a small sweet onion as a substitute.

3 medium-sized ripe
avocados
Juice of a small lime

Remove the pulp from the avocados and mash with a fork or potato masher until smooth. Add the lime juice and minced garlic and stir to mix well. In a small cast-iron skillet, toast the cumin and coriander seeds over high heat

1 large clove of garlic,
  minced
1 teaspoon cumin seed
1 teaspoon coriander seed
1 teaspoon kosher salt
1 medium-sized tomato,
  peeled and chopped small
3 tablespoons chopped
  frozen green chile (hot),
  thawed, or 1 (4.5-ounce)
  can chopped green chile
  (hot) and a dash or two of
  ground red chile to taste

for a minute or two to brown lightly and release the flavors. Stir or shake the skillet constantly to keep the seeds from sticking and burning. Crush finely with a mortar and pestle. Add 1 teaspoon of the spice and the salt to the avocados, and mix. Taste and add more of the cumin-coriander mixture as you prefer. Add the peeled, chopped tomato and green chile. (If you cannot get frozen green chiles, substitute a small can of green chile, including the juices, and then spike the flavor a bit more with good ground red chile to taste.) Mix together and serve immediately with tortilla chips. This recipe may be doubled.

Serves 6 to 8 as an appetizer.

NOTE: Avocado flesh turns brown when it comes in contact with oxygen. The acidity of the lime juice and the tomatoes slows the process to some extent, but if you need to store the guacamole in the fridge for a couple of hours before serving, you will need to minimize the contact with oxygen by placing a film of plastic wrap right on the surface of the dip. Despite what you may have heard, an avocado pit placed in the dip won't slow the browning process—except in the spot directly under the pit where the dip is protected from oxygen.

These tamale recipes require some special ingredients you're not likely to have in the cupboard: corn husks for wrapping, masa harina and blue cornmeal, pure ground red chile, tomatillos, and green chiles. Ten years ago these items would have been nearly impossible to find outside the Southwest, but these days a surprising number of markets carry them in Mexican food sections, or they can be easily found in gourmet and natural food stores. If you can't find them in your area, however, here are some good mail order sources:

Josie's Best New Mexican Foods, 2600 Camino Entrada, P.O. Box 5525, Santa Fe, NM 87501, (505) 473-3437, ships corn husks, ground red chile, and blue cornmeal. It also ships frozen New Mexico green chiles, and while the price is steep, the flavor is far better than that of the canned green chile you find in most groceries.

The Chile Hill Emporium, Box 9100, Bernalillo, NM 87004, (505) 867-3294, mail-orders blue-corn masa harina and the finest ground red chile you can get (not to be confused with commercial "chili powders," which have other spices in them as well). It also has a limited supply of corn husks purchased from nearby pueblos.

For the shrimp tamales, you will need white grits, available in many groceries. Arrowhead Mills makes very good-flavored grits available in health food stores. If you can't find white grits in your area, I suggest you order them from Hoppin' John's, 30 Pinckney Street, Charleston, SC 29401, (803) 577-6404, since these coarse-ground, full-flavored grits are the best I've found commercially available.

◇ Making Tamales

If you are familiar only with commercial tamales plucked from a jar with a bland taste and flaccid, doughy texture as disappointing as love gone wrong and beer gone flat, you are in for a surprise. Fresh hot tamales made at home and consumed on the spot will fill your winter kitchen with the sun-drenched fragrance of steaming dried corn husks mingled with the tart bite of green chile or the aromatic sweetness of anise. They will satisfy your creative urges with their malleable shapes and spark your imagination with their clever little ties and wrappings. They will please your eye (especially the *tamales dulces* made of blue cornmeal, which turn to a surprising pale shade of rosy violet after steaming).

But most of all, fresh hot tamales will make you sigh in pure pleasure at their light, delicate textures and subtle but distinctive tastes. These tamales

are no more like the canned tamales you can find in stores than, say, an ear of corn plucked fresh from the stalk, boiled immediately, and devoured as soon as it can be bitten is like a can of creamed corn from the grocer's shelf.

For your New Year's tamale party, you will want to gather together a half dozen or more friends and give yourselves at least 6 hours for making, eating, and celebrating the tamales.

To steam the tamales, you will need 2 large, tall pots with racks that fit inside them on which you will stand the tamales. Use an old-fashioned steaming pan with a 6-inch-high wire rack. In *Authentic Mexican: Regional Cooking from the Heart of Mexico* (William Morrow, 1987), Rick Bayless notes that you can improvise a tamale steamer by balancing a rack on 4 inverted custard cups in a covered kettle. Leo Fernandez says his family often used an enamel canning pot with a cake cooling rack set over an inverted pie plate. What you are looking for is a rack that sits high enough over the water so that the tamales do not touch the water but are steamed by it. You will need about an inch and a half of water in the pan to start. You want the pot to be large enough to accommodate two dozen or more tamales standing closely nestled, but not crammed together, since the corn mixture will expand.

Meghan with tamales ready to steam

• • • • • 🍒 • • • • •

TAMALES ARE A SIMPLE BUT INGENIOUS INVENTION. THEY BEGIN WITH AN outer wrapper that is not eaten. In parts of South and Central America, banana leaves are often used, and you can also use parchment paper, although the taste is not so fine. The tamale recipes here are wrapped in corn husks that have been soaked to make them pliable—as are most tamales made in Mexico and the southwestern United States.

A damp dough, usually made from masa harina, is spread inside the wrapping. Then a well-seasoned filling is spread down the middle of the dough. When the husk is folded over, the filling is enveloped by the dough. The ends of the husk are pinched together or folded over, then secured with ties.

The tamale is placed standing on end on a rack over (not in) hot water. When all the tamales are on the rack, they are steamed, covered, for 1½ to 2 hours. They are done when the husk can be unwrapped cleanly from a firm tamale inside.

The recipes for pork, chicken, and shrimp tamales make about 2 dozen tamales each, while those for each of the fruit tamales included in the Tamales Dulces recipe make about a dozen each. This is more than enough to feed a party of 12 all through New Year's Eve and have leftovers to freeze. If you're holding a smaller party, you may simply halve the recipes.

To make all the recipes here, you will need about 5 (8-ounce) packages of corn husks. At least 3 hours before the tamale-making is to begin, start soaking the husks. They come in clumps, and if you can easily separate them without tearing while they are dry, do so; but if they are too brittle or tight, just drop them in a large kettle in small clumps. Pour very hot water over to cover and then use a heavy plate to hold the husks under the water.

While the husks are soaking, you may want to cook the pork and chicken, setting the meats in the refrigerator to cool so they can be handled easily later. Wait to make the shrimp broth and Creole sauce after the guests have arrived, so they can help with the peeling.

While some guests are making the dough and fillings for the meat and shrimp tamales according to the recipes, the others should be draining the corn husks and patting each dry with dish towels.

Separate the husks into two piles, of wide ones and narrow ones. Use the wide ones first until you get the hang of the dough-spreading technique. Later you can use the smaller ones, overlapping them.

Someone will also need to make ties for the tamales by tearing the narrowest husks lengthwise into strips about a quarter inch wide. (You'll need two strips per tamale, or about 100 for all the tamale recipes in this section.) If the strips are too short, you can tie two together with a no-slip knot at the narrowest ends. And, yes, you can use string to tie the tamales, but they don't look quite so charming.

Make one type of tamale and set them to steaming while you tackle the next. That way you can eat and cook as the party goes on. Make *tamales dulces* last and serve with hot chocolate and decaf.

The dough for the pork and the chicken tamales is a little easier to work with than that for the shrimp, so you might want to make one of them first to build up your technique.

Tamales will keep nicely about 3 months in the freezer and can be reheated by steaming them over—not in—simmering water for 15 to 20 minutes. When I want a single tamale for lunch, I put a large metal canning jar ring in a saucepan, pour water in to just below the top of the ring, and lay the frozen tamale across it to steam. Frozen reheated tamales have a coarser texture and less complex flavor than fresh ones, so it's a good idea to freeze any leftover sauce to reheat—or make some fresh sauce or salsa—and pour it over them when you're ready to eat.

Red Chile–Pork Tamales

2–3 pound boneless pork
  roast
4 cloves of garlic
1 teaspoon salt

2 tablespoons olive oil
3 tablespoons flour
4 tablespoons ground red
  chile
2½ cups broth (from the
  pork)
1 clove of garlic, minced
Salt to taste

1 cup vegetable shortening
  or lard
4 cups masa harina
3–4 cups broth (from the
  pork), cooled

Trim the visible fat from the exterior of the roast. Heat a deep pan over medium-high heat. Render the pork fat in the pan to grease it lightly, or use a small amount of olive oil if there is no fat. Brown the roast lightly on all sides, then pour in water to cover. Add the garlic and salt, cover, and simmer for 1½ hours. When the meat is done, remove from the pan and let cool. Set the broth aside to use in the sauce and dough. When the pork is cool enough to handle, use forks and your fingers to shred it. You can also chop it fine, but the flavor is not quite as good.

To make the red chile sauce, heat the olive oil in a heavy saucepan, add the flour, and stir to keep from lumping, then add the ground chile, continuing to stir.

Slowly add the broth to the mixture, stirring all the while to keep from lumping. Add the minced garlic. If the mixture should lump, you can use a whisk or blender to get the lumps out. Taste and add salt to your satisfaction. Cover the shredded pork with the red chile sauce.

While the meat and sauce are melding, make the dough. In a large mixer bowl, whip the shortening or lard until fluffy. (There are many who swear that lard is the only proper ingredient for tamales, that without it they don't have the right flavor. But Leo says his family has always used shortening and that if you are making homemade broth, it will give as good a flavor to the dish.)

Add the masa harina and cooled broth alternately, a little at a time, mixing well after each addition. Use all the masa and as much of the broth as it takes to make a very wet but not soupy dough. You want a consistency that's not quite so runny as cake batter, but wetter than mashed potatoes. If you run out of broth, add water. When the ingredients are blended, continue mixing with an electric beater at medium speed for 2 minutes more.

To assemble the tamales, spread open a large corn husk, about 5 to 6 inches across. You may want to lay it on a flat surface, but when you get really adept, you can make the tamales by opening the husk in the palm of your hand. (When you run out of wide husks, you may use two narrower ones by laying them side by side, overlapping them in the middle.)

Using a large serving spoon, put about 2 tablespoons dough in the center of the husk, leaving at least 1½-inch margins at the top and bottom. Use the back of the spoon to smooth and spread the dough across the tamale, making a rectangle that is 3 to 4 inches wide and about 3 inches long. Leave about an inch or more of husk uncovered on each side of the dough.

Spoon a tablespoon of filling lengthwise down the middle of the dough, then fold the two edges of the husk in toward each other so the dough surrounds the filling. If the bare edges are narrow, you can lap one over the other, but if they are larger, you should fold both in the same direction around the tamale, doubling one back under the other's edge.

Fold the bottom edge of the husk up like the flap of an envelope. Tie with a strip of husk. Loosely pull the top together and tie it also. When all the tamales are made, stand them closely together in the steamer with the folded ends on the bottom.

The steamer should have an inch and a half or so of water in the bottom, but it should not touch the steaming platform on which the tamales sit. You don't want the pan to boil dry, so you may need to add water during the steaming process. To know if the water is boiling away, put a nickel in the water. It will rattle as long as the water is simmering, and when it stops, you should add more hot water. If you need to do this, do it by pouring the water gently down the side of the pan—or through a hole in the center of the steaming platform if there is one—taking care not to get the tamales wet.

Cover the steamer, bring the water to a boil, then turn down to a steady simmer. Let steam for 1½ to 2 hours. The tamales are ready when the wrapping pulls away easily from the tamale dough.

Makes about 2 dozen.

Tomatillo-Chicken Tamales

5 chicken breasts
1 clove of garlic
1 small onion
1 medium-sized stalk of
   celery
1 teaspoon salt

4 cups tomatillos (4 [13-
   ounce] cans or 2 dozen
   fresh)
2 cups chopped green
   chiles
4 cloves of garlic, crushed
½ cup chopped fresh
   cilantro
Salt to taste

Put the chicken, 1 garlic clove, onion, celery, and 1 teaspoon salt in a pot with a lid. Cover with water, bring to a boil, and then turn down the heat and simmer, covered, for 30 minutes. Remove the chicken, and when cool enough to handle, remove the bones and skin, return them to the pot, and continue to simmer for 30 minutes. Strain, chill, and defat the broth. Shred the chicken.

To make the tomatillo sauce, you will need about 4 cups pureed tomatillos. Drain the canned tomatillos and process until smooth in the blender. If using fresh ones, remove the husks and put the tomatillos whole in a heavy saucepan over medium heat. Stir and mash with a wooden spoon until they begin to mush, then process in the blender. Add the green chiles, garlic, cilantro, and salt to taste. Put in

1 cup vegetable shortening
 or lard
4 cups masa harina
3–4 cups broth (from the
 chicken)

a heavy saucepan and simmer over low heat for 20 minutes, before pouring over the chicken.

Prepare the dough as for Red Chile–Pork Tamales (see page 22), using chicken broth instead of pork. Assemble the tamales and cook as for the pork tamales.

Makes about 2 dozen.

TAMALE MEMORIES

When I was growing up, my mother would say sometime before Christmas that we were going to the market. We were looking for a hog's head. The grocer had so many orders that you had to sign up to get one, and sometimes there would be a sign on the hog's head that this head belongs to so-and-so.

After we had got the head, my mother would invite her neighbors and relatives and friends to come in to make tamales. On the day they arrived she would cook the head. She put it in a big pot and boiled it with spices, garlic, whole peppers and cilantro. She kept this broth to mix with the masa.

The corn husks had to be gathered, separated, and cleaned. They are called hojas. My mother would wash and scrape them, and, having separated the husks, she would cut them into uniform rectangular shapes. I learned later that they could be bleached and prepared more easily by putting them in boiling water.

My mother bought her masa at the store . . . Preparing the masa just right took a long time.

Now the meat from the hog's head had to be ground. It took big pots to hold all the meat. After it was ground it had to be cooked again with spices. At this stage everyone wanted to taste it. When it was approved by all the ladies, the meat was said to be ready to be laid on the masa, which had been spread very thinly on the shucks.

The shucks had to be rolled up just right, folded just so and tied. Then the tamales were stood in big pots, but they must not touch the bottom. My mother would lay her tablespoons on the bottom of the pot to support something—maybe a tin pie plate—on which to stand the tamales and lift them out. Then boiling water was poured over them. A clean cloth was laid across the pot for a cover, and they were steamed . . .

Then one of the ladies would take one out and taste it. This was a time for talking, laughing, exchanging dichos. They stopped their work and had coffee. When all was done, everybody would take some tamales home.

My mother liked to have tamales on hand to give as gifts to the peddlers who came regularly to our house, the postman, and all those service people. The tamales and a bottle of her tomato juice made a nice gift.

—"A Conversation with Mrs. Alonzo (Sylvia) Sosa, Native of Harlingen," from Ernestine Sewell Linck and Joyce Gibson Roach, *Eats: A Folk History of Texas Foods*

Shrimp and Grits Tamales

2 pounds medium-sized
shrimp, unshelled
1 teaspoon salt

Rinse the shrimp well. Put 2 quarts water in a large saucepan and add the 1 teaspoon salt, white pepper, black pepper, cayenne, celery, onion, and garlic. Bring to a boil, add the shrimp, and cook just a few minutes, until they

½ teaspoon white pepper
½ teaspoon black pepper
½ teaspoon cayenne
  pepper
1 large stalk of celery
1 small onion
1 clove of garlic

1 (30-ounce) can tomatoes,
  undrained
2 cloves of garlic
1 teaspoon dried oregano
1 teaspoon cayenne pepper
1 tablespoon sugar
1 tablespoon butter
1 medium-sized green bell
  pepper, chopped
1 tablespoon flour
6 scallions, chopped
Salt to taste

4 cups white grits
1 cup vegetable shortening
  or lard
3–4 cups broth (from the
  shrimp)
2 teaspoons salt

are done. Remove the shrimp and leave the other ingredients to simmer, covered. When the shrimp are cooled, remove the shells and return the shells to the pot. Simmer for another 30 minutes, then strain and set the broth aside. Meanwhile, chop the shrimp in small pieces.

To make the Creole sauce, put the tomatoes, garlic, oregano, cayenne, and sugar in the blender and process until smooth. In a heavy skillet, melt ½ tablespoon of the butter over low heat, add the green pepper, and sauté until just beginning to soften. Remove the pepper and add the remaining ½ tablespoon butter. Add the flour and stir until browned. Pour in the tomato mixture, add the green pepper and scallions, and simmer over low heat for 20 minutes, stirring occasionally. Add salt to taste. Use 3 cups of the sauce to cover the shrimp and reserve any remaining sauce. Refrigerate the shrimp and sauce.

To make the dough, put the dried grits in the blender a cup at a time and grind to a fine cornmeal-like consistency. Prepare the dough as for Red Chile–Pork Tamales (see page 22), using grits instead of masa harina and shrimp broth plus salt instead of pork broth. Assemble the tamales and cook as for the pork tamales. Warm any extra sauce and serve on the side.

Makes about 2 dozen.

Tamales Dulces with Pineapple

2 (16-ounce) cans crushed
   pineapple
1 cup vegetable shortening
   or lard
4 cups blue cornmeal or
   blue-corn masa harina
2 cups chicken broth
1 teaspoon salt
2 teaspoons baking powder
1 cup raisins
1 cup dried cherries
¼ teaspoon anise, crushed

Drain the pineapple, setting the fruit aside and reserving the juice. Prepare the dough as for Red Chile–Pork Tamales (see page 22), using 2 cups juice from the pineapple with the 2 cups chicken broth for the liquid. When the shortening, meal, and juice-broth mixture are all blended, sprinkle the salt and baking powder over the dough and mix well. Add the drained pineapple and mix in with a wooden spoon. Divide the dough in half and mix the raisins into one batter, the dried cherries into the other. Add the anise to the raisin tamales and mix well.

These are "blind" tamales, which means the filling (fruit) isn't separate from the dough but mixed in with it. To assemble them, you place the dough in the center of the corn husk just as you do for regular tamales, but instead of spreading it, you pat it lightly into a cylindrical shape and then roll up the husk and tie. *Tamales dulces* should be a little smaller than filled ones. Steam for an hour and a half. These are especially delicious served with *café con leche* or Mexican chocolate.

Makes about 12 raisin and 12 cherry tamales.

The time it takes. Those are the best hours. When the tough has to be made ten-der, but can't be hurried. How often Mother Rusch and I, while the billowing tripe kept the kitchen stable-warm, sat at the table pushing checkers over the board, dis-covering the sea route to India, or catching flies on the smooth-polished table top, and telling each other about the tripe of olden times, when we were Pomorshian and still heathen. And about older than olden times, when elk cows were the only source of meat.

—GÜNTER GRASS, *THE FLOUNDER*

Two

Late Winter Celebrations

Summertime blues are small change compared to those of winter. Summer seems to promise all sorts of pleasures and more than enough opportunity to gather with friends outdoors. It's January and February that throw up the obstacle course of snow and ice and early dark, and that bring the general let-down feeling that follows the preceding holiday season. Finding the energy to celebrate is almost as hard as finding a reason.

Even Valentine's Day, the most universally observed holiday of this time of the year, sends a mixed message. If you happen to be in love, it can be a delight. But if you're without a sweetheart, it's a difficult holiday to get heated up for.

The best care for such late winter's chill is to invent a party warmed by good friends.

THE HOTDISH DOLDRUMS DANCE

Look in the Random House Dictionary and you will find *doldrums* defined as "a state of inactivity or stagnation" or "a dull, listless, depressed mood; low spirits."

Hardly the sort of situation one would expect to inspire a typical celebration. But then, Karen Faster's annual Hotdish Hoedown in Madison, Wisconsin, is not a typical celebration by any definition.

Slated for the last Saturday of January or the first of February each year, the Hotdish Hoedown began as a way to combat the late winter doldrums, Karen says. Since she's a transplanted Minnesotan, it was also her way of celebrating the family of friends she'd created for herself in a new hometown.

"Back when I was nuclear (in Deephaven, Minnesota), my parents entertained a lot. They'd do the host-and-hostess-cook-the-whole-meal thing sometimes. But when it was a family gathering, everyone brought a hotdish," Karen says.

"The Hoedown started the first year as a housewarming party. I'd just moved into this new place, and it was the dead of winter. All the holidays were over. Everybody was feeling kind of let-down and the weather tends to isolate you up here in January. So I thought it might perk things up to have a party.

"I also wanted to bring together all these friends who'd helped me feel welcome and helped me settle in. I thought they should all meet each other and have a good time. They felt like family to me, and I wanted the party to feel like family, so I asked every household invited to bring a hotdish."

And just what, one might ask, is a "hotdish"?

Random House is no help on this one. For this definition, Karen suggested I consult a more exclusive lexicon, Howard Mohr's *How to Talk Minnesotan*.

Mohr says the hotdish is "Minnesota's most popular native food" and describes it as a main course baked in a single pan. An authentic hotdish, he says, begins with canned cream of mushroom soup and a can of some sort of vegetables, then goes from there. And he says there are nearly four thousand variations on hotdish in Minnesota from the ever-popular Velveeta Hamburger to the exotics: Garbanzo Bango Hotdish, Back-of-the-Refrigerator Hotdish, and Turkey Wiener Doodah Hotdish, winner of the 1985 Grand Prix de Hotdish.

Karen says that when she first staged the party, in 1990, she included Mohr's definition of hotdish on the invitation.

"But I discovered that I really didn't need to. There's enough of a shared culture between Minnesotans and folks from Wisconsin that everybody I'd invited understood the concept, even if they hadn't called it by that exact term."

Not everyone sticks to the canned parameters of Mohr's definition, either, Karen says.

"There are enchilada casseroles that show up every year and are really popular. Some people use fresh vegetables or make things from scratch. There's always a dish from Mollie Katzen's *Moosewood Cookbook*, and it's always a hit with the vegetarians.

"But you'd be surprised how many people want to make classic hotdish. They get inspired wondering, 'Now just what can I do with Tater Tots?' And when it comes to eating, it's always the cheesiest Velveeta, hamburger, soup, and noodle concoction that's gone first. I think it has to do with comfort and wanting food that tastes the way food tasted when we were little. I think that really is important, especially when winter has you down."

But for all its popularity, the hotdish buffet isn't the only excitement at this late winter celebration. Karen also instituted the Great Jell-O Contest that first year, and this totally inedible, art-for-art's-sake competition has become something of an annual creative event. Guests are encouraged to make something—anything—out of Jell-O and enter it in a competition judged by the party's attendees, who fill out secret ballots.

Objets d'aspic have included a mirror that actually reflected (thick Smurf-blue Jell-O over aluminum in an ornate gilt frame) and a tropical Jell-O island paradise complete with a celery-stalk palm tree and hula-dancing plastic trolls.

"One of my favorites was the winner for Best Grossest Ingredient one year—a bunch of dead goldfish in a fish mold decorated with a shark nose," Karen says.

To keep things lively, Karen likes to add a new category or two to the

Jell-O contest each year. In 1994, it was "The Best Book or Movie Representation." The winner was *Gone With the Wind*, with a paper-doll Rhett escorting a paper-doll Scarlett clad in a billowing hoop skirt made of shimmering gelatin.

Categories for prizes also include "Best Use of Color," "Most Jiggly," "Most Aesthetic," and "Best Use of Fruit." Plus, Karen has been known to create a category and name a winner on the spot.

"One year I came across a woman I didn't even know, but I could tell she was ready to cry if her Jell-O didn't win something. I think I made a prize for the Jell-O that had traveled farthest—she was from out of town. And when she got her prize—a secondhand store Jell-O mold—she was thrilled."

Another much-coveted prize was the *New Joys of Jell-O Cookbook* Karen found in a used-book store. And all the children who enter seem to win a prize—usually a box of crayons to be used on the big sheets of butcher paper Karen scatters about the room for doodling.

Dancing is also on the agenda, although Karen says that so far that's attracted the least participation. The first years she held the party at her cozy frame house, "but I thought maybe it was too claustrophobic for folks to dance."

Her original guest list of "oh, about forty" has expanded to more than sixty over the years, no doubt partly due to the wording of the invitation, which encourages invited guests to bring along anyone else who "appreciates a good hotdish."

In 1993, the party moved to a nearby community center, and a few more folks were willing to take the floor when the hoedown music began—but still not as many as Karen had hoped.

"I think I may have to buy one of those revolving glitter disco balls in the future," she says. "Maybe that will do the trick. Or maybe folks are just too filled up on hotdish to get up and dance."

A couple of classic hotdish recipes follow, along with some new inventions.

Alice glanced nervously along the table, as she walked up the large hall, and noticed that there were about fifty guests, of all kinds: some were animals, some birds, and there were even a few flowers among them. "I'm glad they've come without waiting to be asked," she thought: "I should never have known who were the right people to invite!"

—Lewis Carroll, *Through the Looking-Glass*

Sometimes things struggle in the skillet, and mushroom soup subdues them.

—"Grace Under Fire" (ABC Television, October 1994)

Funeral Hotdish

This is the quintessential hotdish with browned burger, mushroom soup, and processed cheese. It got its name, Karen says, because it seemed to be the hotdish her mother always made to take to the bereaved family when someone died.

"One night my mom was standing around the kitchen, wondering out loud what to make for dinner, when one of my siblings popped up and said, 'Why don't you make Funeral Hotdish?' We've called it that ever since."

Of course, fine-food fanciers might well die at the thought of serving such a déclassé dish, but others will recognize it as classic comfort food. And when it appears at Karen's party, it's one of the first casserole dishes to wind up empty.

1 pound ground beef
8 ounces egg noodles
¾ teaspoon salt
2 tablespoons vegetable oil
2 medium-sized onions,
  chopped
½ cup sliced mushrooms
½ pound processed cheese
⅛ teaspoon freshly ground
  black pepper
½ cup milk

Preheat the oven to 350° F. Lightly oil a large casserole.

Brown the beef in a skillet, drain, and set aside. Bring 2 quarts water to a boil in a large pot; add the noodles and ¼ teaspoon salt. Return to the boil and cook for 8 minutes, until the noodles are al dente. Drain. Heat the vegetable oil in a skillet, over medium heat, add the onions, and sauté until translucent. Add the sliced mushrooms and continue to sauté until the mushrooms are turning golden.

Cut the processed cheese into chunks about ½ inch square. In a large bowl, mix together the noodles, beef, onions, mushroom, and cheese chunks. Add ½ teaspoon salt and the pepper; stir. Pour the mixture into the oiled casserole, then pour the milk evenly over the top. Bake in the preheated oven for 1 hour.

Serves 6 to 8.

ℜuptial ℌotdish

This hotdish got its fancy name, Karen says, when a friend was looking for a dressed-up rendition of the classic tuna-noodle casserole to take to someone's potluck wedding. The almonds, green pepper, and olives provided the extra punch she was seeking, and pretty soon everyone she knew was requesting this particular hotdish for their weddings. Hence, Nuptial Hotdish.

8 ounces egg noodles
½ teaspoon salt
1 tablespoon vegetable oil
½ cup chopped green bell
  pepper
½ cup sliced mushrooms
½ cup slivered almonds
1 (6-ounce) can solid white
  tuna, drained
1 (10¾-ounce) can
  condensed cream of
  mushroom soup
½ cup mayonnaise
4 ounces grated mild
  Cheddar cheese
½ cup chopped pimiento-
  stuffed green olives

Preheat the oven to 350° F. Oil a large casserole.

In a large pot, bring 2 quarts water to a boil and add the noodles and salt. Return to the boil and cook for 8 minutes, until the noodles are al dente. Drain and put into a large bowl.

Heat the vegetable oil in a skillet over medium heat, and then sauté the green bell pepper until well coated with oil and just beginning to soften a bit. Add the mushrooms and continue cooking until they are golden.

Mix the pepper, mushrooms, almonds, and drained tuna with the noodles. In a small bowl, blend the mushroom soup with the mayonnaise. Add to the noodle mixture and stir until evenly distributed.

Pour half the noodle mixture into the oiled casserole. Sprinkle half the grated cheese over the surface and then sprinkle all the olives over that. Pour in the rest of the noodle mixture and top with the rest of the grated cheese. Bake in the preheated oven for 45 minutes, or until the hotdish is bubbling and lightly browned on top.

Serves 6 and may be doubled.

"I don't cook," Karen Faster says, "so one big motivation in having a hotdish potluck party is that then people bring me something to eat."

When pressed, though, Karen admits there is one recipe she has mastered, a hotdish so low-tech one is tempted to dub it Hotpot:

"You put a can of cream of mushroom soup in a saucepan, and then, while it's heating, you stir about 2 tablespoons of flour in that. Then you add a soup can of milk and mix it up. Bring it to a boil and then dump in a can of tuna. Mix that up and then dump in a bag of potato chips that you've smashed up. Then you eat it right out of the pot because it tastes so good you can't wait to get a bowl."

As for dressing for this dinner, flannel pajamas with feet are de rigueur.

Hotdish Side Dish

Technically speaking, you cannot have a hotdish without cream sauce of some kind, canned or otherwise; so this recipe from Karen Faster's mother, Cecy, must be called a side dish. But you won't care what it's called once you get a mouthful of its earthy, tangy flavors. Cecy says she discovered it when testing recipes for a regional fund-raising cookbook several years ago.

You can actually make this with other varieties of rice—I tried it with brown basmati once and thought it was delicious. But it's finest when made with hand-harvested long-grain, truly wild rice. For more information on getting such rice, see page 40.

The recipe doesn't specify a fancy mushroom—and it's delicious with the plump little white mushrooms offered in most groceries. But more and more stores are carrying a wider variety of fresh mushrooms, so I suggest you substitute any that you like.

1 cup long-grain wild rice
½ teaspoon salt
3 tablespoons butter
1½ cups chopped onions
1½ cups chopped mushrooms
Freshly ground black pepper to taste
1 cup coarsely chopped raw cranberries, fresh, or frozen and thawed

Rinse and drain the rice. Put in a heavy saucepan, with a lid that fits snugly, and add 3 cups water and ¼ teaspoon salt. Cover and bring to a boil, then turn down heat and simmer, covered, for 35 to 45 minutes, until the water is absorbed and the rice is fluffy.

NOTE: Not all long-grain wild rice is the same. These are the proportions and times that Cecy uses for the hand-harvested Minnesota rice she prefers. If you are using another long-grain rice, and if the directions with that rice call for other proportions, follow the package directions. You want to end up with 3 cups cooked rice.

As the rice finishes cooking, preheat the oven to 350° F. and lightly oil a 2-quart covered casserole.

Heat the butter in a skillet, add the onions, and sauté until they soften and turn translucent. Add the mushrooms and sauté until they begin to turn golden. Season with ¼ teaspoon salt and the pepper. Remove from the heat and stir in the cooked rice. (Taste here and add more salt or pepper if needed.) Add the chopped cranberries and toss to mix throughout. Put the mixture into the oiled casserole, cover, and pop in the preheated oven for 30 minutes. Serve while hot.

If you're not taking it to a Hotdish Party, it is especially wonderful with smacking fresh grilled salmon.

Feeds 6 to 8 as a side dish.

Wild rice used to be a rarity, and a very expensive one. But these days you can find wild rice in even the most conventional supermarket. Cecy Faster cautions that all wild rice is not the same, however, making a distinction between rice that is grown and harvested by hand and that which is commercially grown and mechanically harvested. This latter she calls "paddy rice."

"Paddy rice will be almost black in color, while hand-harvested rice is usually a very dark brown. Most packages will say 'Minnesota wild rice,' but much of the paddy rice is actually grown and harvested in California, then shipped to Minnesota for processing, so it may say Minnesota rice when it really isn't," she said.

Cecy prefers rice that has actually been grown in the lakes of Minnesota, harvested by hand, and packaged and distributed by Native American tribes in the region. Her reasons aren't just regional chauvinism. She says truly wild wild rice has a richer, more complex flavor than paddy rice and it will "cook up fluffier." She also believes that buying from Native American businesses is a good way to support indigenous cultures.

It's possible to find the kind of long-grain wild rice Cecy prefers in some groceries, natural food cooperatives, and specialty stores. Most packages will say if the rice is hand-harvested, organic, or traditionally grown, and will also identify if the company is Indian-owned. If the package doesn't, then the rice is probably not.

If you can't find such rice in your area, or if you're curious about the differences between the various sorts of rice, you may want to contact Grey Owl Foods, P.O. Box 88, Grand Rapids, MN 55744. The Indian-owned company sells Minnesota-grown hand-harvested rice, organically grown Canadian lake rice, and paddy rice, along with several varieties of gourmet rice blends. It will send you brochures describing its products and ordering information, and it has an 800 number for free calling: 1 (800) 527-0172.

Show-off Hotdish

Wondering what would happen if you took the fundamental concepts of hotdish, but went back a step and made everything from scratch, I came up with this sensual potato concoction. It actually doesn't take much longer to make than a good tuna casserole and pays off in the rich interplay of flavors. I thought about calling it Le Hotdish de France because it's a jazzed-up version of the classics, but then I worried that the ghost of Django Reinhardt might haunt me and, worse yet, that Karen and her friends might scoff that I was putting on airs. Show-off Hotdish seems to be more to the point.

15 new potatoes slightly
  larger than golf balls
12–15 cloves of garlic
5 tablespoons unsalted
  butter
1½ teaspoons kosher salt
Freshly ground black
  pepper
2 medium-sized onions
½ pound mushrooms
¼ teaspoon powdered
  mace
2 tablespoons flour
1 cup milk
3 oil-packed sun-dried
  tomatoes, drained

Preheat the oven to 400° F. Lightly grease a large baking dish. (I use an ovenproof pasta bowl that's 2 inches deep and a little less than a foot in diameter.)

Wash the potatoes well and quarter. Put them in the baking dish with the cloves of garlic scattered evenly among them. Melt 1 tablespoon of the butter and pour over the potatoes. Sprinkle on 1 teaspoon kosher salt and add a few grindings of black pepper. Toss to mix together, then place in the preheated oven and roast for 30 minutes, stirring once or twice to make sure the potatoes don't stick.

While the potatoes are roasting, cut the onions in half, and slice about ⅛ inch thick. Melt 2 tablespoons of the butter in a large skillet with a lid. Add the onions to the melted butter, cover, and turn heat to low. Cook for 10 minutes, shaking the pan occasionally to keep from sticking. After 10 minutes, remove the lid and turn the heat to high. Cook, stirring gently, for about 5 minutes, until the onions have turned a deep golden color. Remove from the pan and set aside.

Wash the mushrooms. Remove the stems, chop fine, and set aside. Slice the caps. Melt 1 tablespoon of the butter in the same skillet you cooked the onions in. Add the sliced mushroom caps and cook over medium heat for about 5 minutes, stirring occasionally, until they turn golden. Set aside with the onions.

Melt the final 1 tablespoon butter and sauté the mushroom stems over medium heat with ½ teaspoon kosher salt. Mix the mace with the flour. When the mushrooms are softened and juicy, sprinkle the flour mixture over them and stir for a minute or two to season the flour. Add the milk slowly to the mushroom mix, stirring constantly with a wide spoon or whisk to keep the flour from forming lumps. Cook over medium heat, stirring constantly, until the mixture begins to thicken, about 5 minutes. When the sauce has thickened, remove from the heat.

When the potatoes have finished roasting, remove them from the oven and turn the temperature down to 350° F. Add the onions and mushroom slices to the potatoes and garlic. Toss to mix together. Slice the sun-dried tomatoes into slivers and sprinkle these over the potatoes. Pour the mushroom sauce over the whole thing and put it back in the oven to bake at 350° F. for 20 minutes, until the sauce is bubbly and the edges are browning. Serve immediately.

Serves 4 to 6 as a main course with salad, or 8 as a side dish.

Once upon a time Thanksgiving was just the purview of a handful of Pilgrims and their newfound Indian friends. But then the idea caught on and the rest is holiday history. Can national Hotdish Day be next?

Bonita Morse heard about the Madison Hotdish Hoedown from her brother, one of Karen Faster's friends. Bonita decided it was just the thing to brighten up the glum tail end of winter in Bloomington, a suburb of Minneapolis, so she and a friend staged their first hotdish party in March of 1993.

"People loved it," she said—about fifty people, that is, who made hotdishes of nearly everything, but most of all Spam.

"Someone even made an hors d'oeuvre with a square of Spam topped by a cube of lemon Jell-O, speared on a toothpick. That was good. Well, not good, but clever."

Prizes were awarded for a variety of hotdish categories, including "The Most Likely to Be Thrown Out."

Winner Beverly Scully of Stillwater, Minnesota, could not recall the precise recipe but said that it did have Stove Top stuffing mix, browned hamburger, and cream soup. Asked for a championship tip, Beverly said, "I really think I won because I brought it in a lovely blue-and-white crocheted hotdish carryall."

The Mississippi River has its headwaters in northern Minnesota. Maybe the aromas of early hotdishes were carried down its path, for it was that fictional raft rider of the lower Mississippi, Huckleberry Finn, who best described the charms of a meal thrown together and cooked in a single pot: "In a barrel of odds and ends it is different; things get mixed up, and the juice kind of swaps around, and the things go better."

VALENTINE DESSERT PARTY

February magazines are awash with recipes and recommendations for a romantic dinner for two. But don't they realize that most often "Love Is a Many-Splendored Thing"?

Shelley Hamel does. Her annual Valentine Dessert Party is a "sweets for the sweet" event with a guest list that includes some twenty-five or so friends who've won the hearts of Shelley and her husband, David, over the years.

Shelley says the Valentine's party started about a dozen years ago as a way to say thanks to the many friends who'd helped the couple reclaim and refurbish the old house they'd bought on Lake Monona in Madison, Wisconsin. The house was a shambles when they moved in, but now it is distinguished by flowing, open levels, gleaming wood, careful detail work, huge windows, and a sleeping loft that looks out on the lake—all eloquent testimony to the hard work of the Hamels and their friends.

But Shelley decided that even though it was a community spirit she was honoring with the Valentine's party, she wanted to be the event's *auteur*.

"I tried it as a potluck once or twice, but it's not nearly as much fun for me. I like the idea of doing something very special for my friends all by myself and, to be honest, I like it when all the praise and thanks come back to me, too.

"Besides, I also like to lick all the bowls."

Certainly there are bowls enough to lick each year as Shelley bakes, makes, mixes, and fixes some dozen desserts. It takes five days to put the party together, she said, and the first is spent simply deciding what to make.

"On that day I sit down with my box of recipes and relive my past. I was an only child and I had all the attention of my mother. I got to be in the kitchen with her when she cooked, and every recipe I have has a memory or a story."

On the recipe for her mother's chocolate fudge there's a nine-year-old's scrawl saying "real good."

"One of my favorite childhood memories is that fudge," Shelley says. "Once my mother made a mistake in the recipe and so she gave me the whole pan. Not to lick just the leavings, mind you, but a whole pan of that mistake to eat by myself. And when I look at that recipe card, I always think of that. I like to take each recipe out and savor reading and thinking about each one."

As she decides on which recipes to make, Shelley makes a list of all the ingredients she'll need. Then, on the second day, she shops.

"Normally I don't much like grocery shopping, but this day is different. See, the great part is I don't have to put anything away. I can just bring it home and set everything out on the counters because I'm going to use it right away."

Days three and four are spent baking and preparing. She looks the recipes over and makes some mental notes about what should be fixed first and what next based on the ingredients, techniques, and times. But Shelley confesses, "When it comes down to it, I usually make things in the order that I want to lick the bowls. I call this whole thing 'licking the bowls of my child-hood,' and that's what's so fun to me about it."

Having the party in February in Wisconsin is a plus, because things that have to stay chilled can just be popped in the attached garage.

"I might not be able to carry this off if I didn't have that extra chilled storage space. But, bottom line, it's so much easier than having a dinner party because you don't have to do anything at the last minute."

In fact, all the food is finished on day four, and day five is spent cleaning the house top to bottom and then relaxing. On the day of the party, Shelley arranges all the desserts on one table, complete with cards telling what each is so people can know what they're carving into.

"Contrary to what people may think, it's really not a children's party," Shelley cautions.

"Children don't discriminate with sweets—a big cookie is the same as a four-layer chocolate torte for them. And what happens when children come is they gorge on sweets right away and then are wild for the rest of the party. So I try to gently discourage folks from bringing their children."

On the other hand, Shelly encourages her adult guests to let out the child in them all: "There's something very exciting when someone first walks in and looks at that table and realizes, 'Oh my, all those goodies, and I can have whatever I want.' It's like being seven years old again and spying the tree on Christmas morning."

Tropical Cake

This was a traditional Christmas cake in Shelley Hamel's family, her mother using both green and red maraschino cherries in the mix. Shelley uses only red cherries, which she says not only make it appropriate for her Valentine's Day bash but look more appetizing.

Fresh Brazil nuts already shelled were a little hard to find, but I finally discovered them at a nut and grain store. Health food shops and vegetable markets often have them, too.

This cake has an unusual flavor—and a very sneaky addictive quality. The first bite I took didn't convince me it was worth the trouble. But I found myself going back for more and more, and determined to make it again once the last crumb was gone. It's not too sweet but very satisfying and is especially lovely with a nice cup of tea.

3 cups shelled whole Brazil nuts
16 ounces pitted whole dates
1 cup drained maraschino cherries
¾ cup all-purpose flour
¾ cup sugar
½ teaspoon baking powder
½ teaspoon salt
3 eggs
1 teaspoon vanilla extract

Preheat the oven to 300° F. Lightly grease a large loaf pan (9½ × 5½ × 2½ inches) and line with waxed paper.

In a very large bowl, mix the nuts, dates, and cherries. Sift the flour, sugar, baking powder, and salt over them, then mix together with your hands until everything is well coated.

In a separate bowl, beat the eggs until frothy, then mix in the vanilla. Pour over the nuts and fruit and again mix with your hands. Lightly pack the mixture into the loaf pan and bake in the preheated oven for 1 hour and 45 minutes.

Set on a wire rack and let the cake cool completely before removing from pan. Because of its chunky texture, this cake is difficult to slice even when it's thoroughly cooled, so use a very sharp knife. Shelley recommends that you turn the loaf upside down, since that seems to make the slicing a little smoother. The cake keeps nicely for several days if covered well and placed in refrigerator.

Serves 12.

Chocolate and Sea-foam Cake

Shelley's recipes sparked a longing in me to re-create my favorite cake from girlhood—a dense, moist chocolate layer cake with ethereal sea-foam icing. I remember coming home from school and slipping into the dark cupboard just to sniff the heady brown-sugar-and-chocolate fragrance of this dessert. My mother didn't bake often, but when she did, she wasn't stingy. She would cut a large piece for me and then pour a big glass of milk and let me sit at the kitchen table and ruin my supper if that's what I wanted. And I did.

CAKE

2 eggs
1 cup strong coffee, freshly
    brewed
½ cup unsweetened cocoa
2 teaspoons vanilla extract
¾ cup (1½ sticks) butter,
    softened
1¼ cups sugar
1¼ cups all-purpose flour
½ teaspoon baking soda
½ teaspoon salt

Take the eggs out of the refrigerator so they can come to room temperature before you use them. Preheat the oven to 350° F. Grease 2 (8-inch) cake pans and line with waxed paper.

Prepare the coffee, and while it is piping hot, combine with the cocoa in a small bowl, stirring until smooth. Allow to cool until almost room temperature (stand bowl in ice water to hasten), then whisk in the vanilla.

In the large bowl of an electric mixer, cream the butter at medium speed, slowly adding the sugar and beating until the mixture is very fluffy. Add the eggs one at a time and beat well after each.

Sift the flour, baking soda, and salt together, then add the flour and the cocoa alternatively to the butter-sugar mixture while running the mixer at low speed. Beat until blended, scraping down the sides of the bowl as you do.

Pour the batter into the pans, dividing evenly. Use a spatula to spread and smooth the batter into the pans. Bake on the center rack in the preheated oven for 25 to 30 minutes, or until the cake layers test done.

Cool in the pans on wire racks for 10 minutes, then invert onto the racks, remove the pans, and cool completely before icing.

ICING

3 egg whites
¼ teaspoon cream of tartar
1 cup granulated sugar
1 cup brown sugar, packed
¼ cup Karo light corn
  syrup
½ teaspoon vanilla extract

As soon as the cake layers have cooled thoroughly, place one on a serving platter and begin making the icing.

Using an electric mixer at medium-high speed, beat the egg whites and cream of tartar in a large bowl until the whites begin to form stiff peaks. Turn off the mixer, but leave the bowl of stiffened egg whites ready to be beaten again.

Put the sugars, syrup, and ¼ cup water in a heavy saucepan—one that has a handle so you can pour from it easily.

Bring the sugar mixture to a boil while stirring. Continue to boil, stirring occasionally, until a candy thermometer registers 250° F. (This usually happens rather quickly, so keep an eye on the mixture.)

Remove from the heat and immediately start beating the egg whites again with the mixer on medium. Pour the hot syrup in a thin stream into the egg whites, taking care not to splash. When the syrup is in the egg whites (don't bother scraping the saucepan), scrape down the side of the bowl with a spatula to make sure everything is well mixed. Add the vanilla extract.

Use a wooden spoon to beat the icing vigorously. When it begins to lose some of its gloss and to hold its shape, you are ready to ice the cake. Ice the top of one layer first, then carefully position the second layer on it. Ice the sides, then the top of the cake.

Serves 10 to 12.

When she finished beating the meringue, it occurred to Nacha to lick some of the icing off her finger to see if Tita's tears had affected the flavor. No, the flavor did not seem to have been affected; yet without knowing why, Nacha was suddenly overcome with an intense longing. One after another, she thought back on all the wedding banquets she had prepared for the De la Garza family, ever cherishing the illusion that the next wedding would be her own. At eighty-five, there was no longer much point in crying, lamenting the wedding banquet she'd been waiting for that had never come, or the wedding she had never had, even though she had had a fiancé. Oh yes, she had! But the mama of Mama Elena had sent him packing. Since then all she could do was enjoy other people's weddings, as she had been doing for years without grumbling. So why was she complaining now? There must be some joke in all this, but she couldn't find it. She frosted the cake with the meringue icing as well as she could and went to her room, a terrible aching in her heart. She cried all night, and the next morning she didn't have the strength to help with the wedding.

—LAURA ESQUIVEL, *LIKE WATER FOR CHOCOLATE*

Tunnel of Love Fudge Cake

Not quite a flavor from childhood, since I didn't taste my first Tunnel of Fudge Cake until I was in high school, but this is a dessert whose mysterious ways can delight the child in us all. And made in this interesting variation—using rich, dusky black walnuts instead of their bland English cousins—it has a flavor that will appeal mightily to those of us with even the most jaded adult palates.

The trick to the original Tunnel of Fudge Cake (a recipe devised originally by the Pillsbury Company to showcase several of its products) was that the cake made its own icing inside, a creamy tunnel of gooey frosting that seemed to appear magically. Actually, it was a box of frosting mix added to the batter that created the tunnel. In this recipe, based on the current official version from Pillsbury, it's confectioner's sugar that does the trick.

I first tasted black walnuts in this classic cake at a Louisville restaurant called Apron Strings that specializes in down-home foods. It takes the flavor of the cake to a whole new level—like the difference between puppy love and a genuine long-term relationship. I suggest you find the freshest black walnuts you can.

1¾ cups (3½ sticks) butter
1¾ cups granulated sugar
6 eggs
2 cups confectioner's sugar
1 teaspoon vanilla extract
2¼ cups all-purpose flour
¾ cup unsweetened cocoa
2 cups coarsely chopped
    black walnuts

Preheat the oven to 350° F. Grease and flour a 10-inch tube pan. In the large bowl of an electric mixer, cream the butter and granulated sugar at medium speed until light and fluffy, then add the eggs one at a time, beating well after each. Add the confectioner's sugar gradually and blend well. Add the vanilla and blend.

By hand, mix in the flour and cocoa. When well blended, stir in the black walnuts. Spoon into the prepared pan and smooth evenly with a rubber spatula. Bake for 1 hour. Remove from the oven and allow to cool on a wire rack for 1 hour before inverting over a plate.

Serves 12.

FOOD FOR LOVE 1

Red, through what advice I can never know, a few days later slipped into my desk the first nickel candy bar I had ever seen, called, I think, a Cherriswete.

It was a clumsy lump of very good chocolate and fondant, with a preserved cherry in the middle, all wrapped up in a piece of paper that immediately on being touched sent off waves of red and gilt stain. It was, to me, not only the ultimate expression of masculine devotion, but pure gastronomical delight, in a household where Grandmother disapproved of candy, not because of tooth decay or indigestion, but because children liked it and children should perforce not have anything they liked.

I sniffed happily at the Cherriswete a few times and then gave each girl in my retinue a crumb, not because I liked her but because of her loyalty. Then I took it home, showed it to my little sister, spun it a few times more past her nose to torture her, and divided it with her, since even though young and savage we loved each other very much.

My heart was full. I knew at last that I loved Red. I was his, to steal a phrase. We belonged together, a male and female who understood the gastronomical urge.

—M.F.K. FISHER, *AN ALPHABET FOR GOURMETS*

Peanut Butter Krinkles

Shelley Hamel's recipe for peanut butter cookies is the same one her mother used when she was growing up, but next to "½ cup peanut butter" in the ingredients list is the word "Fresh!" written in red.

"One time when I was making them I wondered what would happen if I ground my own peanuts. The result was a cookie that was even better than the one I remembered—really light and peanutty-tasting," Shelley reports.

To make the cookies with fresh peanut butter, shell a little more than half a cupful of roasted, unsalted peanuts and put them through your blender or food processor until they form a slightly lumpy paste. Of course, if you have a grocery or health food store that grinds peanut butter fresh, you can use that. And they're awfully good cookies with plain old jar peanut butter, too.

1½ cups sifted all-purpose
   flour
1 teaspoon baking soda
½ teaspoon salt
½ cup vegetable shortening
½ cup peanut butter
½ cup brown sugar
½ cup granulated sugar
1 egg, unbeaten
½ teaspoon vanilla extract

Preheat the oven to 375° F. Sift together the flour, baking soda, and salt.

With an electric mixer at medium speed, blend the shortening and peanut butter in a large bowl, then add the sugars gradually and cream. Add the egg and vanilla and continue to cream until the mix is light and fluffy. Turn the mixer to low speed and gradually add the flour, beating until just blended. (Don't forget to scrape the sides of your mixing bowl with a spatula during the beating process.)

Drop the cookies by the tablespoonful onto ungreased cookie sheets, spacing at least an inch apart. Bake in the preheated oven for 12 minutes.

Makes about 3 dozen.

FOOD FOR LOVE 2

I have friends who begin with pasta, and friends who begin with rice, but whenever I fall in love, I begin with potatoes. Sometimes meat and potatoes and sometimes fish and potatoes, but always potatoes. I have made a lot of mistakes falling in love, and regretted most of them, but never the potatoes that went with them.

—Nora Ephron, *Heartburn*

Ultimate Bread Pudding

No chapter on Valentine's desserts would be complete without a recipe for my sweetheart's favorite sweet, bread pudding. Nowhere does the rule of *de gustibus* seem to apply so strongly as it does to bread pudding, though. Folks tend to either love it or hate it. But when my friend Sarah Fritschner, food editor of the Louisville *Courier-Journal*, brought her version to a large party recently, virtually everyone begged for the recipe.

It's a gem not simply for its intoxicating taste but because it's so adaptable. Sarah used very dry, very crusty French bread, noting that the overnight soak makes the crusts tender so there's no need to cut them off (and waste them), as most bread pudding recipes advise you to do. She encourages you to use any sort of bread you have around, however, including leftover Danish or muffins, even toasted pound cake, if you're feeling decadent. (Sarah recommends you lessen the sugar added if you're using sweet breads, however.) You can also substitute buttermilk for the milk and cream.

But most of all, I wanted to include this recipe so I could share a story told me by my friend Molly Furlong of Louisville. About five decades ago, during World War II, Molly and a bunch of her friends were sitting on someone's front porch one Sunday afternoon, discussing ways to keep a frugal kitchen. Specifically, they were talking about what to do with stale bread.

"I think it was Shorty Jansen who spoke up and said that she always made her stale bread into bread pudding," Molly recalls.

"Then one of the other women in the group said, 'Well, nobody in my family will eat bread pudding.'

"And Shorty said, 'Neither will mine, but it takes care of the stale bread.'"

Had Shorty had this recipe, however, I doubt we'd have such a delightful story.

PUDDING

12 ounces day-old or fairly
  dry bread (8–12 cups)
4 eggs
2 teaspoons vanilla extract
1 cup sugar
3 cups milk
1 cup heavy cream
1 teaspoon cinnamon
½ cup raisins or currants
3 tablespoons bourbon
2 tablespoons butter,
  softened

Cut the bread up or use your hands to break it into small pieces. In a large bowl, beat the eggs, then add the vanilla and sugar and beat only enough to combine. Beat in the milk and cream, then stir in the cinnamon and raisins. Add the bread and the bourbon. Cover with plastic wrap and refrigerate at least 8 hours, preferably overnight.

When you are ready to bake, preheat the oven to 375° F. Lavishly grease a 9×13-inch baking pan with butter. Use your fingers to break up the bread some more. Pour the bread pudding into the baking pan and bake for 40 minutes, until set. Serve warm with bourbon sauce.

SAUCE

½ cup (1 stick) butter
1 egg
1 cup sugar
¼ cup heavy cream
¼ cup bourbon

For the sauce, melt the butter in the top pan of a double boiler. Beat the egg and sugar in a small bowl. Add to the butter along with the cream and heat gently over boiling water, stirring often, until the sugar is dissolved and the mixture is just beginning to thicken. Add the bourbon and serve immediately.

Makes enough pudding and sauce for 8 or more.

*O*range Chablis

This light, tart treat is a pleasant contrast to the heavier, richer sweets of the Valentine dessert orgy. It is also refreshing served ice-cold in the dead of summer. Ladle it from a cut-glass bowl into stemmed sherbet cups for a pretty presentation.

1½ cups Chablis or any
   light-bodied dry white
   wine
⅓ cup sugar
¼ teaspoon ground nutmeg
1 cinnamon stick
4 whole cloves
6 medium-sized oranges

In a serving bowl, stir the Chablis, sugar, and nutmeg until the sugar dissolves. Add the cinnamon and cloves and set aside. Peel the oranges with a knife so there is no white pith remaining on the outside. Slice into thin rounds, removing any seeds and center pith as you do. Place the oranges in the wine, cover tightly, and refrigerate for at least 6 hours, or overnight. Remove the cinnamon stick and cloves before serving.

Serves 12 or more.

"You kid!"

"Kiss me."

"Be mine."

What's Valentine's Day without these directives printed on tiny, chalky candy hearts? Not much, says Shelley Hamel, who admits that these are the one dessert she buys for her annual Valentine dessert party.

"I put them in bowls around the house and people pick them up and giggle over them and show them to each other. It's not that they really taste that great, although some people like them. But it's just not a real Valentine's celebration if you don't have those little fortune hearts."

Hot Pink Peppermint Ice Cream

What could be better for a Valentine's dessert than pink peppermint ice cream? Its color is festive, but even better is the taste, with a zippy bite that spreads pleasurably in the back of the mouth and lingers long after the ice cream is gone. If you like chocolate with your peppermint, melt 4 ounces semisweet chocolate in the top of a double boiler just before serving. Drizzle the hot chocolate over the ice-cold cream. It will harden into a tasty glaze. But frankly, I like this ice cream just as it is.

It's best to make the custard the day before you want to freeze it. If you want to make several batches, you can put the finished ice cream in plastic containers and keep in the freezer for a day or two.

2 eggs
3 cups half-and-half
1 cup sugar
⅛ teaspoon peppermint
 extract
3 drops red food coloring

Prepare a Donvier (see "Freezing Ice Cream," below) or other hand ice-cream maker with a capacity of 1 quart.

Heat water in the bottom of a double boiler until it boils.

Meantime, beat the eggs to blend the whites and yolks, then beat in the half-and-half until all is blended. Pour into the top pan of the double boiler and place over the boiling water in the bottom pan. Add the sugar and mix, stirring constantly. Keep the water in the bottom pan at a low boil as you stir the custard for 10 minutes, until it begins to thicken.

After 10 minutes, remove from the heat and pour into a ceramic or glass bowl. Add the peppermint, stir, and allow to come to room temperature. Cover securely and refrigerate for 8 hours or more.

When you are ready to freeze, add the red food coloring and stir the mixture well so it spreads evenly. Freeze according to your ice-cream maker's instructions, but allow at least 45 minutes to 1 hour for a good consistency.

Makes 1 quart; serves 4 to 6.

FREEZING ICE CREAM

We have an electric crank/bucket ice-cream maker, but it has been gathering dust in the basement ever since I picked up a hand-cranked Donvier Ice Cream Maker several years ago. I found it at a secondhand store, and since it was only ten dollars, I thought I'd give it a whirl even though I had my doubts about what it could produce. Now I would gladly pay the full retail price for a replacement, although it doesn't seem as if we'll be needing one for this sturdy little appliance, even though we use it frequently.

The Donvier and other ice-cream makers of its ilk don't use a mixture of ice and salt packed around a cylinder to freeze like their old-fashioned predecessors. Instead, it has a quick-chilling, nontoxic chemical sandwiched between the aluminum walls of its cylinder. You must freeze the cylinder for a good 7 hours before it is ready to use, and some folks complain that this is a problem. But I just keep mine in the freezer all the time.

Since mine is always ready, it's become the deus ex machina *that's resolved countless impromptu dinner parties with a stunning dessert. Although the peppermint ice cream here, like any ice cream using fresh eggs, requires cooking and then chilling several hours in advance, there are plenty of other ice creams and sorbets that can be made on the spot. Pureed fresh strawberries with sugar are simple and stunning. Add some half-and-half and you have strawberry ice cream. And with a can of cream of coconut in the cupboard, I am always prepared to serve unexpected guests a tropical treat (see page 157).*

The ice cream takes about 45 minutes to chill, needing to be stirred every 3 or 4 minutes. I find that guests like to watch the process, and though the stirring is child's play (especially compared to the hard work of the hand-crank machines of yore), most folks like to take a turn or two.

Three

Persian
New Year

Like many ancient cultures, Iranians celebrate the new year not on an arbitrary calendar date but on the day of the vernal equinox. And because of this, the traditions and rituals of the holiday focus on the idea of rebirth and new life.

The equinox arrives sometime between March 20 and 22. In the days prior to it, the house is cleaned thoroughly and a table or carpet is covered in a richly textured cloth and set with symbolic items including seven foods.

Each food represents a principle of life. A plate of fresh sprouts symbolizes rebirth, an apple dish represents health and beauty, and a dish of vinegar is for age and patience.

The Koran and a book of poems by Hafez, the most revered

of Sufi poets, are part of the setting. There is a bowl of colored eggs for fertility, coins for prosperity, a mirror for reflecting on creation, candles, and a goldfish in a bowl.

In her beautiful book *The New Food of Life* (Mage Publishers, 1992), Najmieh Batmanglij says the fish is there to represent not only life but the end of the astral year in the sign of Pisces. Nowruz, which is the name of this holiday, honors both the beginning and the end, destruction and rebirth.

For Anoosh Shariat and other Iranians now living in the United States, separated from a homeland that has changed dramatically in their lifetimes, the New Year becomes a celebration of both the powerful and ancient culture that is a part of them and the new life they have established here.

WAITING FOR THE EQUINOX

Anoosh Shariat left Iran at the age of fourteen. This was in the early 1970s, and the law at that time was that boys fifteen and older could not leave the country without serving time in the military. So families that could sent their young sons to Europe before conscription time. Anoosh went to Germany to study and live with a brother who was already there.

But though he left his native country behind, he didn't leave his passion for Persian food and culture. He carried those things with him, and they influenced him deeply as he came of age, both as a person and as a chef.

Anoosh began cooking out of need. He doesn't eat meat and was used to the subtle and delicious vegetarian dishes his mother, an accomplished cook and hostess, made in Iran.

"I was a picky eater. I didn't want to eat the hot dogs of Germany, so I had to learn to make my own food," he says.

But soon it became his vocation.

He studied with traditional Continental chefs in Germany, then moved to Texas, where he added Southwestern flair and the Southern American cooking of his wife, Sharron, to his repertoire. New American cuisine with its emphasis on fresh and scrumptious local produce appealed to his eye and palate both. And when the couple finally opened their restaurant, Shariat's, in Louisville, Kentucky, in the early 1990s, it was an eclectic blend of all of these elements that made up the menu.

But it's not eclecticism that calls the shots when the Shariats set the festive table to celebrate the Persian New Year. It is tradition, with just a few contemporary twists.

The Shariats met in Dallas, and as a young married couple there in the 1980s, they often celebrated the New Year with friends in the Iranian community.

"Sometimes it was a gathering of friends at someone's home," Sharron says. "One year it was a really nice party at a Dallas hotel where they brought in a band from the L.A. area—there's a huge Iranian population in Orange County—and everyone danced to traditional music."

In addition, the couple would set the symbolic Persian New Year's table and usually have a celebration in their home with friends.

"A lot of our friends were in mixed marriages, plus Iranian couples and American couples," says Sharron. "But this is a celebration that everyone could respond to, no matter their background. Instead of being a big, loud party like the traditional New Year in the United States, the Persian New Year is quieter and more family-oriented. It's a celebration of friends.

"Instead of drinking and carrying on, Anoosh and his Iranian friends like to read poetry for the New Year, Persian poetry, which is so philosophical."

When they moved to Louisville, however, the pressures of running their own restaurant and starting a family overwhelmed the Shariats at first. The New Year was still acknowledged, but their celebrations were less elaborate.

Now, however, that their children, Arian, five, and Danielle, three, are old enough to participate, the Shariats are emphasizing the celebration in their home.

"In part I want to celebrate the Persian New Year so our children will share their father's background, but there's something about the event that is very aesthetically and spiritually satisfying to me as well," says Sharron, whose background was fairly eclectic, including formative years on the fringes of the arts counterculture in Woodstock, New York.

"A few weeks before the holiday, we sprout seeds—mung beans, lentils, or wheat. There is a plate of sprouts for each child, and so they get involved in that even before the New Year is here," Anoosh says.

The sprouts will be placed on the ceremonial table along with the other foods. They will definitely have a goldfish on the table, purchased by Anoosh just for the occasion, although he confesses, "I forget exactly what it is the goldfish stands for, but it is so beautiful on the table, swimming in the water. And there is a belief that at just the moment when the New Year is here, the fish stops swimming and stands still in the water. When we were kids we would watch for that."

The exact moment of the turning of the Persian year is anticipated much as revelers anticipate the exact stroke of midnight on the January 1 New Year. But the equinox may not arrive until sometime in the wee hours of the morning.

"When I was a child, sometimes they would get us up in the middle of the night for the New Year. And everyone would jump out of bed and change quickly into new clothes bought just for the year. You must greet the year in brand-new clothes," Anoosh says.

That this tradition is still important to Anoosh is something Sharron marvels at: "My husband simply does not shop for clothes. It is not something he ever does. But at the New Year, he always takes the kids out and buys them new clothes, which for him to do is a major event."

Poetry is still Anoosh's favorite way to spend those hours of waiting for the New Year: "It is very beautiful and moving, the poetry of Persia. And for us, the poetry of Hafez is also sacred. It is usually his poetry which we read for the New Year. And some people use the book as a way of telling your fortune. You open it randomly and put your finger on the page, and whatever you find there is a message for you about the coming year.

"We also celebrate the longest night of the year, and then we get together with friends and read poetry all through the darkest part of that night. And you eat the last of the harvest's vegetables on that night."

For the New Year, though, it won't be the last of the vegetables that the family eats. Instead it will be foods from Anoosh's childhood, prepared with new variations—a blend of both the ancient and the new life.

Saffron Chicken

This is a subtly seasoned chicken dish, just right for spring eating. The skewered chicken can be grilled on a regular grill but is perfectly suited for a small hibachi, which can be tucked up on a porch should the weather turn unpredictable. If the weather is just downright ornery, grill these under a broiler flame.

½ teaspoon saffron threads
2 tablespoons plain yogurt
¼ cup onion, chopped very fine
6 chicken breast halves (about 4 ounces each), bone removed but skin on
Salt to taste
Freshly ground black pepper to taste

Crush the saffron with mortar and pestle and soak for a few minutes in 1 teaspoon warm water. Mix with the yogurt, and mix in the onion.

Toss the chicken in the yogurt, coating each breast, cover, and marinate at room temperature for 20 minutes. Lay the chicken on the grill over medium coals and cook until done, turning carefully once. It should be done in 10 to 12 minutes. Add salt and pepper to taste. Serve with Saffron Steamed Rice (recipe follows).

Serves 6.

Saffron Steamed Rice

Saffron is one of Iran's most esteemed exports and an essential ingredient in many traditional dishes. This is a classic with a slightly more complicated method of preparation than usual. The point is to create a pot of perfectly fluffy rice fragrantly suffused with the flavor of saffron and accented by the crisped crust that forms on the bottom of the pot and is served on the side.

2½ cups basmati or long-grain rice
3½ tablespoons salt
½ cup (1 stick) unsalted butter
¼ teaspoon crushed saffron threads in 1 tablespoon warm water

The night before you are going to prepare the rice, rinse it 3 times in warm water, then soak overnight in cold water to cover with 1½ tablespoons salt.

When you are ready to prepare, set 2 quarts water with 2 tablespoons salt to boil in a 4-quart pan with a snug-fitting lid. Pour off the soaking water from the rice, then add the rice to the boiling water and cook, uncovered, for 10 minutes. Pour into a strainer and rinse the rice with warm water.

Wipe out the pot and add enough water to just cover the bottom (about ½ cup) and the butter. Bring to a boil over medium-high heat. As the liquid begins to boil, lower the heat and sprinkle the rice into the pot, distributing evenly and creating a slightly mounded cone shape with the rice. Be careful not to pack the rice closely, since you want the steam to circulate freely. Use a chopstick or the handle of a spatula or mixing spoon to make 5 or 6 vent holes in the mound of rice.

Put the lid on, and when the pan starts to steam, turn the heat low and cook for about 15 minutes.

The rice can be served immediately or, if you want, can be removed from the heat and kept tightly covered for up to 30 minutes.

When ready to serve, use a spatula or wide spoon to carefully scoop the rice onto a platter, being careful not to break apart the grains. Drizzle the saffron water over the top of the rice and fluff lightly with a fork.

The crust at the bottom of the pan is also scooped out and served on the side.

Serves 6.

NOTE: Anoosh says this dish "serves 6 healthy persons," but there may well be leftovers. It is delicious for breakfast the next day mixed into soft-scrambled eggs.

Grilled Eggplant with Pomegranate-Walnut Sauce

Smoky eggplant set off with the sweet tang of pomegranate-walnut sauce can be a meal in itself with rice. But it's also the perfect accompaniment to Saffron Chicken. Toast the eggplant as soon as the coals are ready, then grill the chicken. If grilling over coals isn't possible, you can do the eggplant, like the chicken, under the broiler flame.

Some cooks dismiss the tradition of salting and pressing eggplant slices to remove excess moisture and diminish bitter taste as an old wives' tale. But as is often the case with old wives' tales, recent research shows this one has merit. It is also a tradition with this dish.

Pomegranate juice is available in many groceries and health food stores. If you simply can't find it, use unsweetened cranberry juice.

3 medium-sized eggplants
Salt

1 medium-sized onion
Olive oil
½ cup walnuts, finely
　ground
½ cup pomegranate juice
1 tablespoon red wine
　vinegar
1 tablespoon honey
2 teaspoons tomato paste
2 cups water (or chicken
　stock)
Salt to taste
Freshly ground black
　pepper to taste

Olive oil

Peel the eggplants, cut in half, and slice ½ inch thick. Sprinkle salt liberally on both sides of slices and place in a colander over a bowl or pot. Let sit for 1 to 1½ hours.

While the eggplant is "sweating," prepare the sauce. Chop the onion fine and sauté in a little olive oil in a medium-sized saucepan over medium heat until lightly browned. Add the walnuts and sauté just a few minutes, enough to coat with oil and bring out the fragrance. Mix the pomegranate juice, vinegar, honey, tomato paste, and water to blend, then add to the pan with the onions and nuts. Let cook, uncovered, over medium-low heat for 35 to 45 minutes, until the liquid has thickened. Add salt and freshly ground pepper to taste. Process in a blender until smooth.

When you are ready to prepare the eggplant, rinse to remove the salt. Lay the slices on 3 thicknesses of paper towels. Cover with more paper towels, 3 thick, and press gently but firmly to remove moisture. Brush with olive oil and grill over moderately hot coals for 10 to 15 minutes, turning every 5 minutes or so, until tender and browned.

Lay the eggplant in a shallow casserole. Spread the sauce over the eggplant and serve immediately.

Serves 6.

Four

Easter

Pastel bunnies and gaily decorated eggs are the most common contemporary symbols of Easter. Both hark back to ancient spring equinox celebrations, ritual reminders of the cycle of rebirth and the fecundity of the earth.

Modern Easter observances are often festive parties whose main purpose is to celebrate the promise of warm weather. Egg hunts are staged outside in the first spring grass. New clothes for the new season are worn with pride. Children (and their parents) gorge themselves on baskets of candy, and family dinners have a picnic feel about them.

In the hoopla, the finery, the sugar surges, it is sometimes easy to lose track of the religious import of this holiday. For Christians, however, it should be the most significant of all.

Christmas garners the lion's share of attention, and there is something particularly magical in a holiday that marks the birth of a child. But it is Easter that commemorates the most important tenet of the Christian belief, the promise of resurrection, of life after death.

EASTER OF LIGHT

"I am the light of the world," Christ said.

For Sandra Mlinarcik, growing up in a Polish Catholic family on the South Side of Chicago in the 1950s, the annual Easter celebration was, in fact, a literal celebration of darkness transformed to light.

"When I was growing up," Sandra recalls, "you would go on the Saturday before Easter to make your confession, and stand in a darkened church; the church cold and smelling of incense. The statues would be shrouded in purple cloth, and it would seem as if the people were shrouded, too. Everyone was solemn and silent—more so than at any other time. And everything was so dark. You would stand in line and try to make the best confession of the year.

"Then when you came back on Sunday—oh my! The lilies! The candles! The statues unshrouded! The church was full of light and the fragrance of flowers, the feeling of spring. That contrast between darkness and light, from fasting to the feast, from death to rebirth—that is what Easter is to me."

The drama of the holiday was underscored by the Easter food ritual in the Mlinarcik household and neighborhood.

"Where I grew up was kind of like an ethnic ghetto—everyone around was Polish and mostly Catholic. My mother's parents spoke seven different languages. My grandmother was raised in a convent. We lived with my mother's parents for some time when I was a child, and then we lived nearby, so the rituals were ingrained in our family and also a part of the community.

"Prior to Easter Sunday, there was the forty-day Lenten fast. We didn't eat meat then, but it wasn't so much what you gave up—it was that the meals altogether were simpler. The adults would have one meal a day and then the other two meals that they ate were so small, they didn't even add up to a meal together. And there was a very real sense of doing without.

"But along with it, there was this extraordinary sense of anticipation.

"It's the custom to fast the night before Easter and until after the Mass on Sunday. And I guess your sense of deprivation and your anticipation are heightened because on that Saturday the house is filled with the smell of food cooking for the next day, for the big Easter buffet after Mass.

"On Saturday you would take to church a basket with bits of all the foods that you were going to serve the next day. These baskets would be shrouded, too, covered with a cloth and dark and mysterious. And, inside, you would have a little bit of everything so the priest could bless it. And this was called the Swieconka.

"On Sunday after Mass, you break your fast with first a bite of these blessed foods. And everyone who comes to your house for the buffet would do the same, taking a bit from the Swieconka. People in the neighborhood would go from house to house all day, eating from one another's buffets.

"And after all the darkness and the fasting, and the smelling things being prepared, but not tasting—oh, to suddenly look on that buffet! There was butter in the shape of a lamb, and good rye bread, with horseradish and boiled eggs and the salt for them. When I got older and had Jewish friends, it struck me: the similarities between our Easter meal and the seder for Passover.

"And then there was my grandparents' homemade Polish sausage. We would have all helped to make it, and the whole time have been dreaming of eating it. It was very simple—just pork, salt, pepper, and garlic. None of these spices or celery salt or that stuff like you get at the store now. But it was so delicious and it was always served with the horseradish.

"And we'd have pickled beets, cold, and then, of course, *kapusta*, which is sauerkraut the Polish way. It would have been cooking all Saturday with sliced onion in it, and vinegar and brown sugar, garlic and pepper. And your nose would have been filled all that day and night with the anticipation of tasting it with the sausage.

"But most incredible for a child was the array of sweets—all these candies and delicacies you'd denied yourself during Lent. And best of all, we would always have a cake in the shape of a lamb. It was standing up: pound cake baked in a mold and decorated with this thick white butter-cream frosting, with eyes and nose of raisins or black jelly beans. I can picture it, with a red ribbon and a bell around its neck and the flag of Poland in the tail. And it was such a wonder to look at and then to taste.

"And that whole ritual of first fasting and then putting all these tastes and foods into your mouth was like coming alive again. That Easter feast was the resurrection for me."

And it still is, Sandra says, although her understanding of what the feast means and how she presents it has changed as her life has changed.

"I left home at eighteen to live on campus at Loyola, graduated in June 1968, and married in March of '69. We lived in Rochester, New York, for a while and then in the Finger Lakes region, way out in the country. I remember being afraid to go outside and hang my wash because I couldn't see anybody when I was out there, and that made me, a real city girl, scared.

"After that, we moved to a remote cove in Nova Scotia, then to Syracuse, New York, where my husband and I divorced."

During that odyssey, Sandra was not the devout Catholic girl of her Chicago childhood. In fact, for a few years before her divorce, her husband was a member of an Eastern religious sect, and the religious rituals they practiced reflected that more than those of Sandra's traditional upbringing. But even when she was not practicing the other aspects of her faith, Sandra observed the Easter meal.

"Somehow I always managed to have a meal that echoed that buffet of my childhood. Even once when we were camping in the snow in Shenandoah National Park, I still brought sausage, bread, and hard-boiled eggs. And when I was growing up, we would always have *krupnik*, a spiced sweet vodka. Of course, I didn't have that with me in the park, or any way of making it, but I had blackberry brandy instead. And I took this food and blessed it myself and ate."

It was after her separation from her first husband that Sandra began to reclaim the full traditional meal of her youth, and the concept of resurrection took on a new meaning for her.

"During my marriage, the Easter celebration was something I did almost privately. My husband didn't really understand it or share in it, and I couldn't bring it out in the open, but I also couldn't give it up. Then that first year we were separated, I realized it was something I wanted to share with other people. So I crammed friends into my little apartment in Syracuse, and I tried to remember the recipes and to re-create them—and in a way it was like I was taking back my life again, being resurrected as myself. And in the process, I was creating a family for me, too."

The tradition continues today at Sandra's home in Louisville, Kentucky, with some twenty to thirty friends and family members there for the traditional Polish buffet each Easter.

"For me, the celebration of Easter is as big or bigger than the celebration of Christmas. I have a box of decorations. I put little wooden eggs on the fig tree and have candles with Easter symbols. I cut branches and put them in bud vases, forcing them to bloom—like the flowers in the church when I was a child. And the house is full of Easter lilies and sparkling with the candles' light.

"The preparation of the food itself is for me a part of preparing for Easter. It's kind of like prayer in movement—the chopping, the getting it together, the anticipation of what the holiday means. And in the process, I feel myself growing spiritually, coming to terms with my beliefs."

In recent years the holiday has taken on yet another dimension, another interpretation of rebirth, for Sandra.

"Now that a lot of the older people in my family have died, I am the person that the food traditions have evolved to. My mother usually comes to my house for Easter every year, as well as my sister's and my brother's families.

"In some ways, I've become my grandparents. And it's true to say that as I prepare for the meal, I feel the presence of my grandparents *in* me when I do it. It is very much a ritual of continuance, of resurrection. And because they continue on in me, it is literally a celebration of everlasting life."

◇ **Easter Polish Sausage**

The Polish sausage Sandra Mlinarcik's grandparents made was not the coarsely ground, very spicy hard sausage you find sold in most grocery stores as kielbasa.

"It had a finer texture and there was no spice. It was just fresh pork, garlic, salt, and pepper ground together with handfuls of chopped ice thrown in to give it a good consistency, then stuffed into the pig intestines," she says.

If you live in Chicago or another city with a large Polish population, you can likely readily find just such sausage. Or you may be able to do what Sandy has done in Louisville: find a local sausage maker who will make the links to those specifications.

("But I have to really ride herd on him," she sighs. "Every year or so he tries to sneak just a little of some spice or another in there. It's hard to keep a good sausage maker from putting his own personal stamp on his product.")

If you have no luck on the handmade sausage front but want to serve a Polish-style Easter buffet, I had very good results by simply buying fine-quality plain pork bratwursts and simmering them very lightly for 30 minutes with several split cloves of garlic in the water. Slices of the meat with slivers of rye bread, followed by bites of sauerkraut or beets and a sip of sweet, lethal *krupnik*, make for a festive meal indeed.

Kapusta

Sauerkraut the Polish way is one of those recipes that defies reduction to cups and teaspoons, Sandra says. So much depends on the quality of the kraut you begin with and the preferences of the cook who presides. What she does say with conviction is that the dish must cook for a full day, simmering on the back of the stove, being stirred and tasted and doctored several times in the process.

"A lot of Polish cooks throw in pork bone or sausage, and some people make a paste of browned flour to thicken it," Sandra says.

"But that makes it heavy, and that's not what you want. What you want is for the *kapusta* [kuh-POOHS-tuh] to have a crisp, clean bite that's a contrast to the rich sausage."

The proportions here are meant to be merely guidelines. Add more or less to your taste and as you go.

1 quart glass jar of
  sauerkraut
1 cup (2 sticks) butter
¼ cup brown sugar
¼ cup apple cider vinegar
1 large onion, diced
Salt to taste
Freshly ground black
  pepper to taste
½ cup vodka

In a colander, rinse the sauerkraut and let it drain.

In a large saucepan, melt the butter over medium heat. Add the sugar and vinegar and stir until the sugar dissolves. Add the kraut, onion, and 1 quart of water and cook over medium heat until the kraut mixture just begins to bubble.

Turn the heat to low, cover, and simmer for about an hour. Taste and add salt and freshly ground pepper. Continue to simmer for 6 hours or so over low heat, adding more water if necessary and adjusting the seasonings to your taste. Sandra says that the kraut should have an interplay of sweet and sour and that it should taste "clean."

Add the vodka in the last hour of simmering. Taste again and adjust the seasonings for the final time.

Kapusta can be made the day before, stored in the refrigerator in a covered glass or ceramic container, and gently warmed before serving.

Makes a side dish for 8 or more.

NOTE: It's important to use kraut that is packed in a jar, not in cans, Sandra says, and I'm inclined to agree. The canned kraut not only seems to have a funny whang in its taste but doesn't seem to be as crisp and sturdy as the glassed kraut, so it doesn't stand up to the long, slow cooking as well. Since Passover and Easter are close in time, you may be able to find kosher kraut, which is almost always of good quality.

The presence of clay eggs in prehistoric tombs suggests that since earliest time, people have regarded the egg as a symbol of immortality. Ancient Persians gave one another eggs at the spring equinox—a token of the earth's rebirth during that season. Christians incorporated the symbol into their Easter celebration, along with other pagan rituals. (Even the name Easter is derived from Eostre, the Anglo-Saxon goddess of dawn and rebirth.)

Dyeing the eggs of Easter is a universal practice among Christians, although styles vary from the blood-red eggs of Greece to the intricate patterns and designs of Ukraine.

Contemporary Americans seem to favor pastel hues and bunny decals from dye kits purchased at the store, but it hasn't always been so. When Margaret Harding was a young girl in southwestern Louisiana, she and her Cajun cousins still dyed eggs the old-fashioned way.

"The first thing we'd do is gather together leaves from trees. The chinaball tree would make the prettiest greens. And then there were certain flowers that would give you colors. And of course, the juice from beets would make the most beautiful purple-red. And you'd boil these things in water, with a little vinegar, and then just drop the egg in and take it out when it was as dark as you wanted."

But her favorite was the delicate ecru patterns made when an egg was dyed wrapped in golden onion skin.

"You use a room-temperature egg and you wrap the onion skin around it as best you can. Then you put that in the toe of an old sock, or wrap it up with some light cloth or cheesecloth, being careful that the onion skin stays wrapped around the egg. You tie that little package up—you can use those plastic twist bread ties now. They work just fine. And you lay it gently in a pan of water with some vinegar in it and bring it all to an easy boil. Let it boil for fifteen or twenty minutes, then take it out with a big spoon and let it cool before you unwrap it. Pat it dry real easy like—just buff it so you don't mess the patterns. See, it looks like old lace."

Cwikla

3 cups sliced cooked beets (canned beets are fine)
8 whole cloves or ½ teaspoon caraway seeds
1 tablespoon grated fresh horseradish (if not available, prepared horseradish that is not creamed can be used)
2 cups white vinegar
1 tablespoon brown sugar
2 teaspoons salt

Drain the beets. (Set the juice aside to use for dyeing eggs, if you wish. See page 74 for instructions.)

Lay 1 cup of the beets in the bottom of a large glass bowl and scatter four cloves or half the caraway seeds on them. Sprinkle half the horseradish over the beets. Lay another cup of beets over the first, and top with the rest of the spice and horseradish. Top with the third cup of beets.

In a saucepan, mix the vinegar, sugar, and salt and bring to a boil. Boil for 2 minutes, then pour over the beets. Cover the bowl and refrigerate for at least 24 hours.

Serves 12.

Poppy Seed Kluski

"Curiouser and curiouser," Alice once said. She might well have been talking about this noodle dish. Its slight sweetness seems strange at first, and the crunch of the poppy seeds is quite unusual, but the flavor is oddly appealing.

Sandra Mlinarcik says Poppy Seed Kluski was not a family recipe but was popular with others in her Polish Catholic community in Chicago. It is still served in Poland—most often on Christmas Eve. But Sandra has added it to the Easter buffet, and its unique sweet/tart flavor really works nicely with the rich sausage and the bite of both sauerkraut and beets.

There is a shortcut version made with canned poppy seed pastry filling, but I found it far too sweet and cloying. This variation harks back more closely to the traditional old-country way and really isn't much trouble at all, although everything should be assembled just when you are ready to serve.

Kluski noodles are available at most supermarkets. They're an egg noodle about ⅛ inch wide and about 2 inches long. Any similarly sized pasta can be used.

2 tablespoons poppy seeds
2 cups dry kluski egg
   noodles
2 tablespoons butter
1 tablespoon honey
1 teaspoon lemon juice
½ teaspoon grated lemon
   zest

In a small saucepan, bring ½ cup water to a boil; pour in the poppy seeds. Stir and remove from the heat. Cover and let sit for 10 minutes. Strain. (Nope, I don't have a strainer with holes small enough to keep the poppy seeds from falling through, either. I use a coffee filter in my strainer. A paper towel would also work.)

Cook the noodles in 2 quarts boiling water for approximately 10 minutes, to al dente stage. While they are cooking, prepare the poppy seed dressing.

In a small saucepan, melt the butter and honey together over low heat. When the mixture begins to bubble, add the strained poppy seed. Remove from the heat and, using a heavy wooden spoon, mash the seed in the butter-honey mixture, lightly crushing it. Add the lemon juice and zest; stir.

When the noodles are ready, drain and turn out into a flat, wide bowl. Pour the poppy seed dressing over them and toss to coat the noodles. Serve immediately.

Serves 6 as a side dish.

In Sandra Mlinarcik's Polish neighborhood in Chicago, the old folks called it bicz jajki, *which meant, literally, "beat eggs." But the kids often referred to it as "war eggs." In Lafayette, Louisiana, Margaret Harding and her Cajun kin called it "pah-kay," although in other parishes it might be called "pahk-pahk," both a corruption of the French word for Easter,* Paques. *And my Italian-American sister-in-law from Baltimore, Debbie Jones, née Buono, grew up saying she and her cousins were going to "pick eggs."*

But no matter how you say it, the ritual is the same. Each person chooses a hard-boiled Easter egg to be his or hers. (Sandra said her grandfather would test them by tapping the eggs against his front teeth to find the hardest.)

Two contestants proceed to tap the ends of their eggs against each other until one of the eggshells cracks. The tapper with the unbroken egg is the winner and can claim the other's egg as a prize. You continue tapping until all the eggs but one are broken, and the holder of that one is declared champion.

In my family, we'd call it egg salad.

Krupnik

The honey and spices in this traditional vodka drink "soften it just a little bit so it feels really good going down," Sandra says. She is right. I made this for a buffet one Sunday and watched a fifth disappear in no time. The sweet heady flavor was a perfect complement to the savory smoked trout appetizer it sat next to. I suggest serving it in cordial glasses, since it packs a deceptive wallop. And keep just a little hidden in a cupboard so the cook is sure to have a sip or two when the guests have all gone home.

1½ cups honey
1 teaspoon vanilla extract
¼ teaspoon ground nutmeg
2 cinnamon sticks
2 whole cloves
3 strips lemon peel, each
  about 2 inches long
750 milliliters very good
  vodka

In a large saucepan, combine the honey with ⅔ cup water, the vanilla, spices, and lemon peel. Bring to a boil over high heat. Cover, turn the heat down to medium, and simmer for 5 minutes. Remove from the heat and immediately add the vodka. Stir and then pour into a large ceramic or glass pitcher. Cool, then cover. Let it stand for at least 24 hours, up to 3 or 4 days. Strain to remove the spices. May be warmed very gently or chilled for serving.

Makes enough for a dozen folks to sip.

Crusty Rye Loaf

If you are serious about baking breads, or if you are enraptured by crisp crust on your bread or homemade pizzas, then you want to have a baking stone. This unglazed ceramic-tile circle or square is used instead of a baking pan, and the crust you achieve with one is worth the investment.

Sandra says it was the quality of the crust—dense and chewy—that distinguished the rye bread she had as a child from the less crusty rye bread you find in most grocery stores and American bakeries today. If you don't want to bother with baking the bread, I suggest you try to find a European-style bakery where chewy crust is considered an art.

This recipe is based on the Round Country Bread recipe in Franco Galli's *The Il Fornaio Baking Book* (Chronicle Books, 1992). It also owes much to *The Tassajara Bread Book* by Edward Espe Brown (Shambhala, 1970), which taught me *why* we need homemade bread as well as *how* to knead it. Both are essential texts if you are serious about bread.

STARTER

½ teaspoon active dry
  yeast
¼ cup warm water
  (105°–110° F.)
2½ cups unbleached bread
  flour
¾ cup water

The day before you are ready to bake, make the starter. Dissolve the ½ teaspoon yeast in the ¼ cup warm water. (Use a candy thermometer to be sure of water temperature.) Set aside for 15 minutes. Measure the 2½ cups flour into a large bowl. When the yeast is ready, make a well in the center of the flour with a wooden spoon. Pour the yeast and the ¾ cup water into the well, then stir until thoroughly combined. The dough will be sticky and difficult to stir, but all ingredients must be well blended together. Put in a container that can be covered tightly and store in the refrigerator

BREAD

¾ cup starter
1½ teaspoons active dry
  yeast
½ cup warm water
  (105°–110° F.)
7 cups rye flour
1 tablespoon salt
2¾ cups water
½ cup unbleached bread
  flour for kneading (about)
¼ cup caraway seed
Olive oil
1 tablespoon cornmeal

for 24 hours, allowing it to ferment slowly.

On the day you are ready to bake, dip out ¾ cup of the starter. Set aside so it can come to room temperature. (Leftover starter can be frozen in ¾-cup portions and used in future recipes. Thaw before using.)

Dissolve the 1½ teaspoons yeast in the ½ cup warm water (again, use a candy thermometer to be sure of temperature) and set aside for 15 minutes.

Measure the rye flour into a large bowl, sprinkle the salt over it, and use a wooden spoon to mix together. Make a well in the center of the flour. When the yeast is ready, put it in the well with starter and water. Mix together with a wooden spoon until you can't stir it easily anymore.

Lightly flour one hand with the unbleached bread flour and begin kneading the dough in the bowl. With your floured hand, lift the edge of the dough farthest from you over the rest, then press down firmly with the heel of your hand. With your other hand, turn the bowl one quarter rotation clockwise, then repeat the kneading motion with your floured hand. Continue briskly for 5 minutes, occasionally picking up the whole ball of dough and slapping it back into the bowl. Enjoy yourself. (The dough will be sticky, but that's okay. You can sprinkle a little flour on your kneading hand if too much dough starts to stick to it, but don't use too much.) When the dough pulls away easily from the sides of the bowl, you're ready for the next step.

Lightly flour a sturdy work surface (a big wooden cutting board is good) and turn the dough out onto it. Add any dough stuck to your hands to the dough ball.

Knead the dough for 15 to 20 minutes, until it is soft and elastic. Knead by folding toward the center the edge of the dough closest to you, pressing it in firmly with the heel of your hand as you do. Then turn the dough a quarter rotation and repeat. I like to alternate hands so it doesn't get tiring. You need to rest for a minute every 5 minutes or so, and so does the dough. (Lately I've been using a kitchen timer to gauge how long I've been kneading and when to rest. But in the days of vinyl records, I used to put on a favorite up-tempo disc and knead for the duration of a side, stopping every two songs to rest a bit. If you want to try this, bear in mind that most New Age music is too mellow and head-banging music too intense for good kneading. I think some solid rhythm and blues is best.)

The final time you knead, sprinkle the caraway seeds over the dough and work them in. When they are incorporated, shape the dough into a ball.

Oil a large bowl and place the dough in it, turning it so it is well coated with the oil. Cover the bowl with a clean cloth and place someplace warm (75°–80° F.) and draft-free to rise for 1½ hours.

Fold the edges of the dough in toward the center, pressing down lightly. Turn over so the top is smooth, cover again with the cloth, and let rise until doubled—about an hour.

Lightly flour the work surface and turn the dough out onto it, then divide into 2 roughly equal portions. Working with one at a time, fold the edges of the dough in toward the center, much as you did when kneading the bread, but not pressing down much this time. Do this several times around each portion of bread, creating a ball with a smooth side.

Sprinkle cornmeal lightly over a baking sheet with no sides and place the loaves on it, rough sides down. Cover and allow to rise for 45 minutes. While the bread is rising, place the baking stone (if you are using one) in the oven. Preheat the oven to 425° F.

If you are not using the baking stone, you may simply place the baking sheet with the loaves in the oven. If you are using the baking stone, you need to slide the loaves carefully off the baking sheet and onto the stone without removing the stone from the oven. You can pull the rack the stone is on out some to give you access. Leave ample space between the loaves so the hot air can circulate evenly around them.

Allow the loaves to bake for 5 minutes, then turn the temperature to 400° F. Bake for 40 to 50 minutes more, or until the loaf sounds hollow when rapped on top with your knuckles. Remove the loaves to wire racks and allow to cool completely before slicing or wrapping in a clean cloth to store. Because it is crusty, this bread keeps nicely for a day or two.

Makes 2 loaves.

The Tassajara Bread Book could be subtitled Zen and the Art of Bread Baking. It has wonderful recipes, but is most important because it gently instructs the reader in the spiritual lessons to be learned and practiced while making bread.

Zen teaches its practitioners not only to accept mistakes and learn from them but to love them.

When I made my first batch of this rye bread (with no caraway seeds), my house was too cold and my time too limited to give the bread a good, full rise. Consequently, the loaves I baked were squat and hefty, not full and light. But when we cut into one, the bread itself was extremely dense and moist and earthy with the fragrance of the rye and the sour of the starter all mingled together. Sliced super-thin and topped with fresh creamy butter, it was delicious and satisfying. It also served well as a base for slices of Polish sausage; and with a bowl of steamy fresh vegetable soup, it made a perfect evening meal. And much as I like the loaves I later baked properly, it was that dense and fallen failure that I loved the most.

Lamb Cake

This is a traditional pound cake that for Easter was baked in a pan in the shape of a lamb, then frosted with butter cream. Some cookware stores still carry the lamb pans, but if you don't have one, you can bake this in a 10-inch tube pan and decorate it with colorful Easter candies.

Pound cake got its name from early recipes that used a pound each of the main ingredients. Some adjustments in measuring yield a better cake, however.

Perhaps it's still called pound cake to remind you that if you tried to beat this cake by hand, you would most likely feel as if your arm had been pounded by the time you were done. It really shouldn't be attempted without an electric mixer. There is no rising agent in the batter—the cake rises from the air that is beaten into it. Because of this, it's important to complete each step quickly and move promptly on to the next one and to pour the batter into the pan as soon as it is ready.

Sandra Mlinarcik's cake was plain, but this one has orange added for citrus zip.

CAKE

10 large eggs

2 cups (1 pound) unsalted butter

2 cups sugar

4½ cups sifted all-purpose flour

½ teaspoon salt

1 teaspoon vanilla extract

¼ cup fresh orange juice

1 tablespoon grated orange zest

Butter the lamb pan or 10-inch tube pan and line with waxed paper. Preheat the oven to 325° F. Get out the large bowl for your electric mixer and an even larger bowl for mixing the final batter.

Separate the eggs into 2 smaller bowls and allow them and the butter to come to room temperature. (Butter shouldn't be mushy, however, just malleable.)

In the large bowl of an electric mixer, cream the butter and sugar until fluffy and very light. Add the egg yolks a few at a time, beating well after each addition. Mix the flour with the salt, then add about 1 cup at a time, beating well after each addition and scraping down the sides of the mixing bowl to make sure the batter is thoroughly blended.

Add the vanilla and then drizzle in the orange juice, mixing all the while. Add the orange zest and mix in.

Transfer the batter to the larger bowl, wash the large mixer bowl, and dry thoroughly. In the cleaned mixer bowl, beat the egg whites to stiff and shiny peaks. Using a large rubber spatula, fold half the whites into the rest of the batter. Make sure the whites are thoroughly incorporated, but don't overbeat. Repeat.

Turn the batter out into the pan. Bake on the center rack in the preheated oven for 1½ hours, until the top is brown and the sides have pulled away from the edges of the pan. Cool in the pan for 10 minutes on a wire rack, then invert and remove the pan. Cool completely before frosting.

ICING

3 cups confectioner's sugar
⅓ cup butter
3 tablespoons half-and-half
1 teaspoon vanilla extract

Sift the sugar into a bowl. Heat the butter and half-and-half over low heat until the butter is melted. Whisk in the vanilla. Pour over the sugar and beat until the mixture is very smooth and spreadable. Ice the cake. If using the lamb mold, decorate with chocolate or black licorice candies for the eyes, nose, and toes, red licorice whips for the mouth. (Paper Polish flag in the tail is optional.)

Serves 10 to 12.

THE COSMOS HAS TEETH

We have come together as we do every Sunday at 7:30,
At Dooley's farm, to discuss the Bible,
Specifically, the Book of Hosea,
Prophecies uttered around 740 B.C.
Many meals ago.
"Like grapes in the desert, I found Israel;
Like the first fruits of the fig tree
In its prime," Kevin reads.
Mary brings in food—cheese, crackers,
apple slices, peanuts.
The reading stops as Kevin, in his Big Smith overalls,
leans forward. He eats.
We all lean forward. We eat.
Outside in the barn, the chickens lean forward
And their blood red combs, the reddest combs in Missouri,
Dooley claims, lean forward with them, of course,
And the chickens eat.
And Dooley's collie leans forward. She eats.
Her pups lean forward, nuzzling. They eat.
In the yard, the elms lean forward.
They are eating the earth.
And the earth, which has been eating the sun all day,
Leans forward toward the moon.
It would devour it if it could.
"Your belly is your God," Dooley says,
Leaning forward in an attitude of reverence
Over the God called Wisconsin Cheddar.
It seems obvious to me that the Creator has large, perfect teeth,
That the Big Bang was in fact the Big Belch,
And that the galaxies are in reality plates of steaming roast beef.

But I don't say this.
For one thing, I won't risk offending someone's religious sensibilities,
And for another, I have been taught that it is impolite
To express profound philosophical truths
With my mouth full.

—JOHN GILGUN

LOAVES-AND-FISHES EASTER

Like the egg, the fish is also a symbol of rebirth—particularly in the Judeo-Christian culture. Jonah's journey into the whale and out again is representative of spiritual death and resurrection. The earliest Christians adopted the fish as a symbol for Jesus because the letters of *ichthys*, the Greek word for fish, formed the initials of the Greek words for "Jesus Christ, Son of God, Saviour." For early Christians, the fish was also a symbol of deep mystery, of the world of the spirit that lies beneath the surface of appearances.

This symbolism was on the mind of Deane Patton when she and her husband, Phil Wakeman, set out to create a new Easter menu a few years ago. Deane, who converted to Catholicism as an adult, wanted the meal to have some religious connection. A meal with fresh fish as its centerpiece seemed perfect.

But there was another inspiration for the choice of main course as well. The couple live just outside Westport, Kentucky, a small Ohio River town. Their house perches on a grassy hill overlooking their pasture, garden, and a creek. With a couple of horses and a huge garden to tend, they spend a lot of time outside, particularly when the weather is warm.

"We were finding every year that we were already well into a spring frame of mind by the time Easter rolled around," Deane explains. "And all that winter hibernation stuff—eat big meals, get plenty of sleep—was over. It just seemed like the traditional Easter meals—a big old ham or roasted lamb—were winter food. We wanted something light and fresh like the weather outside, like spring."

Fish was a natural, and salmon became the choice because of its availability and because its pretty color was most appealing to the couple, who are professional photographers. Phil suggested grilling so he could maximize the time outdoors. While he readied the wood fire, Deane came up with a springlike stuffing of scallions, mushrooms, and artichokes.

As for the loaves, a fine crusty wheat bread is perfect with the meal—and you can create one using the recipe for Crusty Rye Loaf on page 79, substituting wheat flour for the rye. And what could be a better Easter ritual than breaking bread for dessert as well? The Jamaican Easter Bun recipe that follows is perfect for that.

Blessed Salmon

The Wakeman/Patton grill is actually a metal fire ring set in the ground and topped with a grate—like the ones you see in campsites at state parks. They laid the 4½-pound fish on a broiler pan with vents in it, so the smoke could permeate, and topped the whole thing with a metal washtub to create a covered grill. A few years later, when they asked a bunch of us out to break bread and fish on Easter, the salmon was twice as big and Phil cleaned out the wheelbarrow (or at least, we prayed that he did) and inverted it over the fire. You can do this at home using a covered grill, however.

1 (4–4½-pound) whole salmon, butterflied

1 (14½-ounce) can artichoke hearts

2 tablespoons olive oil

4 scallions, chopped

2 cloves of garlic

1½ cups sliced fresh mushrooms

1½ teaspoons dried cilantro

½ teaspoon dried oregano

1 tablespoon minced fresh parsley

Juice of 1 large lemon

2 tablespoons dry white wine

1 tablespoon capers, drained

Salt to taste

Quarter wedge of lemon

½ cup (1 stick) butter

¼ cup cooking sherry

¼ cup white wine Worcestershire sauce (substitute white wine if Worcestershire unavailable)

1 teaspoon minced fresh parsley

½ teaspoon dried basil

½ teaspoon dried cilantro

Start a charcoal or wood fire. Make sure the grill is brushed clean. Oil it lightly and lay over fire to heat.

Lay the fish on a large plate or tray.

Drain the artichokes and cut in half. Place in a large bowl.

Warm 1 tablespoon of the olive oil in a skillet over medium heat, add the scallions and garlic, and sauté gently until the scallions are softened but not browned. Add to the artichokes.

Warm the remaining 1 tablespoon olive oil in a skillet and sauté the mushrooms over lively heat until golden. Add to the bowl. Sprinkle on the herbs. Add the lemon juice, white wine, and capers. Mix together lightly, taste, and add salt.

Stuff the fish from stem to stern with the vegetable mixture, then use heavy thread or dental floss to lightly stitch the cavity shut. Pop the lemon wedge in the salmon's mouth.

Heat the butter in a saucepan to melt. Add the sherry, Worcestershire, and herbs and mix well. Baste the top side of fish with this.

When the coals are covered in white ash, lay the fish with basted side down on the hot grill about 5 inches above the coals. Baste the top side of the fish and cover the grill.

After 15 to 20 minutes, baste the exposed side again and turn the fish: Use one or two well-oiled spatulas. Slide them under the fish from the cut side. Gently roll the fish over, then use the spatulas to scoot it back more toward the center. Baste the exposed side again and grill until the flesh is firm and flaky, about 10 to 20 minutes more.

Transfer to a warm platter and serve immediately.

Serves 8 to 10.

Ginger Carrot Salad

I confess, I hate the limp, listless carrot salad that shows up on virtually every cafeteria line in the Western world. The flavor is neither sweet nor savory to me, and not worth the effort of chewing. But my friend Deane Patton once confided it was a secret passion of hers, so for my contribution to the Patton/Wakeman Easter feast I set out to make a carrot salad that could please us both.

Rarely does compromise achieve greatness, but we both agree that this version is sensational. The crisp flavor is a perfect contrast for the rich, smoky taste of the Blessed Salmon (preceding recipe), and visually the deep orange of the carrots makes a beautiful complement to the main course.

The party quantity here can easily be reduced by halves or thirds, but if you're doing that, I suggest you go ahead and make up the full amount of ginger vinegar dressing, using about 3 tablespoons for each pound of carrots. The rest will keep in the refrigerator for weeks (you can remove the ginger after a couple of days) and is a yummy condiment to toss on vegetables, rice, or—and this is the best—a freshly sliced, very ripe pear.

DRESSING

4 tablespoons brown sugar
Pinch of salt
¼ cup rice vinegar
5 very thin slices fresh
  ginger

SALAD

3 pounds carrots
1 inch fresh ginger
1 (15-ounce) box golden
  raisins

In a glass jar, dissolve the sugar and salt in the vinegar. Add the ginger slices and marinate for at least 3 hours, or overnight.

If the carrots are organic, scrub them well; if not, peel them. Chop off the tops and bottoms. If you are using a food processor (a good idea if you are grating this quantity), peel the ginger and chop into several small chunks. Grate the carrots in the food processor, using the shredder blade and processing a small chunk of ginger every other batch or so to distribute it well through the carrots. If you are grating by hand, don't chop the ginger, but leave it in a larger piece to make it easier to grate a little into the mix after every couple of carrots.

Mix the raisins with the carrots. Remove the sliced ginger from the dressing, then pour the dressing over the carrots and toss well. Refrigerate for at least an hour before eating. This is one of those rare salads that will maintain its crispness and taste even better on the second day.

Makes enough for a dozen.

Much Greek philosophy, Dr. Johnson's best one-liners, and the inauguration of the Christian religion happened at supper tables.

—GUY DAVENPORT, THE GEOGRAPHY OF THE IMAGINATION

Simple Spring Peas

There is nothing so delicate and springlike as fresh peas, available in the pod in most groceries by Easter. The guests can shell the peas while waiting for the salmon to come to terms.

To my mind, most cooks overcook fresh peas. This recipe produces a vegetable that is both crisp and creamy.

About 1 pound of peas in the pod will yield 1 cup of shelled peas. Plan on a ½-cup serving per person. You may double this recipe, which makes enough for 6.

3 pounds unshelled fresh
   peas
4 tablespoons butter
Salt to taste
Freshly ground black
   pepper to taste

Shell the peas. When ready, melt the butter in a skillet with a snug-fitting lid. Add ¼ cup water, and just as it comes to a boil, add the peas. Toss with a spoon until all the peas are coated, then cover and cook over medium-low heat for 5 minutes. Shake the peas several times during the process. Check after 5 minutes and add a tablespoon or two of water if the pot looks as if it might boil dry. If not, cover and cook for another 3 to 5 minutes, still shaking, until peas are just tender.

Salt and pepper to taste. Some may wish to add more butter as well.

Serves 6 as a side dish.

Jamaican Easter Bun

Jessica Harris's flavorful Caribbean cookbook *Sky Juice and Flying Fish* (Simon and Schuster, 1991) introduced me to the traditional Jamaican Easter bread called simply "bun" and usually served with a slice of cheese. This recipe makes a couple of changes in the original—eliminating currants and substituting fresh lemon for dried fruit peel—to make a lighter, more dessert-like dish. It is lovely served after dinner with very hot, very strong coffee—or a nice cup of tea.

½ cup (1 stick) butter
½ lemon
1 pound all-purpose flour
½ teaspoon baking powder
½ teaspoon freshly grated
  nutmeg
1⅓ cups brown sugar
2 eggs, lightly beaten
⅓ cup milk
½ cup raisins
¼ cup chopped dried
  cherries

Preheat the oven to 300° F. Oil a 10-inch loaf pan.

Allow the butter to soften in a large bowl. Remove the seeds from the lemon and mince very fine, peel and all.

Sift together the flour, baking powder, and nutmeg. Cream the butter with the brown sugar until fluffy. Add the beaten eggs and mix until just blended. Add the flour mixture and mix to blend, then add the milk. Mix in the raisins, cherries, and lemon.

Pour the mixture into the loaf pan and bake for 1½ hours in the preheated oven. The bun is done when a cake tester or knife inserted in the middle comes out clean. Let cool in pan for 5 minutes, then invert on a wire rack, remove the pan, and cool completely before slicing.

Serves 12.

Five

Passover

Passover celebrates the Exodus of the Jewish people, their liberation from slavery in Egypt during biblical times. Over the centuries, it has also come to represent the survival of a people and a belief system through numerous eras and types of persecution. For this reason, it has a powerful resonance, and although it is not necessarily the most significant religiously, it is the holiday celebrated by most Jews.

The Passover seder is a ritual bound by traditions. At most holidays, food is an adjunct, a repast to be shared after the business of worship is done, but here the table and its food, the ritual way it is consumed, is a part of the ceremony itself.

It is not merely tradition, passed on from one generation to the next, that informs this holiday. There are matters of Jewish law that must be observed. There are the restrictions of kosher dietary law—no pork, no shellfish, no consumption of meat and milk together. And there are the dietary strictures of Passover itself—no yeast breads, no fermented products.

Yet even these rules, which seem cut and dried, are open to interpretation. In Ashkenazi households, the strictures against products made with yeast are usually interpreted to mean that any grain is forbidden. In Sephardic homes, however, noodles and grains are often consumed. Olive oil is not used in some households because of the possibility of slight fermentation in the process of extracting the oil from the fruit, but in others it is allowed.

And, of course, there are countless non-kosher homes where Passover is still observed, where the meaning of this festival of endurance and liberation is still profound.

Up in the dining room a holiday atmosphere reigned. The table stretched the length of the room, a white Seder cloth reflecting the glow of the red wineglasses. Candlesticks shone, bearing tall white candles . . .

Heaps of matzahs were covered with napkins that looked like little prayer shawls. The plump white cushions on the chairs seemed embarrassed to contemplate the flat unleavened bread. The Haggadahs—the books containing the story of the exodus from Egypt—were resplendent with the golden letters on their bindings . . .

But the table was not quite ready. It was still being set. No one thought to wonder whether it could bear all the weight.

"Chaya, have you shelled the eggs? Where's the salt water?"

Mother bustled around the table, trying to take everything in and see that nothing was missing.

"Fetch another cushion—there's a guest I'd forgotten. Put a clean cover on!"

"Who's coming, Mother? How many will there be of us?"

"Oh," said Mother, "why count? Especially on a holiday . . . Ssh, they're back from the synagogue."

—BELLA CHAGALL, *FIRST ENCOUNTER*

ECO-KOSHER PASSOVER

In the Philadelphia neighborhood where both Jackie and Leon Olenick grew up, everyone was Jewish.

"Everyone. The mailman, the shopkeepers, the teachers—all," Jackie says. "You didn't have to think about being Jewish. You didn't have to do anything to be Jewish. You just were a Jew, like everyone else."

But although both Jackie and Leon were surrounded by the culture, neither had a strong religious background.

"My parents were lox-and-bagel Jews. Our Jewishness was primarily defined by what we ate," Jackie says.

And Leon recollects, "On Shabbat morning I ate bacon and eggs for breakfast and went to work. Worship was discouraged in my family. You didn't waste money or time on that."

"Our parents were good working-class parents who were tired from the work they had to do just to keep their families fed and sheltered," Jackie explains. "We were raised Jewish, but without any ritual."

The couple became sweethearts in their early teens and even then, Jackie says, they knew they wanted a stronger spiritual life. When they married in 1964, they were determined to make ritual a vital part of their marriage. Establishing those rituals has been a process of evolution.

"In the beginning, we weren't always happy with the institutions that we found for giving our three kids a concept of their Jewishness," Leon says.

"So we began studying with Orthodox Jews and learned about Jewish law and got a framework from them. We've also studied with and have been involved with members of the Jewish Renewal movement."

Jackie explains, "Even though we wanted to honor the centuries of Jewish teaching, we also wanted to honor what was important to us, what was going on in our lives right now. For instance, we wanted our ceremonies to reflect our sense of community, not just the one we live in immediately, but also how we fit into the larger community of the world. We started with the tradition of the Sabbath every week."

"Starting Thursday night, we go to several stores to get just the right ingredients for the dinner. We are mostly vegetarians now, and we try to buy organic produce as often as possible, because we don't believe it is responsible to put pesticides into the earth," Leon says.

"We start preparing Thursday, too. We put on Shabbat music and crank it up really loud. And the stress of the week begins to fall away as we work together in the kitchen."

They work well together, Leon says, completing chores much as they talk—with one picking up the thread just as the other lets it go. And this, Jackie notes, makes the Sabbath not only a celebration of their spiritual lives but a celebration of their relationship with each other.

In 1976 the Olenicks moved to Bloomington, Indiana, and there found a like-minded community of Jewish friends. They met together to study and sing, and the Olenicks began the Sabbath ritual of a potluck dinner at their house with this group of friends. The weekly dinners often lasted late into the night with dancing and singing.

"When our kids were little, they loved it," Jackie says. "Of course, when they hit their teen years, they were a lot more ambiguous about it. And we didn't really pressure them to be there, but let them choose to be with their friends instead if they wanted. The funny thing is, their friends found out about the dinners and started wanting to come. So it stayed a family ritual even then, and our community came to include their friends as well as ours."

When the family moved to St. Paul, Minnesota, in 1984, the Sabbath celebrations continued, including the community of friends they established in the new town. But in time, both Jackie and Leon felt that the stress of a weekly party was becoming too much.

"We both work full-time now," Jackie said. "And on the Sabbath, you're supposed to rest. That is the point. Having everyone over once a week was too much, so now we have everyone here once a month and call it 'the Big One.' Everyone brings a dish. We start about seven and sing until midnight. It's refreshing, and then the other Sabbath days are for our immediate family."

Like their Sabbath observance, the Olenicks' other rituals have evolved with one eye to traditional teachings, but also with a desire to create ceremonies that are personal and meaningful in a modern context.

The Olenicks' Passover seders also began in Bloomington. Some Jews have seder meals on the first two nights of Passover, and for the Olenicks, having two meals was the only way they could accommodate all the friends who wanted to be included. After they moved to St. Paul, their seder table kept expanding, with new friends made in the new community and old friends from Bloomington who would still make the long drive to the Olenicks' seder.

The Olenick seder table now extends from the dining room of their comfortable Craftsman-era house into the living room, filling most of the combined rooms' 25-foot length. On each night, it is surrounded by about forty friends and family members—different friends on each night so everyone can be included. Not all the celebrants are Jewish, but all are members of the community that the Olenicks see as their larger spiritual family.

To begin the meal, they read from the Haggadah, a booklet that traditionally contains the order of the seder service, the blessings and prayers, and the story of the Israelites' deliverance from Egypt.

The Olenicks have written their own Haggadah, a spiral-bound work that observes the rituals of a traditional Passover, but also addresses their personal commitment to creating a world that is ecologically sound and blessed with peace. Their Haggadah includes a Navajo folk prayer, "Amazing Grace," the Shaker hymn "Simple Gifts," and a poem from novelist Richard Bach that advises how to discover if your mission on earth is completed—if you are alive, he says, then it isn't.

A meditation on the meaning of "kosher" from Rabbi Zalman Schachter-Shalomi is included in the Olenicks' Haggadah. In it he suggests expanding the term to mean foods and actions that are considerate of others, and of the world. The rabbi notes that the Bible forbids the unnecessary torment of animals. He then questions if eggs, generally considered kosher, can be so if they are taken from chickens who "spend their entire lives imprisoned in a cage one cubic foot in size."

Noting that fruits and vegetables are considered kosher, he questions if they should be if the produce is grown and harvested by migrant workers living in exploitative conditions very akin to the slavery that Passover is meant to celebrate release from.

Accepting these broader, more thoughtful definitions of kosher has meant changing the food served at their seder table, Jackie says.

The Olenicks' menus focus on simplicity. They define kosher as "a sense of responsibility to the world, to the future of our children, three grandchildren, and their children to come.

"Now we define ourselves as Eco-Kosher. We try to be conscious of where our food comes from and to be responsible in the choices that we make, and also to be aware of how we prepare it."

Their Passover seder menus reflect that awareness. And Jackie says that trying to create interesting, nourishing food that meets traditional kosher laws, the strictures of Passover, and their own personal guidelines has become a challenge. But it's one she has embraced with enthusiasm.

"THERE IS A HEBREW WORD: *KAVANAH*," JACKIE SAYS. "IT MEANS INTENTION.

"The intention of making the meal for seder or Shabbat a holy work comes out in the food, and that is more important than just what food we are preparing. It is our intention to bring it to a sacred place. And that intention is more important than dogma. What is the point of dogma if it isn't sacred?"

A political component keeps the Exodus message alive for us. That's the gift of the Jewish people to the world, that you can take an oppressed situation and alter it. If God intervened in history then we can alter history, because we're supposed to imitate God.

—LETTY COTTIN POGREBIN

ℳatzo Soup sans Chicken

Matzo ball soup is made with chicken broth so frequently that we have come to think of it as intrinsic to the recipe. In fact, matzo balls are a wonderful addition to many simple soups and stews—particularly the savory, herb-filled matzo balls in this recipe. (Serve them up in a bowl of cold borscht sometime—forgoing the usual dollop of sour cream—for a yummy treat low in saturated fat.)

For the Olenicks' Passover seder, Jackie wanted a soup that echoed the traditions of the Philadelphia neighborhood where she and Leon were raised but also adhered to the vegetarian beliefs they had adopted. It needed a broth with the rich, golden resonance of chicken, but without the actual bird.

The mushrooms give this broth its meaty flavor while the turmeric and achiote (annatto) seasonings give it a rich red-gold color and tang. There is enough here for the matzo ball soup plus a couple of cups left over to be used as seasoning in other recipes, including the Manna-from-Heaven Stuffed Vegetables on page 102. The broth can be made a month or two in advance and frozen. The matzo balls can be made the day before and refrigerated, and then the soup made on the day of the seder.

CHICKENLESS BROTH

2 tablespoons vegetable oil

1 medium-sized onion, coarsely chopped

2 cloves of garlic, sliced in half

½ pound mushrooms

2 teaspoons kosher salt

1 medium-sized potato

½ pound carrots

1 large stalk of celery

1 small yellow squash or zucchini

½ tablespoon annatto (achiote) seed

½ teaspoon turmeric

1 large leaf of fresh sorrel

4 sprigs of fresh parsley

Heat the oil in a soup kettle over medium heat, adding the onion and garlic as it becomes warm. As they sauté, clean, then quarter the mushrooms. Add them to the oil, sprinkle with ½ teaspoon of the salt, and cover. Turn the heat to medium-low and let them simmer for 10 minutes.

While the pot simmers, clean the potato well but don't peel. Cut in half, then chop each half into 6 pieces. Peel the carrots and split in half lengthwise. Trim the celery tops and bottom, then cut stalk into 3 pieces. Trim squash and split in half lengthwise.

Sprinkle the annatto, turmeric, and the remaining 1½ teaspoons salt on the sautéed mushrooms, onion, and garlic. Stir to coat with the oil and juices, then add 4 quarts water and the rest of the chopped vegetables, the sorrel leaf, and parsley. Bring to a boil, cover, and turn heat down to a lively simmer. Cook for 1 hour.

Strain the broth through a large sieve and gently press the cooked vegetables with the back of a wooden spoon to extract juices. Add the juices to the broth and discard the vegetables. Set aside 2 cups broth for use in other recipes. You can use the rest of the broth for matzo soup immediately, or refrigerate it overnight to use the next day. It freezes for up to 2 months.

Makes 3 to 4 quarts broth.

SAVORY MATZO BALLS

¼ cup finely minced
  scallions
1 tablespoon finely minced
  fresh sorrel leaves
1 teaspoon finely minced
  fresh marjoram
1½ teaspoons kosher salt
½ cup matzo meal
2 eggs
2 tablespoons vegetable oil
½ tablespoon Chickenless
  Broth

In a small mixing bowl, mix the scallions, herbs, 1 teaspoon salt, and the matzo meal together. Beat the eggs lightly with the oil and add to the meal mixture. Blend, then add the broth to make a thick paste. Cover and place in the refrigerator for at least 30 minutes.

When you are ready to make the matzo balls, bring 1½ quarts water with ½ teaspoon salt to a boil in a 3-to-4-quart saucepan. Remove the matzo dough from the refrigerator. Use a dessert spoon to scoop up balls of the dough, then roll each lightly between the palms of your hands to smooth them—but don't compress them. (If the dough sticks, wet your hands lightly with cold water.) Matzo balls should be about an inch in diameter, and the dough should yield 1 dozen.

Gently drop each ball in the boiling water, then adjust the heat so that when the pot is covered, the balls are cooking at a lively simmer. (A pot with a glass cover is ideal for keeping an eye on the progress of the matzo balls, but if you don't have one, use a heatproof glass pie plate.) Let cook, covered, for 30 minutes, then remove from the water with a slotted spoon.

Use immediately or cool to room temperature, cover, and refrigerate overnight.

Makes 1 dozen.

MATZO BALL SOUP SANS CHICKEN

2½ quarts Chickenless Broth
2 large carrots
1 medium-sized parsnip
12 Savory Matzo Balls

In a large soup kettle, bring the broth to a boil. Peel the carrots and parsnip. If the parsnip is older, it may have a woody center; remove this. Cut the carrots and parsnip into strips about an inch long and ¼ inch thick. Add to the boiling broth and turn the heat down until the soup is at a lively simmer. Cover and cook for 30 minutes.

If the matzo balls have been refrigerated, let come to room temperature. When you are ready to serve the soup, gently place the matzo balls in the bubbly soup and let warm for 5 minutes. Ladle up, 1 matzo ball to a serving.

Serves 12.

Manna-from-Heaven Stuffed Vegetables

Non-vegetarians often think giving up meat is a sacrifice, but vegetarians who know their way around a kitchen more often see it as a blessing in disguise. Coming up with tasty entrees—especially ones dramatic enough to serve as the centerpiece for a ceremonial meal such as Passover—is a challenge, but one that can be met well and tastily.

These stuffed vegetables are a good example. They are wholesome and healthy, to be sure. And they are lovely to look at with the bright red and yellow peppers, the ebony eggplants, and the green zucchinis arranged on a large platter. But best of all, they are fragrant and surprisingly rich with the nutty sweetness of the almond meal. The spicy tomato sauce (rather whimsically named Red Sea Sauce here) is superb on them, but I admit I could not decide if I liked them better with it or plain.

And if you're wondering how this plays with the carnivores, let me tell you that my brother-in-law, Mr. Meat-and-Potatoes himself, pronounced it "outrageously good," cleaned his plate twice, and was disappointed when there was no more. Make plenty!

1½ cups matzo meal

1½ cups almonds

2 cups Chickenless Broth (page 100) OR other vegetable broth

¼ cup vegetable oil

2 cups finely chopped onion

1 clove of garlic, minced

1 large eggplant, 8–9 inches long and about 6 inches thick

2 zucchinis, 7–9 inches long

1 large red bell pepper

1 large yellow bell pepper

Kosher salt to taste

Freshly ground black pepper to taste

Preheat the oven to 350° F.

Put the matzo meal in a large bowl. At medium speed in a blender, grind the almonds to a coarse meal. Mix with the matzo. Warm the vegetable broth, then pour over the meal mix and stir. Set aside.

Heat 1 tablespoon of the oil in a skillet over medium heat. Add the chopped onion and sauté until softened. Add the minced garlic to the remaining 3 tablespoons oil and set aside.

Wash the vegetables, but do not peel. Remove the stems and cut in half lengthwise. Scoop out the flesh of the eggplant and zucchinis, leaving a shell about ⅓ inch thick all around. Mince the removed pulp and set aside.

Remove seeds and any white pith from the peppers. Rub the hollowed vegetables with the garlic oil inside and out, then lightly salt the insides. Place with cavities up on lightly oiled baking sheets.

Add the remaining oil and garlic, the minced vegetable pulp, and the sautéed onions to the matzo meal and almonds. Mix well and add salt and pepper to taste. The consistency should be like wet clay, but not soupy. Add more broth or water if you need to.

Fill the vegetable cavities with the meal mixture. Place in the preheated oven and bake for 30 minutes. Test the flesh of the zucchinis and eggplant with a fork to make sure they are soft. The zucchinis may take 5 or so minutes longer.

Let the vegetables cool so that they can be handled, then cut into serving-sized portions: halve the pepper and zucchini pieces and cut the eggplant pieces into sixths or fourths. Arrange on a serving platter and serve either warm or at room temperature with Red Sea Sauce on the side, since some guests may prefer the delicate flavor of the stuffed vegetables unadorned.

Serves 12.

RED SEA SAUCE

½ tablespoon cumin seed
3 whole cloves
1 cup unseasoned tomato
  sauce
1 tablespoon minced fresh
  ginger
½ tablespoon sugar
½ tablespoon lemon juice

In a small, heavy saucepan, toast the cumin over high heat until the fragrance is released. (This takes only a minute. Shake the pan and keep a close eye on it so the cumin doesn't burn.) With a mortar and pestle, crush the toasted cumin and cloves together to make a pungent powder.

Pour the tomato sauce into the saucepan and set over low heat. Add the cumin-clove mix, minced ginger, sugar, and lemon juice. Stir well, then simmer, covered, over low heat for 8 minutes. Serve warm on the side with a very small ladle or spoon, since a little of this pungent sauce goes a very long way.

Serves 12.

Israeli Salad

Salads are a major part of the Olenick family seder. Fresh vegetables and fruit are kosher and, of course, meet the vegetarian needs of the family. Jackie varies the salads from year to year, trying new recipes that sound appealing, but this salad, from a recipe given to her by Israeli friends, is always on the table.

"This dish is so popular in Israel that my friends told me they often eat it for breakfast," Jackie says.

"The secret is to chop the vegetables in very small pieces, but not make them mushy. The Israelis I know would pride themselves on how small they could chop."

To keep the vegetables from getting mushy, it's necessary to serve the salad very shortly after chopping. If you need to prepare some parts of the salad a couple of hours before the meal, you can chop the cucumbers, peppers, onion, and scallions separately, then refrigerate, mixing them together and adding the freshly chopped tomatoes and dressing when ready to serve.

5 cucumbers
1 large green bell pepper
1 large red bell pepper
1 sweet white (Vidalia or Walla Walla) or purple onion
6 scallions
4 large tomatoes
1 cup chopped fresh parsley
¼ cup chopped fresh dill (or more)
2 tablespoons vegetable oil
Juice of 1 lemon
Salt to taste
Freshly ground black pepper to taste

Peel the cucumbers. Chop them, the peppers, onion, and scallions into pieces about one-quarter inch square (or the size of the nail of your little finger).

Peel the tomatoes by plunging for a few seconds in boiling water, then rinsing with cold. The skins should come right off. Chop in pieces the same size as the other vegetables.

When you are ready to serve, mix the vegetables, parsley, and dill. Add the oil and lemon juice and toss. Add the salt, pepper, and more dill to your liking.

Serves 12.

The shank bone of a lamb is traditionally placed on the ritual seder plate as a remembrance of the sacrifices made at the Temple and of its destruction. But in the Olenicks' vegetarian seder they substitute a beet.

"We have a big, plump beet whole on the large seder plate and then we have cooked beets sliced on the table so everyone gets a little on their plate," Jackie says. The substitution was recommended by Rabbi Arthur I. Waskow in his Seasons of Our Joy *(Beacon Press, 1991).*

"We think the beet works perfectly because of its red juice, which can symbolize the blood," Jackie said.

*O*asis Salad

This salad is zesty and fragrant, and the colors look beautiful on the table. It is best if made with a sweet onion—Vidalia or Walla Walla varieties preferred.

4 thin-skinned, juicy
oranges
2 ripe, firm avocados

Peel the oranges over a bowl, making sure to catch all the juice. Slice in half crosswise. Remove the seeds and the center pith. Break into sections.

Peel the avocados and cut into chunks

1 medium-sweet white
 onion
½ cup chopped fresh
 cilantro leaves
1 head romaine lettuce
Juice of 1 lime
2 tablespoons vegetable oil
2 teaspoons sugar
½ teaspoon kosher salt
⅔ cup sweetened coconut
Freshly ground black
 pepper

about the same size as the orange pieces. Halve the onion and chop into pieces about as wide and long as the avocado and orange chunks. Toss together, then sprinkle with the chopped cilantro and toss again.

Wash and dry the lettuce, remove the core, and cut or tear into salad-size pieces. Place in a large bowl.

Mix the lime juice with the oil, sugar, and salt, and sprinkle over the lettuce, tossing lightly. Add the orange/avocado mix, including the juice, and toss lightly again. Sprinkle with the coconut and toss once more. Serve with fresh black pepper on the side so guests can season as they wish.

Serves 12.

The bitter herbs on the ritual seder plate symbolize the bitterness the Israelites endured in Egyptian bondage, while the bowl of salt water symbolizes the tears it provoked. For Leon Olenick and his son, the bitter herbs bring real tears.

"Jackie calls it a Jewish macho thing," Leon says with a laugh. "We don't buy prepared horseradish for the meal. Instead I call my son and he comes over and we grate the root ourselves in the kitchen. As we work, the pungency of it gets to us and pretty soon we're mixing our real tears with the horseradish, but smiling, too, with this father-son tradition we are sharing. It's something I especially look forward to."

Ḥaroset

While most of the ceremonial foods on the ritual seder plate don't reappear in the actual meal, the haroset does. Haroset is a mélange of fruits and nuts representing the mortar the Israelites used to build Egyptian cities while in captivity. It comes in many guises—apples, walnuts, wine, and spices are the most frequent ingredients in American homes, but it may be made with dates, figs, or other nuts and fruits. And its earthy sweetness is a perfect foil for the savory flavors that characterize so many Passover dishes.

This recipe comes from Arthur Cohen, a friend of the Olenicks, and the only person outside their family who contributes a food to their seder.

"I asked Jackie and Leon one year if they wanted me to bring haroset, and they said no, they would make it. But I was persistent and told them I had this unusual recipe. So I made it that year, and every year since. I make it at their house, though, so they know that it is kosher," he said.

Arthur's recipe, using dates and walnuts, is from Syria, one of the Middle Eastern countries his Sephardic Jewish ancestors hailed from. Like many family recipes handed down, it did not come with specific measures, but is mixed from what is at hand, ingredients being added and increased until it "looks right." Right, in this case, is a consistency similar to a thick apple butter.

The wine, Arthur explains, "is to give it a bit of a bite and also to remind us of the blood the Israelites shed into the mortar." It is added after the dates have cooked down into a thick paste, and it thins the mixture somewhat, hence the matzo meal added to thicken it up again.

For Passover, Arthur makes enough to serve eighty people for the two nights of the Olenicks' seder. It is eaten on matzo wafers and as a side relish on the plates. And there is often enough left over to be taken home and used much as one would use apple butter.

The recipe here should easily serve 12 and have some left over.

3 pounds pitted dates
2 cups chopped walnuts
(chopped in ¼-inch
pieces, or smaller)
1½ cups kosher Concord
grape wine, or more
¼–½ cup matzo meal
Cinnamon to taste

Put the pitted dates in a large, heavy saucepan and cover with water. Bring to a boil, then turn the heat down to a simmer. Cover and simmer, stirring occasionally, for about an hour. You want the dates to cook into a paste, so it's best to stir with a large wooden spoon, mashing the dates some each time you do. You also want most of the water to evaporate. If it has not by the end of an hour, uncover the pot and cook for a while like that to hasten the evaporation—keeping a close eye on it so the dates don't stick.

When the water has mostly evaporated, making it a damp, but not soupy, paste, add the chopped walnuts.

Stir in the wine and taste, adding more if you like. Then add the matzo meal a little at a time until the mixture is the consistency of a thick apple butter. You want a paste that will not "run" when spooned onto a plate and that can be spread on matzo wafers.

Add cinnamon to taste. Refrigerate until ready to use. Haroset will keep for several weeks covered tightly in the refrigerator.

Serves 12.

Fruit Fool

The Olenicks often end the Passover meal by passing a platter filled with fresh fruit. Because their meal has no meat, they may also put out wedges of ripe cheese. The Orange Blossom Pralines (page 207) are a crunchy, zippy accompaniment as well.

When you can't find enough truly fine fresh fruit to serve simply on its own, however, Fruit Fool makes an excellent close for any dairy Passover meal.

4 cups fresh or frozen
  blueberries, strawberries,
  or raspberries
1 cup sugar
2 pints heavy cream
Mint leaves for garnish
  (optional)

Blend the fruit and half the sugar to a fine puree. (If you are making with fresh fruit, you may want to set aside some whole berries to use as a garnish.) Whip the cream and the rest of the sugar until they form stiff peaks. Fold the fruit puree into the whipped cream. Don't mix to blend, but leave dark streaks of the fruit in the cream. Spoon into individual glass serving dishes (bowl-shaped wineglasses are perfect), cover, and refrigerate until ready to serve. Garnish with berries or a sprig of mint.

Serves 12.

A land of wheat, and barley, and vines, and fig trees, and pomegranates; a land of oil olive, and honey;

    A land wherein thou shalt eat bread without scarceness, thou shalt not lack any thing in it.

—Deuteronomy 8:8–9

And the people sat down to eat and to drink, and rose up to play.

—Exodus 32:6

THE MOTHERS' PASSOVER

Bobbie Krinsky, fifty-eight, is a silversmith in Madison, Wisconsin, who creates Judaica—objects to be used in Jewish rituals. Her work is a reflection of her background: the descendant of Russian Jews who migrated to Milwaukee at the turn of the century, she has thought much about what it means to her to be Jewish. Yet when she first considered talking about her Passover seder, she felt she might not have anything significant to say.

She had only in recent years begun preparing a seder for family and friends again, a tradition that for some time she had let lapse. In addition, hers is not a seder that keeps strictly to the tenets of Jewish law. She does not keep a kosher kitchen, and while she does not use leavened bread, grains, or noodles in her seder menu, she does steep the traditional brisket in a sauce made of ketchup and beer—the latter obviously a product of fermentation.

Even more to the point, Bobbie wondered if there was anything unique about her seder.

"At first I thought, what's to say? I thought this was so pat—a seder is a seder and you serve those traditional foods."

Then Bobbie realized that there were infinite ways to set the seder table, and that the way she has chosen tells much about herself.

The recipes that she says are "musts" reflect her cultural background. She calls the pot roast that is the centerpiece "a Brooklyn brisket" and, indeed, it is an icon of the immigrant community of New York, where an inexpensive piece of meat was a treasure in disguise—one that could be slowly and lovingly transformed into a gourmet treat.

She is adamant that true chicken broth must be made without the back of the chicken in the pot to sully the flavor. It is a law passed on to her by her mother, and one not to be taken any more lightly than the Talmudic law that says no meat may be steeped in the milk of its mother. Her rules for what constitutes a traditional seder are, in fact, personal and arbitrary, but uttered with authority.

"Dinner must begin with gefilte fish, even if you have to buy it in a jar, and it must be accompanied by a beet-flavored horseradish. The next course must be matzo ball soup made with real chicken broth. And there must be haroset and a potato dish and the matzoth."

For this menu, she gathered recipes from a variety of sources, but all with a common thread. The cooks were all mothers: her mother, her husband Ed's mother, her ex-husband's mother, and the mothers of one or two close friends.

"As I pulled those recipes together, I began to realize: there's a liturgy here," she explained.

That liturgy was the preparation of the food in ritual ways, as much defined by the cooks as by scholars. And the women who had created these recipes and then passed them from one hand to another, from one land to another, were the shepherds of the faith.

"I had a sense of myself as a part of this long line of extraordinary women: women who are mothers and grandmothers and mothers-in-law. And I thought, these women rule the world! What I am participating in is a network, a web, a fabric, passed on for generations from one strong woman to another."

But even in that traditional liturgy, Bobbie discovered the need for change.

"When I set out to do the first seder after so many years, I decided I wanted to do it for the people I was closest to, although most of them are not Jewish. At first I was considering having everybody bring something. That's the Madison approach to dinners. But then one friend said something about olive oil and I thought, 'No, no, no, we don't do that. We do schmaltz.'

"So, acting as my own worst enemy, I decided *only* I could *properly* cook the major traditional foods. After all, that's been the tradition of most of the women whose recipes I'd gathered over the years. They were the queens of their kitchens.

"So I did it. And it was a great seder and it only took me two full weeks to prepare for it, pull it off, and recover.

"But isn't religion supposed to help one to grow and to learn? What I learned is that a more important tradition to honor at seder is that everyone contributes a dish to the meal, especially when my friends are such good cooks and so much better than I am at following recipes. So that's my plan now, to give some of the recipes that I want to other people who want to prepare something, and that way we have the traditional food without some of the traditional suffering."

Chicken Soup with Schmaltzy Matzo Balls

You'll need only about half the broth for a dozen appetizer servings of this soup, but you can freeze the rest for use in other recipes or to have soup another day.

Bobbie Krinsky's is a pure, golden broth—the kind of elixir that generations of Jewish mothers have credited with the ability to cure countless ailments from the common cold to a broken heart.

Prepare the broth the day before you are going to serve the soup. (You may want to set aside 1½ cups to make Gefilte Fish with Beet Horseradish: recipe follows.)

BROTH

1 (3–4-pound) chicken, cut up, without the back
4 medium-sized carrots, peeled
1 large whole onion
4 large stalks of celery, cut up
⅓ cup parsley (not chopped)
Kosher salt to taste
Freshly ground black pepper to taste

Rinse the chicken and remove excess fat and skin. Set aside ¼ cup to make schmaltz for the matzo balls.

Put the chicken in a large soup pot. Add 6 quarts cold water, turn the heat to high, and bring to a boil. A grayish foam will rise to the top as it boils. Using a large slotted spoon, skim off the foam. You may have to do this 3 or 4 times, but that is what makes the broth clear and pure-tasting. When the foam that rises is a thin thread and white, add the vegetables. Foam will rise again, and you should skim that once and then reduce to a bubbling simmer. Half cover with the lid of the pot, and let it cook for 1 to 1½ hours, never letting it boil hard again. About halfway through the cooking process, add salt and pepper to taste. The chicken should be fork-tender.

Pour into a colander to separate the meat and the vegetables from the broth. Set the meat and vegetables aside. (Bobbie likes to eat them for a quick supper on the day she makes the soup.)

Chill the broth; remove the fat that rises to the top, and discard.

Makes about 5 to 6 quarts broth.

SCHMALTZ

¼ cup chicken fat and skin
¼ cup finely chopped onion
¼ cup canola oil

Bobbie calls schmaltz Jewish butter, and it imparts a distinctive rich flavor to the matzo balls. Dice the chicken fat and skin with a very sharp knife. Dice the onion to the same size— ¼ inch square or smaller.

Put the canola oil in a small, heavy saucepan, add the chicken fat and skin, and cook over medium-high heat until the mixture begins bubbling and foaming. Turn the heat down to keep at a lively simmer and watch, stirring occasionally, for 3 to 4 minutes, until the fat looks cooked but is still a light color. Add the onion and continue to cook until they and the chicken bits are a deep golden brown. Don't burn! (These are *grebens*, and Bobbie says a traditional treat is to spread them on a slice of Jewish rye bread, salt lightly, and gobble up. However, keep yours in the schmaltz.

MATZO BALLS

2 tablespoons schmaltz
  with *grebens*
1 egg, slightly beaten
¼ teaspoon grated nutmeg
½ cup matzo meal
1 teaspoon plus a pinch of
  kosher salt
2 tablespoons chopped
  fresh parsley
2 tablespoons broth or
  water

In a non-metal bowl, mix the schmaltz and egg together. In another bowl, blend the nutmeg, matzo meal, 1 teaspoon salt, and parsley. Add to the schmaltz and eggs. When well blended, add the broth and mix again until just blended. Cover the bowl and place in the refrigerator for 30 minutes or more.

Fill a 3-quart pot halfway with water, add a pinch of kosher salt, cover, and bring to a lively boil. While the water is coming to a boil, make the matzo balls. Using a dessert spoon, scoop a dollop of the refrigerated matzo dough into the palm of your hand and roll lightly, making a sphere about an inch in diameter. If the dough sticks, dampen your hands lightly with cold water. Place the balls on a plate.

When all the balls are rolled, remove the lid from the boiling water and reduce the heat until water is bubbling slightly. Spoon the balls one at a time into the water. Cover and simmer for 30 minutes. You want the water to bubble just a bit, but not roil so much that it causes the matzo balls to bang around and crumble. To keep an eye on the activity, it's good to use a pot with a glass lid, or you can cover the pot with a heatproof glass pie plate.

Makes 12.

While the matzo balls are cooking, heat 3 quarts of the prepared broth to steaming in a separate kettle. Taste and add salt or pepper if needed. When the matzo balls are done, remove from the water with a slotted spoon and transfer gently to the soup pot. Allow to simmer 5 minutes, then serve, 1 matzo ball in a cup of broth to a customer.

Serves 12.

MATZO MEDICINE

The curative powers of every Jewish mother's steaming chicken soup have been mythologized through centuries of literature, folklore, movies, and television. That we believe in its magic was demonstrated dramatically after the major earthquake that struck Los Angeles in January 1994. Esquire *magazine reported that sales of matzo ball soup skyrocketed not only at delis but at upscale spots. The restaurant Gardens at the Four Seasons Hotel in West Hollywood reported a 50 percent increase in matzo ball soup orders following the big shakeup.*

Esquire quoted La Veranda chef/owner David Slay, who was selling soup for $5.25 a bowl and said, "I guess they figure they need something to soothe their battered souls."

Gefilte Fish with Beet Horseradish

While gefilte fish is a must on Bobbie Krinsky's Passover menu, making it from raw fish is not.

"Ed's mother makes a lovely gefilte fish from scratch, but she is in Brooklyn and gets her fresh fish ground at the market, not something I've been able to do in Madison. Instead I've found some wonderful recipes for 'doctored' gefilte fish, using the kind sold in jars."

This recipe comes from the mother of a close friend.

12 pieces unsweetened gefilte fish in clear, non-gelatinous broth

1½ cups chicken broth (see page 114)

6 medium-sized carrots

1 medium-sized onion

Pinch of saffron

Kosher salt to taste (optional)

Chunk of fresh horseradish, about 3×3 inches

2 tablespoons beet juice

Pour the broth from the gefilte fish into a medium saucepan. Remove the pieces of fish carefully from the jar and arrange in a wide bowl.

Add the chicken broth to the fish broth. Peel the carrots, halve lengthwise, and cut into ½-inch-thick pieces. Chop the onion to comparable size. Add the carrots and onion to the broth, cover, and bring to a light boil, turning down the heat immediately to a simmer. Cook, covered, until the carrots are just tender, usually 15 to 20 minutes. Add the saffron and stir to dissolve. Taste and add salt if necessary.

Spoon the vegetables over the fish and then gently ladle the broth over. When cooled to room temperature, cover tightly with plastic wrap and refrigerate for 24 hours. Serve cold.

Before you are ready to serve, peel the horseradish. (Spring horseradish may be greenish and requires deeper peeling than the beige, more mature root. Cut a cross section, and you will see how deeply you need to pare.)

You may grate the horseradish by hand on a fine grater, weeping as you go. Or you may cut it into ½-inch cubes and grate in a blender at high speed with a teaspoonful of water to a medium-fine texture—but not a puree. If you choose the latter method, be sure to turn the blender container away from your face before you take off the lid, since the first whiff is tremendously pungent. Moisten with the beet juice, tossing to spread it evenly. Serve in a bowl on the side.

Serves 12.

Bobbie's Brisket

"I know brisket is a cut of beef, but when a Jew says 'brisket' it means an oniony, savory pot roast made from that piece of meat, delicious for dinner and fabulous for sandwiches," explains Bobbie Krinsky.

"I have the three best recipes in the world: Fran's, Jo's, and mine."

Fran is Bobbie's mother, Jo is her mother-in-law, and of their recipes, Bobbie says, "I like Jo's seasonings and the beer that she uses in the sauce. But I prefer to bake it in the oven, browning it as my mother's recipe does and using a lot of paprika and garlic. I also tenderize the meat with papaya when I can get it. That's a 'Bobbie' idea, since brisket is notoriously tough. So I grate ⅓ cup underripe papaya into the onions. These disintegrate in the cooking, and my roast is very tender. 'My' roast, hah!"

(Underripe papayas aren't always easy to come by, however, and the briskets I've made with this recipe without it have been fork-tender, so it's not included here.)

Bobbie's Brisket should be cooked the day before you wish to serve it, sliced, and left to soak up its sauce overnight. Then it's reheated just before serving.

4–5-pound brisket of beef
2 large onions, sliced about
  ¼ inch thick
2 teaspoons kosher salt
½ teaspoon ground white
  pepper
1 tablespoon paprika
Pinch of sugar
1 teaspoon turmeric
2 large cloves of garlic,
  mashed
¼ cup ketchup
1 cup beer or water

Trim the excess fat from the brisket if the butcher has not done so, but leave a thin layer on the top of the roast.

Turn on the broiler, and while it is heating, lightly oil a shallow roasting pan and spread the sliced onions evenly in the bottom. Lay the brisket on top with the fat side down. Place under the broiler to brown very lightly, then flip over and brown the other side. You don't want the meat to sear, but simply to turn from pink to a grayish-brown.

Turn off the broiler and turn the oven to 325° F. Mix the salt, pepper, paprika, sugar, turmeric, and garlic together. When the brisket has cooled just enough to handle, remove from the pan and rub the spices into it evenly all around.

Mix the ketchup with the beer or water and pour over the onions. Lay the brisket on the onions, fat side up, and cover the roasting pan with a lid or a tent of foil. Roast in the preheated oven, basting 3 or 4 times and turning the brisket at least once, for 3 hours, or until the meat is fork-tender.

Remove the brisket from the oven, uncover, and let cool until it can be handled. Slice the brisket against the grain, about ½ inch thick. Arrange the pieces in a glass or crockery serving dish that can be heated, and pour the juices and onion over it. Refrigerate overnight.

About an hour before you are ready to serve, remove the serving dish from the refrigerator and let come to room temperature. Place in a preheated 350° F. oven and heat until piping hot throughout, about 20 minutes. (Let the serving dish come to room temperature before putting it in the oven so it won't crack from the temperature change.)

Leftovers make yummy sandwiches or a tasty burrito filling.

Serves 12.

"There are dietary laws you must obey for seder," Bobbie Krinsky says. "You don't eat any leavening. You do not eat noodles. You're not supposed to eat grains like rice or split peas. But unless you're Orthodox, you might have a drink and you surely have wine. It's not logical. It's emotional. And while everyone believes the rules are hard and fast, everyone also interprets them differently and makes exceptions."

Several years ago her temple was involved in an exchange with a black Christian church in Madison.

"We shared services with one another and helped celebrate each other's holidays. And the church decided that they would make a seder meal for our temple. Now, on the seder table is a plate of symbolic foods—the horseradish for the tears of Israel, parsley for hope. And in the center of the plate there is supposed to be the shank bone of a lamb.

"And there we were, surrounding this beautiful table with a feast laid out and the symbolic plate in the center. And slowly we all realized that instead of a lamb shank, the bone in the middle was actually a ham bone.

"I guess they'd not been able to come up with lamb and the ham bone seemed a logical substitute. Of course, we are forbidden to eat pork. But fortunately, you don't eat from the lamb shank either, so no one had to touch it or deal with it directly. And although everyone in the temple realized what was going on, no one spoke up or said anything to the members of the church. Because doing that, in that very beautiful moment of sharing, would have been a violation of the extraordinary gift they were giving to us."

Roast Potatoes and Carrots

Bobbie's Brisket is so rich it is best accompanied by this simple vegetable dish. The baking sheets can be popped onto the top shelf of the oven and started about 15 minutes before you warm up the brisket. These are nice dressed with Sage Vinegar (see page 132).

3 large baking potatoes
6 large carrots
12 cloves of garlic
1 tablespoon corn oil
2 teaspoons kosher salt
Freshly ground black
  pepper to taste

Preheat the oven to 350° F. Lightly oil 2 baking sheets with shallow sides or 2 shallow roasting pans.

Wash the potatoes well. Leaving the skins on, dice the potatoes small—about ½ inch square. Peel the carrots, halve lengthwise, and cut into pieces about ½ inch thick. Peel the garlic cloves and put all the vegetables into a large bowl. Drizzle the corn oil over them and toss lightly to coat. Sprinkle the salt and several grindings of pepper over the vegetables and toss again to season evenly.

Spread the vegetable pieces on the baking sheets in a single layer. Place on the top shelf of the oven, and roast for 15 minutes. Turn with a spatula and place back in the oven for another 15 to 20 minutes, until tender and browned. Serve immediately.

Serves 12.

"*Jewish cooks are such characters,*" *Bobbie Krinsky says.*

"*Even the most sophisticated, internationally savvy, creative cooks fall right in line in the traditional Jewish food department. When it comes to Jewish cooking, they are incredibly opinionated about how it must be done. And how it must be done is usually how they learned to do it at home.*"

She mimics the shocked whispers of her aunts and cousins gathered around a buffet table: "*She uses sugar in that?!*" "*She puts mayonnaise in chopped liver?*" "*Baking powder? In latkes? No!*"

"*A Jewish cook will blanch when someone puts tomato in chicken broth or red wine with a brisket. She silently thanks God she knows better.*

"*And yet some of the best Jewish cooks I know have 'heretical' secrets. Harriet does put a little mayonnaise in her delicious chopped liver, and I couldn't tell, except it is so creamy. Myra puts beef broth in her chicken soup, and it's so rich and wonderful.*

"*The bottom line is no one knows what is actually 100 percent purely traditional because to each and every Jewish cook, her recipes, her mother's are the only ones she really trusts.*"

Ⓜom Fishman's Matzo Popovers

The stricture against using leavening and grain products other than matzo could have squelched the aspirations of less inventive cooks. But for generations of Jewish women, it seems only to have inspired more and more clever inventions.

These matzo rolls are sterling proof. The recipe was passed on to Bobbie by her mother-in-law from her first marriage and has become a part of her seder liturgy. With a delightful airy texture, the rolls resemble popovers, but with a distinctly eggy flavor. They are perfect for soaking up the juices of Bobbie's Brisket, giving it a slightly British air in the process. Or the tops can be cut off, and the centers filled with sweetened fresh berries, then the tops popped back on for a cunning, light dessert.

⅓ cup canola oil
1 teaspoon sugar
½ teaspoon kosher salt
1 cup matzo meal
4 eggs

Preheat the oven to 425° F. Lightly grease the cups of a muffin tin that makes a dozen. Have an electric mixer with a large bowl ready.

In a medium-sized saucepan, bring 1 cup water to a boil. Add the oil, sugar, and salt and stir until the sugar and salt are dissolved. Stirring as you go, slowly pour the matzo meal into the bubbling liquid, then immediately remove from the heat. The mixture will be thick and sticky. Plop it into the mixer bowl and beat at medium speed for about 1 minute.

One at a time, add the eggs to the matzo mixture, beating until well blended after each one.

Put a heaping tablespoonful of the mixture into each muffin tin. (If any dough is left over, divide it evenly among the tins.) Place in the preheated oven and bake for 15 minutes, then turn down the heat to 325° F. and bake for another 20 minutes.

Serves 12.

Apple-Pear Haroset

Like the Olenicks, Bobbie makes plenty of haroset so there is enough to serve with dinner as well as to use in the seder ceremony. Her haroset is usually made with tart apples, but with so many varieties of apples and pears available in the market today, it seems a shame not to make a mélange of many flavors. Pick whatever is freshest and most fragrant from the produce bin.

6–8 apples and pears
1 teaspoon lemon juice
¼ cup kosher sweet grape wine
⅓ teaspoon cinnamon (optional)
Honey to taste
¼ cup chopped blanched almonds

Wash the apples and pears, quarter them, and remove the cores. Chop into pieces about ½ inch square. Place in a large bowl, sprinkle with the lemon juice, and toss together.

Add the kosher wine and, if you like, cinnamon. Mix together and taste. Add honey if the mixture is overwhelmingly tart. You want a mixture of bite and sweetness. Add the almonds, toss, and serve immediately.

Serves 12.

In The Jewish-American Kitchen, *author and food scholar Raymond Sokolov says that a menu of Jewish food defined only by dietary laws or holiday "would cut the heart out of the Jewish menu, which is a conglomeration of dishes borrowed from here and everywhere, dishes that have survived the trials of the Diaspora, dishes born of emigration and resettlement, and finally dishes that grow out of the creative assimilation of American ways."*

Truffle Wedges

Bobbie Krinsky says fresh fruit is also her first choice for a Passover dessert: "That's not traditional at all. In my mother's generation, it was considered something of a challenge to create a great, gooey dramatic dessert without using flour or butter or any leavening powder. Sometimes, though, the dessert looked better than it tasted."

Not these lovely little wedges of nut meal and chocolate, however. They come from the recipe files of Joyce Goldstein, who grew up in New York, where her grandmother, Hannah Weil Greene, had a small cooking school. Truffle torte was one of Hannah's Passover recipes, these same layers with a chocolate icing between them. But Hannah's recipe said that the layers were "very delicious" simply cut into wedges, un-iced, and served as cookie bars. I thought them even better than the torte, and less trouble.

8 eggs

8 ounces semisweet chocolate

1 cup (2 sticks) margarine, softened (you can use butter if this dessert follows a dairy meal)

1 cup sugar

2 cups almonds, very finely ground

Preheat the oven to 350° F. Grease the bottoms and sides of two 9-inch springform cake pans. Line with waxed paper; grease the waxed paper and dust with matzo flour.

Separate the eggs. (Do this step now so the whites can come to room temperature.)

Melt the chocolate in the top of a double boiler over water that is barely simmering. When just melted, remove from the heat and let cool while you proceed with the rest of the recipe.

With an electric mixer, cream the margarine and ¾ cup of the sugar until very fluffy. Add the egg yolks one or two at a time, mixing well after each. Turn the mixer to low speed and add the melted chocolate. When all is well blended, remove from the electric mixer and fold in the nut meal by hand.

Using the electric mixer, beat the egg whites with the remaining ¼ cup sugar until stiff peaks form. Gently fold the egg whites into the chocolate-nut mixture, mixing just enough to blend but no more. Spoon equally into the prepared pans and smooth the tops with a spatula. Bake on the center rack in the preheated oven for 40 to 45 minutes, until a tester comes out clean or with just a crumb or two on it. Be careful not to overbake!

Cool on wire racks for 20 minutes. Open the springs. When completely cool, peel off the waxed paper from the sides, carefully invert on plates, and remove the waxed paper from the bottoms. When ready to serve, invert the cakes onto attractive plates, or onto plates lined with paper doilies. Cut in wedges and serve with hot coffee and fresh fruit. Ripe pears are especially nice.

Serves 12.

Zesty Mango Sorbet

Sorbets can be made from any number of fruits for Passover, but mangoes are especially nice because they accentuate the flavors of other fruits and also cozy up well to sweets like the Truffle Wedges.

Imported mangoes are in season from January through fall, and ripe ones should be available at Passover time. Colors may vary from green to yellow or a dark rose. More important than the color is the tautness of the skin. It should look as if it fits the fruit. If it looks saggy, the mango is too far gone. The flesh should feel tender to the touch, like that of a ripe avocado. And, most important, the stem end should smell sweet and fragrant. If it smells fermented or sour, it's too old. If the only mangoes you find are hard, green, and lacking fragrance, buy them anyway and put them in a plastic bag, close it snugly, and leave at room temperature for 24 hours. They should sweeten right up.

Getting the pulp out of a mango can be a most mystifying experience. For years I would eat mine standing over the sink, sucking pulp from the peel and pit that it so tenaciously clung to. Then Elizabeth Schneider's useful book *Uncommon Fruits and Vegetables: A Common Sense Guide* (Harper & Row, 1986) introduced me to the handy method below.

2½ cups sugar
1 tablespoon grated lemon
   zest
4 pounds mangoes (about
   4 plump ones)
Juice of 1 lemon

Dissolve the sugar in 2 cups water in a saucepan over low heat, add the lemon zest, turn up the heat, and bring to a boil. Remove from the heat and allow to come to room temperature.

Peel the mangoes and remove the pits. The best way to do this is to cut away as much of the flesh from the pit as you can before peeling. The most efficient way to do this is to stand the fruit on end, stem up and the narrow side facing you. Using a good knife, cut a vertical section off the fruit, beginning about ½ inch to the right of the stem. You should just miss the pit. Do the same to the other side. Set these 2 sections aside and then peel away the skin from the pulp left around the seed, and cut off as much of the flesh as you can.

To remove the flesh from the side sections, use a butter knife to score cubes about ½ inch square in the flesh. (Cut to the skin, but not through it.) When the flesh is scored, push up gently on the center of the skin so that the scored flesh pops up, looking like the surface of a hand grenade. The cubes can now be easily sliced off the skin.

Puree the mango pulp in a blender with the cooled syrup and lemon juice. Freeze in an ice-cream maker according to the maker's instructions. Will keep very well for 24 hours in freezer.

Serves 8 to 12.

Six

Summer Celebrations

Summertime and the partying's easy. Grills are popping and the weather is fine . . .

So it seems a little odd that there are so few formal holidays during the summer season. Our ancestors understood the allure of summer. Solstice celebrations were an important part of their ritual year. Solstice observances had a resurgence during the counterculture days of the 1970s and are still celebrated, particularly in the West where New Age philosophy has a strong hold.

But you don't have to be a Druid, neo- or otherwise, to savor the many joys of summer. Summer's luxuriously longer days and weather that entices one to play are reason enough to celebrate.

SUMMER SALAD DAYS

Bobbie Krinsky is one of a dozen or so members of Westwing Studios, an artists' cooperative in the wing of a Civil War–era building in Verona, Wisconsin, just outside Madison. Silversmiths, potters, painters, jewelers, woodworkers, and fabric designers—the Westwing craftspeople bring a quirky artistic perspective to everything they do, including their annual summer salad celebration.

"We don't hold it on any particular date," Bobbie says. "It's just when things start to get ripe and we begin to feel like it's time we all did something together."

If the weather cooperates on the day of the party, it may take place under a bower of apple blossoms in a nearby orchard. Or if it's rainy, the salad makers will set up camp in one of the larger studios.

The centerpiece of the party is a two-foot-long hollowed-out log that has become the official salad bowl. The idea is to fill it with as many "salad" items as artistically and deliciously as possible. Everyone brings an ingredient, and the process of putting them together becomes a collaborative work.

In a very loose way, woodworker Henry Hart has become the designated greens man.

"Henry was always sitting in his studio eating these weeds when you passed by. We thought he might have a passion for lettuce," Bobbie says.

Henry concurs: "I have a little yard at home. I planted a couple of apple trees there once, but they started shading it, so I cut them down. I prefer my salad."

Arugula has been high on Henry's list lately, so the Westwing salad always has plenty, along with tender dandelion greens, whatever lettuce is in full swing in Henry's garden, lots of herbs, and edible flowers for color and perfume.

Color and texture are as important as taste in this artists' salad, Bobbie says. Slivers of red cabbage, chartreuse pea pods, ebony olives, crimson disks of ripe cherry tomatoes are part of the palette. Other flavored ingredients have included marinated artichokes; chunks of cold herbed chicken; sunflower seeds; buttery walnuts and pecans; mushrooms, both fresh and pickled; beans, both green and garbanzo; dried fruits; fresh broccoli; crisp cucumber.

"Sometimes we argue a little. Someone will want to put something in and someone else will think it may be too much. But usually adventure wins out, and we are inclined to say 'Add it in' far more than 'Leave it out.' We've never made a salad that didn't taste delicious in the end," Bobbie says.

The construction of the salad has something of a ritual air about it. The huge log is set up in a spot of honor and the basic greens go in first. Then all the participants take their containers of whatever they've brought and layer it on. When everything is in, it's time to mix—a job that Bobbie savors because "I do it with my hands."

There are usually three or four dressings available, and diners douse their salad with whatever they wish. The Westwing artists eat their salad from paper plates because it's less trouble to clean up. A really good sourdough bread from a local bakery, strong cheese, and bottles of crisp German white wine complete the menu.

"For us, it's partly a celebration of the season, the chance to get outside, to savor things that are green and growing," Bobbie says. "But the salad itself is also very much a creative act, a strangely liberating one for all of us artists.

"You see, when you are focused on your own work—well, making jewelry, for instance, is so exacting and painstaking. So much can go wrong, and detail must be attended to.

"With cooking, though, things don't go wrong, they just go differently. And you can go with them and it can all turn out better in the end."

PART OF THE CHARM OF THE WESTWING SALAD IS THAT IT'S NEVER THE same dish twice. Consequently, there is no recipe for a salad in this section, but there are several recipes for yummy dressings. Carrot-Raisin-Millet Bread is the perfect foil for a greens celebration, and a classic Strawberry-Rhubarb Pie is the ultimate way to celebrate the beginning of summer's coming abundance.

FROM "LUNCH IN THE GARDEN"

We have lived in these bodies
a long time;
they have been our boats and now
we are carried here,
all the abundance of summer
laid out on a white cloth.
Old friends under a roof of braided vines,
we take the garden's tender lettuces,
the fruits
and listen
to the whisper of leafy voices
telling us who we are . . .

—BETH FERRIS, *NORTHERN LIGHTS*

Sage Vinegar

Salad purists believe it is hard to improve on the basic oil-and-vinegar combination that accents but doesn't overwhelm the actual salad. One excellent innovation, however, is seasoned vinegar. Plenty of herbed vinegars are available in the market these days, although just how fresh they may be when you buy them is a matter of speculation. You can easily make your own, however, and the results are spectacular.

This sage vinegar is especially full-flavored—so much so that it can serve superbly as a dressing alone. It also makes a great companion with fruity olive oil. Don't mix the two in advance, but let your guests do it to their own preference. See "Herbed Vinegar Tips," below, for some general hints on making herbed vinegars.

1 cup fresh sage leaves

1 large clove of garlic, quartered

¼ teaspoon whole black peppercorns, lightly cracked

1¼ cups rice vinegar (about)

Rinse the sage leaves and gently pat dry with paper towels. Place in a clean glass bottle with the capacity to hold 12 ounces. (A wooden chopstick makes a handy, gentle prod for pushing the leaves in if the bottle has a narrow neck.) Add the garlic quarters and peppercorns. Pour the rice vinegar in to cover the other ingredients. (Again, you can use the chopstick to make sure the leaves, etc., are completely immersed.) Cap bottle with a cork or plastic lid (don't use metal), and place in a cool cupboard or other place out of the sunlight for 48 hours.

Sage Vinegar is an excellent condiment for the Roast Potatoes and Carrots (page 121).

Makes about 1¼ cups.

HERBED VINEGAR TIPS

The secret to fine herbed vinegar is plenty of herbs. A cup of fresh leaves, augmented by garlic and spices if you wish, is a good amount to add to about a cup and a half of vinegar.

It's not necessary to boil the vinegar—in fact, it's not a good idea, since the hot liquid can have a deleterious effect on the herb oils. Likewise, simmering the concoction in sunlight is also not wise. Instead, put the herbed vinegar away in a cool dark place for about 48 hours. If you have used plenty of herbs, this will be time enough to develop a full-flavored vinegar.

You can buy fancy bottles for putting up the vinegars, or you can simply use bottles you have around. Make sure that they are scrupulously clean and thoroughly dried. Cap them with plastic caps or corks, not metal caps, which can react with the vinegar. Although big bottles look dramatic, I like ones large enough to hold about 12 ounces. By the time I've used most of the vinegar in one, I'm ready to move on to another flavor adventure.

It's easiest of all to use the bottle the vinegar comes in. Decant the contents, stuff in the herbs and any other seasonings, then use a funnel to pour back in just enough vinegar to cover. Then store the rest of the vinegar in a small bottle or jar. As you use your herbed vinegar, you can add the remaining plain vinegar—or any vinegar, for that matter—to the herbs to keep a perpetual supply.

If you decide not to keep adding more vinegar, make sure that the herbs are totally immersed in what remains. A wooden chopstick is a very handy tool for this, and for gently stuffing large herb leaves into the bottle in the first place.

Tarragon, thyme, and rosemary are among the traditional herbs that are used to season vinegars, but you should not limit your repertoire to them. If there's a flavor you especially like and you can imagine it enhanced by tart undertones, try it. Don't be afraid to mix herb flavors, or to use spices such as cloves, caraway, and peppercorns. It's a good idea to crack the spice seeds lightly before adding them to the vinegar, to release their oils most effectively.

Any vinegar can be dressed up with the flavors of fresh herbs, but distilled white vinegar and most commercial apple cider vinegars have a harsh bite and lack the complexity of flavors that other vinegars may have. You can get great results with wine, fruit, and grain vinegars.

I especially like the rice vinegars found in Oriental markets for combining with herbs, particularly the slightly darker organic brown rice brews. They tend to have an almost buttery undercurrent, but are light enough that they allow the full flavor of the added herbs to come through.

Wine vinegars and fruit vinegars have distinctive flavors that work well with many herbs, with the end result a balanced harmony between the vinegar and add-ins.

Balsamic vinegar tastes rich, almost too rich. It can overpower all but a strong herb. Nevertheless, it works well with plenty of rosemary and garlic. If you use a balsamic vinegar, add 1 scant tablespoon brown sugar to each cup for a more complex flavor.

Umeboshi plum vinegar is as salty as it is tart, and, used alone, it overpowers anything it comes in contact with. It's really too briny for making herbed vinegar, but mixed half and half with rice vinegar and then packed with a couple of cups of half a dozen or more minced fresh herbs, it becomes a handy year-round substitute for bouquet garni. I let mine ferment at room temperature for 24 hours in a wide-mouthed jar, then pop it into the refrigerator, adding a spoonful to a sturdy soup or stew when the spirit moves me. (Use it sparingly at first, since it is intensely flavored and salty.) Fresh herbs can be added to the jar from time to time: such a handy thing when you've bought a bunch of thyme for a recipe that calls for a mere tablespoonful, and are wondering what to do with the surfeit. This pickled garni holds its flavor well, refrigerated, for about a year.

Good sources for more information on making herbed vinegars, and for inspired suggestions for good flavor combinations, are Maggie Oster's Recipes from an American Herb Garden *(Macmillan, 1993)* and Herbal Vinegar *(Storey Publishing, 1994).*

There is an old Spanish proverb that says you must have four people to make a good salad. You need a spendthrift in charge of the oil, but a miser for vinegar, a counselor for the salt, and a madman for mixing it all together.

Yin-Yang Vinaigrette

Umeboshi plums are to salty as *habanero* chile peppers are to hot, which means they'll make you pucker with a vengeance. It also means that the vinegar made from them, available in most natural or Oriental food stores, is actually as salty as it is acidic. This double-yin punch makes it the perfect foil for the yang sweetness of honey and orange. The result is a beautiful amber-rose dressing that is at once flowery but sturdy.

This is also an excellent dressing drizzled on avocados or on fruit salad.

¼ cup umeboshi plum
   vinegar
½ teaspoon sesame oil
1 tablespoon canola oil
4 tablespoons pale honey
Juice of ½ lime
Juice of 2 oranges

Whisk all the ingredients together and serve. Makes about 1½ cups.

Saturday morning was come and all the summer world was bright and fresh, and brimming with life. There was a song in every heart; and if the heart was young the music issued at the lips. There was cheer in every face and a spring in every step. The locust trees were in bloom and the fragrance of the blossoms filled the air.

Cardiff Hill, beyond the village and above it, was green with vegetation, and it lay just far enough away to seem a Delectable Land, dreamy, reposeful and inviting.

—Mark Twain, *Tom Sawyer*

Tangy Apple Dressing

This sweetly tart, fruity dressing is a very nice complement to salads that contain grilled chicken or nuts and also makes a pleasant fruit salad dressing. An added bonus is that it's low-fat.

1 cup apple juice
1 tablespoon balsamic
 vinegar
1 tablespoon brown sugar
1 tablespoon thinly sliced
 fresh ginger
¼ cup buttermilk
½ cup plain nonfat yogurt

In a non-aluminum saucepan, mix the apple juice, vinegar, and brown sugar. Add the slices of fresh ginger and bring the mixture to a boil over high heat. Turn down the heat and simmer, uncovered, for 10 minutes. Remove from the heat and allow to cool to room temperature.

When the mixture has cooled, strain into a small mixing bowl. Whisk in the buttermilk and then the yogurt. Serve in a small pitcher.

Makes about 1½ cups.

Avocado Bliss

This sprightly, herbed puree is unlike any other avocado dressing I've encountered. Its texture is light and velvety, and its flavor is at once delicate but zippy. It works equally well as a dip, and I like to serve it in late May or early June with a bowl of the first summer strawberries and a pitcher of thin, raw asparagus spears.

1 medium-sized ripe
  avocado
1 tablespoon pale honey
½ cup canola oil
Juice of 1 lime
½ tablespoon chopped
  fresh tarragon leaves
1 tablespoon fresh dillweed
Salt to taste (optional)

Quarter and peel the avocado, discard the pit, and place the flesh in a blender. Add the honey, oil, lime, herbs, and about a tablespoonful of water. Blend about 2 minutes, until smooth. You may have to add a little more water to ease the blending. Add more water (up to about 4 tablespoons) to get the dressing to the consistency you desire. I prefer it to be like mayonnaise. Taste and add salt, if you wish.

Makes about 1 cup.

Herbed Buttermilk Dressing

Yum! Creamy but tangy and spiked by the crunch of cucumbers and fresh chopped herbs. This is a perfect dressing.

1 cup buttermilk
1 tablespoon mayonnaise
1 tablespoon chopped fresh
    sorrel
1 tablespoon chopped fresh
    dillweed
2 tablespoons chopped
    fresh parsley
2 tablespoons minced
    scallion
2 tablespoons minced
    peeled, seeded cucumber
⅛ teaspoon kosher salt
Freshly ground black
    pepper to taste

Whisk the buttermilk and mayonnaise together until blended. Add the herbs, scallion, cucumber, and salt. Add a little freshly ground black pepper to your liking. Serve with a ladle for spooning it on.

Makes about 1½ cups.

Carrot-Raisin-Millet Bread

This bread is a favorite at Lynn's Paradise Café in Louisville, Kentucky. Baker Michael Smith scaled down the restaurant's multi-loaf recipe to this handy two-loaf size. The result is an intriguingly textured, confidently flavored bread that is the perfect choice for a Summer Salad Days party.

½ cup milk

2 tablespoons canola oil

½ cup honey

2 tablespoons salt

1 tablespoon active dry yeast

2 cups whole wheat flour

½ cup raw millet

¾ cup grated carrot

1 cup raisins

4 cups unbleached bread flour (about)

Mix 1 cup water and the milk in a saucepan and scald. Remove from the heat, transfer to a large mixing bowl, add the oil, and allow to cool to 105°–110° F. When cooled, whisk in the honey, salt, and yeast. When the yeast is thoroughly dissolved, mix in the whole wheat flour, using a wooden spoon. The mixture will be the consistency of batter.

Gently fold in first the millet, then the carrot, and then the raisins, and continue to fold in until they are evenly distributed. ("Folding in" means that you lift a portion of the dough from the bottom of bowl up and over the rest of the dough. Whereas stirring cuts through the dough, folding doesn't, which gives the resulting loaf a better texture.)

Sprinkle about a cup of the unbleached bread flour over the dough and fold it in. Continue incorporating the bread flour until the dough pulls away from the edges of the bowl. You may need slightly more or less than 4 cups of flour, depending on the humidity and other factors. What you want is a moist dough that is still slightly sticky.

Generously flour a firm surface for kneading and turn the dough out onto it. Flour your hands and knead gently but firmly for 8 to 10 minutes. (For notes on kneading, see page 80 in the recipe for Crusty Rye Loaf.) Add flour to the surface and your hands as needed to keep the dough from sticking. The dough will become more elastic as you knead, and you will require less flour to keep it from sticking. When the dough no longer sticks to surface and hands and has become smooth and somewhat shiny, it's done.

Clean the mixing bowl and oil the inside lightly. Return the dough ball to the oiled bowl, turning it over once so the oil coats it all over. Cover with a damp towel and leave to rise in a warm (75°–80° F.) and draft-free place until doubled. Using your fist, gently press down the risen dough 4 or 5 times. Divide in half and place in 2 large (9×5×3-inch) oiled loaf pans. Allow to rise again for 45 to 60 minutes (to approximately double).

Preheat the oven to 375° F. Bake the bread in the preheated oven for 45 minutes, or until the top is shiny brown and the loaf goes "thump" when you thwack it with a finger.

Remove from the pans immediately and let cool completely before slicing. Serve with Scarborough Fair Butter (recipe follows).

Makes 2 loaves.

Scarborough Fair Butter

Any flower child of the sixties will know that this herbed butter is seasoned with a bouquet of (sing along with me!) parsley, sage, rosemary, and thyme. Lime adds just a kiss of zest to the blend. It's grand on any hearty, grainy bread, especially Carrot-Raisin-Millet, and a great accent for simple steamed vegetables.

1 cup (2 sticks) butter
1 tablespoon minced fresh
  parsley
1 tablespoon minced fresh
  sage
1 tablespoon minced fresh
  rosemary
1 tablespoon minced fresh
  thyme
1 tablespoon fresh lime juice

Put the butter in a mixing bowl and leave at room temperature until softened. Sprinkle the herbs and lime juice over it and blend with a fork until all are incorporated. Spoon into 2 small, pretty serving bowls, cover tightly with plastic wrap, and refrigerate. Will keep well for 2 days. When you're ready to serve, allow to sit at room temperature for a few minutes until soft enough to spread.

Makes about 1 cup.

Strawberry-Rhubarb Pie

There is no pie that better salutes the advent of summer than strawberry-rhubarb, with its lively marriage of sweet and tart. Once a seasonal treat only, you can now make this pie virtually year round with shipped-in strawberries and hothouse rhubarb. But it tastes truly outrageous only at the very beginning of summer, made when the first crop of succulent, juice-oozing local strawberries comes in and when the deep red, flavorful stalks of field-grown rhubarb appear.

This version was created and refined by Peg Lehocky, who used it to rack up ribbons at the Kentucky State Fair a couple of years ago. (One demonstration of the classic status of Strawberry-Rhubarb Pie: the fair has an entire category devoted simply to that variety.)

Peg tested several versions on her son, Dan, who cleverly insisted that each was good but might be just a little better with some fine tuning, and so kept himself in pies for most of one summer. Dan, too, is the reason that this pie is made in a 10-inch deep-dish plate instead of the standard 9-inch pie pan.

"He's been known to eat half a nine-inch pie as an after-school snack," his mother sighs. "Besides, I say if I'm going to make a pie, I might as well make a *pie*."

Dan advises that the only appropriate beverage with this pie is a very tall, very cold glass of milk. He's right.

NOTE: Most recipes tell you to make the crust first, then the filling. This is not how Peg assembles her pie, however. She does part of the filling, part of the pastry, the rest of the filling, and then finishes the pastry and assembles the pie. For more crust tips, see page 146.

FILLING

2 pounds fresh
   strawberries, washed,
   topped, and sliced
1¼ pounds rhubarb, sliced
   into ½-inch pieces
2 tablespoons grenadine
   syrup
1½ cups sugar
½ cup all-purpose flour
½ teaspoon ground nutmeg
2 tablespoons butter, cut
   into small pieces

Preheat the oven to 425° F.

Ice water is essential for this piecrust, so before you start assembling anything, get a bowl, pour about a cup of cold tap water into it, and then add a couple of cubes of ice.

Mix the sliced berries and rhubarb in a large bowl. Sprinkle with the grenadine. Set aside while you begin the pastry.

In a large bowl, combine the 3 cups flour with the salt. Use 2 table knives to cut the shortening into the flour until it resembles coarse meal. Set aside and return to the fruit.

In a small bowl, combine the 1½ cups sugar, ½ cup flour, and nutmeg. Toss with the fruit. Set the mixture aside and return to the pastry. (Work steadily and quickly through

PASTRY
FOR 10-INCH PIE

6–8 teaspoons ice water
3 cups all-purpose flour
1 teaspoon salt
1 cup vegetable shortening
    (butter-flavored Crisco
    preferred)
1–2 tablespoons sugar

the next part, because you don't want the fruit to stand too long or it will become too juicy.)

Sprinkle 6 to 8 teaspoons of the ice water over the flour mix, 1 tablespoon at a time, combining lightly with a fork after each spoonful. (Don't plop the water in or sprinkle it in the same area every time, but spread it out over the dough so you'll get better distribution with much less mixing and handling of the dough.)

You may not use all the water. What you want is a dough that is thoroughly moist but not wet. The water is there to make the dough hold together, not soak it.

Divide the dough in half and on a very lightly floured pastry cloth, using a rolling pin with a lightly floured pastry cover, roll out one half evenly in a circle that is about 1½ inches wider all around than the top edge of a 10-inch pie pan.

Gently transfer to the pan and pat in lightly. Now roll out the second ball of dough evenly to a circle that is about 1 inch wider than the pan top.

Pile the fruit mixture into the crust in the pan and dot with the butter. Gently fit the second crust on top. Trim the crusts so there is an equal lip of crust all around, about 1 inch wider than the pan. Tuck the edge of that lip under itself to seal the top, then crimp the crust with your fingers. Cut air vents in the top and sprinkle a light dusting of sugar over the crust.

Place in the preheated oven on the center rack for 10 minutes, then turn the heat down to 375° F. and bake for 50 to 60 minutes more, until the top is light golden and the juice that bubbles out of the top vents is slightly jelled.

Allow to cool completely before slicing. Leftovers make a wonderful summer morning breakfast.

Serves 8.

THE LOBSTERMEN'S RESTAURANT IN JAMESPORT

I wonder what it's like
at 4 in the morning, the lobstermen,
only them and the three German sisters
who cook in the back. Smell of coffee
morning fries eggs just right
they never stick to the pan.
But I would be out of place, an intruder
though I love the sea with a love
close to passion. But these men
know it better, out there alone
I can imagine how they talk to it
though I don't know what they say.

I break no rule of camaraderie
it's well into the afternoon,
they're long into port and I only stop
for the strawberry rhubarb pie
and always the same question
from one of the three: How does it taste
going down? And always the same reply:
Better it couldn't be.
And nothing could be closer to the truth.
I'm sure it's in the lard, the lard
they mix in with the dough
and the cinnamon to appease the bitter rhubarb.
Better it couldn't be.

How pleased they are to get it out of me
a stranger passing through from Stony Brook

but coming into strangeness:
might as well be Hawthorne's Salem
the sea has such a presence here,
like an old uncle's firm hand from behind
on the fin of your shoulder, so firm
it almost hurts.
But I pay my way. I always have.
True, no sea yarns, no talk of currents
and tides. True I can't repair a net
mend a lobster pot. But I know pie,
especially strawberry rhubarb, and this
so pleases them it makes me one like them.
We share a truth together: about the lard and the cinnamon,
as sure as the seasons . . . as sure as the tides.

—VINCE CLEMENTE

"Light hands" is how Southern country cooks refer to the gift of making perfect piecrusts. Like artisans with "potter's hands," those with light hands seem to know instinctively how to handle dough, how to bring it together with the least amount of the mixing that ultimately toughens it.

Her substantial but flaky crusts indicate that Peg Lehocky has the gift of light hands, but she says there are tricks to the trade that can be learned even by those of us with lead fingers. Using ice water is one, and sprinkling it all over the dough instead of dropping it, plop, in one area is another.

But the key to her success with crusts, Peg says, is using the right flour. Although she's originally from Buffalo, New York, since moving to Kentucky a couple of decades ago she's become a convert to the Southern creed of White Lily Flour enthusiasts.

"It makes the best crusts imaginable, and you just can't get the same texture with other flours, especially those made with hard wheat," she says.

White Lily and many flours from Southern mills, such as Martha White flour, are milled from soft winter wheat. Most other flours—particularly those milled north of the Mason-Dixon Line—are made of a hard, protein-rich wheat that is superb for bread baking. Williams-Sonoma now sells White Lily mail order from its catalogue. Otherwise, flours that are labeled "cake flour" usually have a high ratio of soft wheat and are also good for flaky crusts.

PIG PARTY

Like so many contemporary young working couples, Pat and Dean Murakami rarely have time to call their own. Dean teaches psychology at American River College in Sacramento and does research at the University of California at Davis. Pat is a hardworking pastry chef at Chinois East-West, a popular Orient-meets-California-style restaurant in Sacramento.

Both are intelligent, gregarious people who savor the pleasures of good conversations that take unexpected turns. And both are "foodies" who love the creativity of cooking and the joy of sharing the results with good friends.

Dinner parties for a half dozen or so judiciously tossed-together couples would have been their thing in another era, but because of harried contemporary work schedules, they find it hard to pull off that kind of classic entertaining with any frequency.

Instead they've created an annual celebration that lets them tumble all their friends together in one big gossiping, getting-to-know-one-another mass, and allows them to put on a spread of foods so fabulous their friends talk about it for a whole year.

Referred to as the "Pig Party," it's a bash that's earned its name in part because the centerpiece each year is a golden-crisped, savory-seasoned whole roast pig from a local Chinese market. But it's a Pig Party most of all because of the unprecedented chance it offers the guests to pig out on the plethora of dishes that fill the dining room, kitchen, and yard of their small Sacramento house.

The party began as a housewarming, Pat says: "We wanted everyone to come and see our cute little house."

By now the guest list has reached seam-bursting proportions, with a pleasant seventy-five or so in attendance each year; but the bustle and jumble of so many folks are part of the fun.

The pig is ensconced on a platter in the center of the table in the dining room, a vast bowl of Vietnamese noodles at his snout and side dishes arrayed like supplicants around his throne. There's a dessert station in the laundry room (between the kitchen and the yard) and a grill station where Dean, whose barbecue labors begin the day before and often last through the night, presides.

Most hosts would opt for a stand-up, eat-on-the-hoof format for feeding such a large group in a small space, but Pat says, "It's very important to me that everyone should sit at tables to eat. That way everyone gets to mingle. The academics meet the foodies, the doctors dine with the busboys. And everybody discovers how much they have to talk about."

The Murakamis rent chairs and borrow tables, which are covered with gaily patterned cloths. The yard itself is a food lover's paradise, every inch of its tiny space turned over to growing something either tasty or beautiful. There's a lemon and an apricot tree, irises and hibiscuses blooming, a grapevine over a tiny fence, and tomatoes planted in the grass crevices where the concrete drive has cracked.

Scheduled for the Sunday before Memorial Day, the party coincides with the hiatus between spring and summer semesters at the university. Dean says there's something freewheeling and exhilarating about the event:

"It's like the first days of summer vacation when you were a kid. There's that sense of release and freedom, even though most of us do go back to work now through the summer."

Even so, the party has become a send-off for the summer season, a signal that it's okay to kick back and relax whenever you can. And for the guests, the Pig Party is meant to be a totally relaxing event.

"By and large, this is a gift to our friends. No one is allowed to work. No one is allowed to contribute. They just come and sit back and savor," says Pat.

Of course, pulling off a totally laid-back event requires work, work, work on the part of Dean and Pat.

Organization helps a little. Pat keeps a folder called "The Pig File" from year to year. It's crammed with recipes, notations on what worked and what didn't, what to get more of, what to do differently, and even receipts from what they purchased where. It's also crammed with lists.

One such list charts errands and chores for each day, beginning early in May and extending until the party. They include ordering the pig, renting chairs, printing invitations.

The next, crammed tighter with notations that appear to have been written a bit more urgently, outlines chores for each day of the week before the party. And then there is one very important page with things that must be done the day before.

"Don't be too impressed with all this apparent organization," Pat says with a laugh. "What you don't see is that we often don't even decide what other foods we're serving until the week of the party. We always cook chicken and have several things that are strictly vegetarian to accommodate friends, but the way we prepare them varies from year to year. A lot depends on what we've been cooking at the restaurant recently, what new tricks or tastes I've learned."

Those neatly ordered lists also don't tell you what other demands there are on the Murakamis as the Pig Party approaches. Dean is always in the last-minute bustle that accompanies the end of a semester, including a psychology department picnic that frequently falls the day before the party. And one year Pat was also making a multitiered wedding cake on commission the day before. But instead of getting flustered by the activity, the Murakamis seem to relish it.

"Food frenzy is second nature to me," Pat says. "I grew up in New Jersey, where my dad owned a northern Italian restaurant. I spent my teenaged years sitting in the kitchen peeling shrimp, doing the dishes—all those great chores the daughter of a restaurant owner gets to do. And I just got used to people being able to produce great food and serve it under totally frantic circumstances."

And Dean, who grew up in Los Angeles, says that the work is also part of the fun.

"Pat and I get to do a lot together to pull the party off, the planning and organizing. I grill, she does the sauces. She makes the lists and hands them to me, I go get the stuff. The energy that builds up leading up to it carries right over into the party."

◇ **The Pig**

The secret to the Murakamis' superb roasted pig is a simple one: they buy it already roasted.

"The pig comes done. Done, done, done. It's a done deal from the Chinese Market here in Sacramento," Pat explains.

"We roasted a pig ourselves once, and frankly, it came out sort of bland. They do a great job with it. It's juicy and looks outrageous. Sometimes it comes with an apple in its mouth. Once it had red-and-white pom-poms. We called it the Stanford pig, since those are Stanford University's colors."

Because Pat and Dean don't have to fool with the pig, they have more time for making all the other dishes that make their annual party a genuine pig-out.

My advice for pulling off a pig party on your own is either to order a pig already roasted or to forgo the little porker and put on a buffet of pig-out proportions.

If you live in an area with a first-rate Oriental market, you may be able to order a whole roasted pig from it; or if there is a nearby Oriental restaurant that does catering, it may do roast pigs as well. Meat markets and butcher shops, particularly those that cater, will often roast a pig for you with enough advance notice.

Another option is to order a roasted suckling from Smokehouse Inc., a family-owned butchery in Roxbury, Massachusetts, that will air-express a plump smoked porker to you overnight. Their piglets range from 20 to 80 pounds.

A 40-to-45-pound one is a good size for good eating and will serve about 50 folks as the sole main course. That's the size that the Murakamis get. Their pig is sufficient for 75 with the abundant buffet—and there are always leftovers.

The Smokehouse pigs are first soaked in brine, then smoked over natural woods for about 8 hours, so the finished flavor is something like that of a cured ham. The butchery needs at least a week's advance notice, and its number is (617) 442-6840.

If your heart is set on roasting a pig of your own, *The Grilling Encyclopedia* by A. Cort Sinnes (Atlantic Monthly Press, 1992) is a superb source of instructions—not to mention a great book about grilling in general.

Note, though, that Sinnes cautions that roasting a pig (even a suckling that can be done on a rotisserie instead of in a pit) is a full day's work. Since the chef will need to baste the pig every 15 minutes or so and closely monitor its progress, you should plan your party accordingly.

One thing Sinnes doesn't tell you is how to carve the pig when it's done. Pat Murakami offers this advice: "You just hack it up. Go for whatever looks good to you. Last year one of our friends got really carried away and even ate an ear."

Joey's Jamaican Jerk Chicken

The Murakamis always serve at least one chicken dish at the Pig Party, varying the recipes from year to year. But this recipe for Caribbean-style jerk chicken has been such a favorite that some years they make it even when there's another chicken dish on the menu.

The marinade recipe is adapted from a recipe originated by San Francisco restaurateur Joey Altman. It is an impressive blend of hot and tangy flavors with an undercurrent of sweetness and a knock-out punch of spice. When I served it the first time, the only complaint I heard was that I'd not made enough sauce for sopping. This version should have plenty.

I used the jerk sauce on boneless, skinless chicken breasts, and that's how the recipe is written here. You can also use pieces of whole chicken, however. Just remember that its weight also includes the skin and bones, so buy about 6 pounds total. This is also a fabulous sauce for pork chops. See the variation at the end for cooking instructions.

3 bunches of scallions
¾ cup thinly sliced fresh
  ginger
6–8 cloves of garlic, sliced
¾ cup fresh lime juice
3 tablespoons whole
  allspice, freshly ground
1½ teaspoons cinnamon
¼ teaspoon ground nutmeg
¾ cup cider vinegar
⅓ cup brown sugar
⅓ cup sorghum molasses
½ teaspoon freshly ground
  black pepper
3 tablespoons olive oil
¾ cup soy sauce
3 fresh *ancho* or *jalapeño*
  peppers, coarsely
  chopped

Trim the scallions, chop coarsely, and place in a blender with the ginger, garlic, and lime juice. Blend until smooth. Add the remaining ingredients except for the peppers and chicken and blend until smooth, then add peppers a bit at a time. Blend after each addition, taste, and add more pepper if you want it even hotter. Remember, this is supposed to be very, very spicy. (See page 195 for tips on how to handle hot peppers.)

When the marinade is smooth, set aside half. Use the other half as a marinade for the chicken. Because it's a thick marinade, use your hands to spread it, making sure the marinade coats each piece of chicken. Put the chicken in a non-metal container with a lid (a heavy-duty Ziploc plastic storage bag may also be used), cover well, and refrigerate overnight. Refrigerate the extra marinade in a tightly covered jar.

About an hour and a half before you're

5 pounds split boneless,
skinless chicken breast

ready to serve, take the chicken and extra marinade from the refrigerator and let them come to room temperature.

Light enough coals to make an even layer in the bottom of a covered grill. When the coals are covered with light gray ash, put the cooking grill over them and allow it to heat for 3 or 4 minutes. When the grill is hot, brush lightly with oil to grease. Lay the chicken breasts on the grill close together, but not touching. If your grill isn't large enough to hold them all at once, grill in 2 batches.

Grill for 5 minutes with the cover on and vents open. Turn carefully. The breasts have a tendency to stick, but if you gently work a thin spatula under them, you shouldn't have much trouble. Tongs tend to break the breasts before you can turn them, although they're handy for resituating the breasts once they are turned. When you turn them, it's a good idea to move the breasts that have been in the center to the rim of the grill and vice versa.

Grill on the second side for 5 more minutes, uncovered. A little blackening is not a problem, but watch carefully so the breasts don't char. The sugar and other ingredients in the marinade do have a tendency to burn. Ten minutes should be enough to cook the breasts. Use a sharp knife to cut into the center of one to make sure they are done through. If the juices run pink or the flesh seems not quite done, cook a little longer.

When the breasts are finished, place on a large serving platter and pour the extra marinade you set aside the night before over them as sauce. (DO NOT use the marinade the breasts have soaked in, since it contains raw chicken fluids and could be deadly. It should be discarded.)

Serve at room temperature. This recipe can be doubled or tripled.

Serves 12 to 15 as a main course.

VARIATION: If you use pieces of whole chicken instead of the boneless, skinless breast, they'll need to cook an additional 10 to 30 minutes, depending on the size of the piece of meat. Use the cover throughout the cooking process. Also, you will need to turn the meat every 5 to 10 minutes to ensure that it doesn't burn.

VARIATION: Instead of chicken, you may use 12–18 pork chops ¾ inch thick. Marinade procedures are the same as for chicken. Cooked in a covered grill, chops should take 10 to 12 minutes. Turn them 3 or 4 times during the grilling process. Check for doneness by cutting into the center with a sharp knife.

JERK BY MAIL

Joey Altman went to Jamaica at twenty-five with an enormous appetite and an even greater curiosity about what makes great Jamaican food.

"I hung out with some guys who had an open-air place called the Pork Pit and learned as much as I could from them."

The most important thing Joey learned is that a great jerk sauce has to have a lot more than hotness to recommend it.

"There has to be a combination of sensations: the sweet and tangy and salty have to be all intermingled, none of them outdoing the others. When you get that right, you get what I call the 'Dorito Effect.' You know, something in the taste that makes you keep going back and back and back until the whole bag is finished."

Joey perfected his jerk sauce at Miss Pearl's Jam House, a restaurant he opened in San Francisco. These days he also markets it bottled through several mail order sources as Jamaican Jerk Sauce. You can order it from Mo Hotta, Mo Betta at (800) 462-3220 or Salsa Express, (800) 437-2572.

RICE IS NICE

The Pig Party buffet always includes a platter filled with a mound of fragrant jasmine rice. This delicate grain with a blossomy scent can be found in many Orien-

tal or specialty markets. If it's not available, substitute basmati rice, which has a sweet, nutty fragrance.

Prepare the rice according to package directions, since cooking times and water amounts will vary with the grain. Plan for ½ cup cooked rice per person.

The rice will be less starchy and the grains not so likely to stick together if you rinse it 2 or 3 times before cooking. And remember to cook with the lid on throughout for perfectly steamed rice.

If you want to put a little dash in basmati rice, you can add dried, sweetened blueberries after it has cooked. About 3 ounces blueberries is about right for every 4 cups cooked rice. Remove the rice from the heat, remove the lid, and, with a fork, toss the rice lightly, mixing the blueberries in as you do. Put the lid back on and let sit for at least another 10 minutes so the blueberries will moisten in the steam.

Rice is the ideal foil for the pork, chicken, shrimp, and vegetable dishes that star in this buffet. And it's traditionally been a food of celebration. In Bengali families, a child is initiated into the art of eating rice with a ceremony called mukhe bhat, or "first rice." And in India, when a bride arrives at her husband's house and cooks the first meal for her in-laws, it is called bou-bhat, or "wife rice."

Tropical Shrimp Bowl

The marinade and sauce that work so beautifully for the shrimp here are also perfect for grilled chicken, a variation that Pat Murakami frequently uses, described at the end.

This recipe calls for two special ingredients, coconut milk (see page 157) and fish sauce. All Oriental groceries should have fish sauce, since this lightly briny extract is an essential ingredient in most Asian cooking. If you absolutely can't find it, use a mild soy sauce instead.

60 fresh jumbo shrimp

MARINADE

4 cans coconut milk
Juice of 4 limes
½ cup brown sugar
2 tablespoons fish sauce
½ cup minced shallots

GREEN SAUCE

4 cups fresh cilantro,
   packed
10 fresh *ancho* or *jalapeño*
   peppers
½ cup chopped garlic
¼ cup sugar
1 tablespoon kosher salt
1½ cups rice vinegar

Devein the shrimp and remove the shells to the tail.

In a large non-metal container, mix the marinade ingredients, whisking to combine them well. Place the shrimp in the marinade, making sure they are immersed. Cover and refrigerate for 2 hours.

While the shrimp marinate, prepare the sauce by processing the ingredients in a blender until pureed. Just leave the sauce in the blender cup until you're ready to use it.

When you are ready to cook, light enough charcoal to fill the bottom of the grill evenly. Skewer the shrimp, 4 or 5 to a skewer. When the coals are burning with an even white ash, lay the shrimp skewers on the grill, positioned 3 to 5 inches above the coals. Grill for approximately 10 minutes, turning once and removing the shrimp from the grill when the meat turns opaque. Don't overcook.

Slide the shrimp off the skewers and into a wide serving bowl. Whir the sauce in a blender quickly just to mix everything, then pour over the shrimp. Serve with a big spoon so guests can scoop up plenty of sauce with the shrimp. The sauce is also scrumptious over rice.

Serves 12 as main course.

VARIATION: Instead of shrimp, marinate 15 pounds boneless, skinless chicken breasts overnight. Grill according to directions for Joey's Jamaican Jerk Chicken (page 151). After you remove the chicken from the grill, slice in 1-inch-wide strips, toss in Green Sauce, and serve at room temperature on a platter garnished with sprigs of cilantro.

Serves 18 as main course.

NOTE: Both versions of this recipe can be doubled or tripled.

◇ **Coconut Groove**

Coconut milk is not the same thing as sweetened cream of coconut, an ingredient used in desserts and cocktails and the product you are most apt to find in a grocery store.

Coconut milk is an extract made from shredded fresh coconut and water. It is not sweetened, so if the can you pick up has the word "sweetened" on it or sugar included in its ingredients list, put it back.

You can find coconut milk at Oriental groceries and specialty food shops. When it can be found in regular supermarkets, it's apt to be in the section with Oriental foods, while sweetened cream of coconut is more likely to be with shredded coconut and other baking goods.

If you can't find coconut milk, you can make your own for Tropical Shrimp Bowl (preceding recipe) by simmering equal parts unsweetened shredded coconut and water until the mixture becomes frothy. Strain through cheesecloth in a sieve, pressing the coconut to extract all the juice.

If, despite these explanations, you find yourself the owner of a can of sweetened cream of coconut, you may toss it in the blender with twice that amount of pineapple juice and rum to taste for piña coladas.

Better yet, if you have a Donvier ice-cream maker, mix the sweetened cream of coconut with enough milk to equal 4 cups, put it in the Donvier, and make ice cream according to the instructions. Allow at least 45 minutes to 1 hour for proper consistency. Just before you are ready to serve, melt 4 ounces semisweet baking chocolate in a double boiler until completely softened. Spoon the ice cream up in 4 bowls, then drizzle (don't plop!) the melted chocolate over it. The chocolate will harden instantly and you'll want to eat it immediately. The flavor will bring back memories of a favorite candy bar from childhood. And if sometimes you feel like a nut, you can sprinkle a tablespoon of chopped almonds over each serving of the ice cream before the chocolate drizzle.

Murakami Veggies

I've grilled some deliciously marinated vegetables in my time, but none to equal these, which have the fragrance of seductive Far East spices.

You soak the eggplants last, after the other vegetables have had a head start, because it is a notorious suck-up. Start soaking the vegetables about 30 minutes before you're ready to put them on the grill and about an hour before you're ready to serve. The vegetables can be cooked as soon as you've taken Joey's Jamaican Jerk Chicken and/or Tropical Shrimp Bowl off the grill.

MARINADE

2 tablespoons soy sauce
2 tablespoons water
3 scallions, chopped fine
1½ teaspoons Chinese Five
  Spice powder
¼ cup chopped cilantro

In a wide, flat glass or crockery bowl (a pasta serving bowl is perfect), whisk together the marinade ingredients until well blended.

Trim the ends off the onions, leaving the skins. Place in the marinade with the cut ends down. Slice the peppers into quarters lengthwise and add to the marinade, turning to coat evenly. Trim the ends off the squash and cut in half through the middle, then split each half

3 tablespoons minced fresh
  ginger
3 tablespoons honey
3 tablespoons brown sugar
1 tablespoon hot sweet
  mustard
1½ teaspoons sesame oil
¼ teaspoon Tabasco sauce
3 cloves of garlic, minced
½ teaspoon freshly ground
  black pepper
2 cups peanut oil
½ cup rice wine vinegar

12 (1-inch-diameter)
  boiling onions
3 medium-sized red bell
  peppers
3 medium-sized green or
  yellow bell peppers
3 (9-inch-long) yellow
  summer squash or
  zucchini
2 medium-sized or 4 small
  eggplants

into quarters lengthwise. Toss in the marinade, turning to coat evenly.

After 15 minutes, turn all the veggies so they soak evenly. Cut the eggplants into rounds ½ inch thick. Place in the marinade and turn so they are coated on both sides. Leave for an additional 10 minutes, turning the eggplant once during that time.

String the onions on 2 or 3 skewers.

Arrange all the vegetables on a grill over hot to medium-hot coals. You'll have the best luck if you put the peppers on the outside edges. Turn the veggies frequently until the outsides are crisped and the insides are tender. The peppers and summer squash should finish a few minutes before the eggplant, followed by the onion. Arrange the vegetables on a serving platter (use a sharp knife to remove the skins from the onions) and allow to cool for at least 5 minutes before serving. They are delicious served at room temperature.

Serves 12.

NOTE: The marinade recipe can be doubled or tripled.

Pickled Ginger Mayonnaise

This is a condiment so delectable I'm tempted to lick it right out of the bowl every time I make it. If you serve a roast pig, you must have a couple of bowls of this on either side. If not, it's a lovely accent for Murakami Veggies (preceding recipe). It is also a delightful dip for crisp raw vegetables and sliced tart apples. And it makes a sensational turkey sandwich. In fact, I might try just about anything with this tingly mayonnaise except dabbing it behind my ears as perfume.

The ginger is that lovely pink pickle you are served in sushi restaurants. You can buy it in Oriental markets or many natural food stores. One friend suggested also adding a dab of wasabi, the green-hued Japanese horseradish that also accompanies sushi, or chopped green chili.

3 cups good-quality
  commercial mayonnaise
3 tablespoons minced
  pickled ginger with juice
3 tablespoons minced
  cilantro
2 tablespoons minced red
  onion

Blend together, cover, and store refrigerated until ready to use. Makes enough to serve as a condiment for a 40-to-45-pound roast pig. This recipe may be halved or quartered.

Makes a little more than 3 cups.

Vietnamese Noodle Salad

This is one of those foods you just simply can't stop eating until they're gone. The refreshing minced herbs and crunchy vegetables make it a fine harbinger of summer eating pleasures to come.

The fish sauce is essential for the Nuoc Chom dressing and can be found at any Oriental grocery and some health food stores, if not at a supermarket.

8 ounces rice noodles (also called rice sticks)

½ cup julienned carrot
¾ cup julienned cucumber
½ cup julienned red onion
¼ cup julienned red bell pepper
¼ cup bean sprouts
1 tablespoon minced fresh mint
1 tablespoon minced fresh cilantro
1 tablespoon minced fresh basil

In a large kettle, bring 6 quarts water to a boil. Toss in the rice noodles, stir a few times with a wooden spoon or chopstick, and let cook at a boil for approximately 5 minutes. This is a bit longer than the recommended time on most packages, and what you are looking for is a noodle that is actually softer and more "done" than the al dente stage we usually prefer. (That's because the noodles have a tendency to crisp when transferred to cold water, so cooking them beyond the al dente stage will make them ultimately just right.)

When the noodles are very tender, drain and immediately run cold water over them. Transfer to a container and cover completely with cold water until you are ready to use.

When you are ready, drain the noodles, transfer to a large serving bowl, and mix in the julienned vegetables, sprouts, and minced herbs.

In a small bowl or pitcher, mix together all the ingredients for the Nuoc Chom sauce. Use a whisk or fork and blend until the sugar is dissolved. Taste

NUOC CHOM

2 cloves garlic, crushed

1–2 teaspoons ground red
  chile

2 tablespoons sugar

2 tablespoons fresh lime
  juice

¼ cup rice vinegar

¼ cup fish sauce

GARNISH

¼ cup chopped roast
  peanuts

and add more chile if you want, or water if the sauce is too strong. Pour the sauce over the noodles and toss to coat them well. (Pat suggests you add part of the sauce and taste, then add more if you wish, but I thought it was just perfect with all of the sauce tossed in.)

Sprinkle the peanuts on top and serve immediately. This recipe can be doubled or tripled, but you will want to cook the noodles in batches, 8 ounces at a time.

Serves 12 as a side dish.

◇ **Fruits of the Season**

California is the land of perpetually ripe fruit, so the Murakamis create a cornucopia fruit salad, served in hollowed-out watermelon bowls.

You may want to opt for a giant serving bowl instead. Fill it with pieces of the freshest, ripest fruit you can find. Late spring brings the first crops of local strawberries, and nothing can compare with their flavor. Cherries may also be in season and are worth the trouble of pitting for the flavor, texture, and color they contribute to a fresh fruit salad.

Pineapples, bananas, and kiwifruit should be available. Good oranges to look for in late May or early June include Valencias and navels. You may also be able to find ripe blood oranges, the last of the winter crop, or Jaffas imported from Israel, or winy Minneolas. All have distinctive flavors, and the blood orange has that outrageous color.

Peaches begin to appear in groceries around this time, but their flavor doesn't usually hit its peak until later in the summer. To ensure the best peach taste, look for a background that is yellow or cream in color with no hint of green and choose peaches that feel firm but juicy.

Imported Bartlett pears can be a wonderful late spring choice, as are Gala apples or another flowery, sweet variety. Truly tasty apricots are hard to find even at the peak of their season, later in the summer, unless you live near an apricot tree. Most commercially harvested apricots are picked before they are fully ripened because they are so difficult to ship otherwise. But you can add enticing hints of apricot flavor to your salad by mixing in slivers of dried apricots.

Cut all the fruit into bite-sized pieces no larger than the first joint of your thumb. Pieces that are too large make it hard for the flavors to mingle, but pieces that are too small turn quickly to mush. The salad should be made and refrigerated no more than a couple of hours before serving. The citrus juice will keep the other fruits looking fresh for that short time, but if you keep them hanging around much longer, the fruits will start to brown.

I like fruit salad best without dressing, the juices creating a heady natural one. But if you want, offer Tangy Apple Dressing (page 137) or Yin-Yang Vinaigrette (page 136) on the side. Also, it's nice to have a bowl of broken pecans or walnuts available for guests to add, if they wish.

Every fruit has its secret.

—D. H. LAWRENCE

My advice is not to inquire why or whither, but just enjoy your ice cream while it's on your plate.

—THORNTON WILDER

Three Creams in One

Homemade ice cream is the quintessential summer treat. Pat and Dean Murakami aim to please and offer their guests a choice of vanilla, chocolate, and strawberry. At the annual Pig Party, the ice cream is dished up from a dessert station in the laundry room of the house, a pass-through that connects the kitchen to the backyard. Colorful cloth turns appliances into serving tables, and Pat takes decorating one step further by custom-making chilled ice containers.

Using a large stockpot for each ice container (or making one ice shell at a time) and the freezers at the restaurant where she works, Pat pours a couple of inches of water into the bottom of the pot and submerges bright, beautiful blossoms from whatever flowers are in bloom in the Murakamis' yard in it. When that base layer is frozen, she rests a container on it large enough to hold a half gallon of ice cream. She sprinkles more blossoms around it and then pours a few inches of water to cover and freezes that, repeating the process until the shell of flower-filled ice comes to the top of the container.

When she's ready to use each ice shell, a little hot water applied to the outside of the stockpot will thaw the ice enough so it easily slides out. Ice cream is scooped into the container and then stays frosty as guests come and go, serving themselves.

Pat's method of making ice cream is equally efficient. She's devised a fundamental base that works for all three flavors. The cream is frozen in a large electric freezer that holds half a gallon (not the small Donvier ice-cream maker, which makes only a quart). You can use an electric freezer or, if you've got one, an old-time hand-cranked model.

NOTE: The type of ice you use affects the quality of the finished product. A fine crushed ice is what you want for smooth cream. If all you can get is those small cubes sold commercially, wrap the bag in a towel or light blanket, take a hammer to it, and crush the cubes more.

Layering ice and rock salt into the container is a little like the process Pat goes through to create her ice containers filled with flowers. You want to put in a couple of inches of ice, then sprinkle a handful of rock salt evenly over that, then add a few more inches of ice, another handful of salt, until the ice reaches the bottom of the freezing-can lid. Be careful not to get ice or salt any higher so you won't run the risk of the brine seeping into the can.

ICE CREAM BASE

4 cups half-and-half
8 egg yolks
4 cups sugar

In a heavy saucepan over medium-high heat, heat the half-and-half until it is just about to boil. While it's heating, blend together the egg yolks and sugar. When the half-and-half is hot, pour just a little into the egg mixture and stir. Then continue adding more, a little at a time, until all the half-and-half has been added and they are blended.

FOR VANILLA: Scrape the seeds from 2 vanilla beans and toss both seeds and the scraped pods into the half-and-half while it's heating. Remove the pods before blending with the eggs. Chill the mixture thoroughly in the refrigerator; add 1 to 2 teaspoons pure vanilla extract. Freeze in an ice-cream freezer.
Makes ½ gallon.

FOR CHOCOLATE: Chop about 6 ounces good-quality bittersweet chocolate into very small pieces. Add to the base while it is still hot and stir until the chocolate is thoroughly blended in. Chill thoroughly in the refrigerator. Freeze in an ice-cream freezer.
Makes ½ gallon.

FOR STRAWBERRY: Slice 1 quart strawberries. Sprinkle with 3 tablespoons sugar and heat for a few minutes in a saucepan until the strawberries just begin to release their juices. Add to the ice-cream base and chill thoroughly in the refrigerator. Freeze in an ice-cream freezer.

 Makes ½ gallon.

You, icy sweetness of strawberry, chocolate, or vanilla, melting stickily into your inverted duncecap; ravisher of appetites, leading the younger generation from the straight and narrow paths of spinach; pilferer of the pennies that might go to make a fortune; destroyer of the peace of homes; instrument of bribery and reward of virtue.

—H. L. MENCKEN, BALTIMORE EVENING SUN (1926)

Seven

Independence Days

S ummer brings an intoxicating sense of freedom. We are liberated from the shelter of our houses, so comforting in the winter, but so confining. We are liberated from layers of clothing and even our shoes, if we desire. Children are liberated from the daily routine of school, while adults take vacations from work or simply savor those lovely daylight hours of the evening.

No wonder, then, that our celebrations of freedom fall during the summer months. For centuries we have marked our country's independence on July Fourth with outdoor picnics and outrageous feeds on quintessentially American fare.

Juneteenth, the celebration of the Emancipation Proclamation, has also been around for more than a century, although it is only in the last few decades that it has become a popular celebration outside Texas and the neighboring states where it began.

A SOULFUL JUNETEENTH

The Fairfield Four is a traditional black gospel group from Tennessee. When these elderly men take the stage in tuxedo jackets over crisp-pressed indigo overalls and open their mouths to sing, it isn't simply gospel music that their audience receives. In the blending of African syncopations, Southern white vocal harmonies, field hollers, European hymns, tribal chants, and coded lyrics that talk about freedom on earth as much as heavenly rewards, their music offers an encapsulated history of the black experience in America.

Annie May Walker, Charlestine Daniel, Doris King, and Pat Davis of Madison, Wisconsin, are a gospel quartet of another sort. Their art form is food—soul food cooked in big quantities and dished up for African-American celebrations, such as Juneteenth.

Like the Fairfield Four, the Madison quartet dishes out much more than what appears on the surface. When you sit down to a plate of their collard greens, hoppin John, cornbread, short ribs, and fried chicken, you are getting not only food for the body and soul but a mini–history lesson as well.

"Soul food is who we are," Pat Davis says. "When you eat greens and short ribs, you're eating a whole story. Greens cooked with peppers are what we ate in Africa, and when our people were brought here as slaves, collard greens and the like became what we ate here, cooked much the same way.

"Short ribs were the part of the hog the masters didn't want. So they gave them to the slaves. And we cooked them slow over a fire and seasoned them to taste good. And the joke is, pretty soon the masters and their families were eating our food, it tasted so good."

The celebration of Juneteenth is also a mini-history of the African-American experience. Emancipation was declared by Abraham Lincoln on January 1, 1863, but it wasn't until after the Civil War had ended that slaves in Texas were formally told of their freedom. On June 19, 1865,

Major General Gordon Granger made the pronouncement in Galveston.

Legends have it that the news was withheld by white planters who wanted the slaves to get crops in first; or that an earlier messenger was killed; or that a black man riding a mule from Washington brought the news and it simply took him that long to get to Texas. The legends underscore how hard-won freedom was for American slaves, even when it had been officially declared.

Jubilation followed, and the tradition of a community picnic became firmly established among African Americans in Texas, seeping over to neighboring Louisiana, Arkansas, and Oklahoma. Later, the holiday cropped up in California as Texas blacks migrated there. And in recent years, Juneteenth celebrations have become popular around the country.

"We started ours maybe a half-dozen years or so ago," says Pat. "It's something that has been moving steadily across the nation for several years now. Juneteenth is appealing because the African American doesn't really feel that July the Fourth is his. We feel much more akin to Juneteenth, which is really all about our freedom, our emancipation."

Juneteenth had been celebrated by the black community in Milwaukee for many years, Pat says, and folks from Madison often made a trip to that city to participate. When Madison civic leaders decided it would be good to have a celebration of their own, they contacted the members of the Mary McLeod Bethune Club to spearhead it. These four women, members of the ways and means committee, soon became the cooks behind the classic soul food supper that is served at the event.

The club itself is another mini–history lesson. Named after the black educator and civil rights advocate who was an adviser to President Franklin D. Roosevelt, it was begun in Madison to provide scholarships for local students and to contribute to the education of the community. The club is the local chapter of the National Association of Colored Women, but it has Jewish, Hispanic, and white members, as well as one man.

The crowd that flocks to Penn Park in south Madison to eat the savory foods cooked up by these women is not all one ethnic group either.

"It draws people from the whole city, not just the south Madison area, where the majority of African Americans live," Pat explains. "We see it as a chance to celebrate our culture and to introduce other people to it, too."

The picnic in the park includes dance performances, poetry readings, artwork, and demonstrations by the neighborhood Boy Scout troop, which uses kente cloth as part of its uniform.

"Our cooking is an art form, too," Pat says. "It took great skill to create these good-tasting foods from the scraps thrown out of the big house and the things slaves could find in the woods and around the plantation."

The cooking is a collaborative art among these four women, but there is no question who is their spiritual and tactical guiding force.

"Granny is in charge," Doris King says with no equivocation. Granny is Annie May Walker, well into her eighties but still preparing a meal each day for the homeless who come to the South Madison Neighborhood Center.

The center is where the Juneteenth feast is prepared, and Granny has a chair right in the middle of the kitchen.

"She directs traffic," Doris says. "Even when she's sitting down, she tells us where to go, what to do, and when. She showed me how to make her peach cobbler and taught me a way of doing the crust so it came out just perfect. My crust had always been tough before."

And when Granny picks another person to do one of her regular tasks, it's a little like being anointed.

"We all say 'Yes, ma'am,' to everything she says," Pat said. "And we feel so honored when Granny asks us to make something. You walk around the center a little up in the air saying, 'Granny asked *me* to make the cornbread. Or Granny asked *me* to make the rice.' It's like you've achieved a new status."

And although the Juneteenth celebration is a civic event, there is a very personal, family aura around the women who cook for it.

"In some ways, these women are like surrogate mothers to me," Doris says. Her own mother, Lily, was a member of the Mary McLeod Bethune Club and a remarkable cook. When she died several years ago, the women who had been her colleagues encouraged Doris to step in.

"I knew she loved to cook," Pat says. "Her ribs are a legend in the neighborhood with her 'kitchen sink' sauce. And she has a real hand with greens."

The way the women prepare the food is distinctive both to the African-American culture they come from and to their own personal style, Pat says.

"I have found that all cultures use basically the same foods—beans and rice or a grain, chicken, some form of greens. But what distinguishes the culture is how they cook it. How African Americans cooked reflected the foods of Africa. It was spicy. It was hot.

"It added spice to life is what it did."

The crowd that comes to Madison's Juneteenth numbers in the hundreds and the women cook the food in vats and kettles. The recipes here are reduced to family size.

What is patriotism but the love of good things we ate in our childhood?

—Lin Yutang

Soul Fried Chicken

Pat Davis started frying chicken as a young woman.

"My second job right out of high school was frying chickens for my uncle at Jones Chicken Shack in Louisville, Kentucky, where my family went to live right after World War II. I learned how from my grandmother, and we really did it from scratch. I mean, she'd bring home live chickens and we'd hear them screech when she'd wring their necks."

Pat says she fries her chicken "soul food style, and that means with seasoning in the batter. Most African-American cooks want some flavor in there. It makes it taste better, and it makes it yours. I like to use dried garlic, lots and lots of it. Get that garlic in there and that makes it mine."

The seasonings in this chicken give it a light, mildly spicy tang that is amplified with hot sauce added after it's served. Pat looks for bottled sauces that have a slightly thick consistency to pass with her chicken.

"You want something that's going to stick to the meat a little, not dribble right off," she explains. One exceptionally good choice is the dark roasted *chipotle* pepper sauces that have been showing up in groceries lately. Their slightly sweet, musky fire is the perfect complement to Soul Fried Chicken.

4 pounds chicken, cut up

1 quart buttermilk

1 cup all-purpose flour

1 teaspoon dried minced
   garlic, finely crushed

1 teaspoon dried minced
   onion, finely crushed

½ teaspoon turmeric

2 teaspoons paprika

¼ teaspoon cayenne
   pepper

½ teaspoon kosher salt

¼ teaspoon freshly ground
   black pepper

Canola oil

Wash the chicken and trim off the visible clumps of fat. Lay the chicken pieces in a glass or other non-metal dish and pour the buttermilk over to cover. Cover tightly with plastic wrap and refrigerate for 30 minutes to 1 hour. (If the chicken is not totally submerged, turn the pieces over halfway through the soaking process.)

Mix the flour with the garlic and onion flakes. Add the other spices and seasonings and stir to blend thoroughly. Pour into a wide shallow bowl or plate with a rim.

In a deep, wide skillet or shallow stew pan with a tight-fitting lid, pour canola oil about an inch and a half deep. If you want to fry all the chicken at once, you will need to do 2 pans simultaneously. Or you can fry the chicken in 2 batches. Heat the oil over high heat until a little flour flecked into the oil pops and dances around the pan, crisping quickly.

While the oil is heating, remove each piece of chicken from the buttermilk, making sure it is thoroughly coated. Dredge through the seasoned flour mixture, rolling it gently and sprinkling flour over it to coat thickly and completely. Lay each piece of chicken in the hot oil, skin side down. Don't crowd so closely that you will have trouble using tongs or a spatula to turn the pieces.

When the skillet is full, turn the heat down to medium and fry until the chicken begins to turn dark gold around the edges. Gently and carefully, so as not to break the crust, turn the chicken pieces over. (I like to use tongs for this operation, but if the crust is sticking to the bottom of the pan, it may be necessary to slide a thin metal spatula underneath to keep the crust intact when you turn.)

When the chicken is turned, cover the pan, turn the heat down just a little bit more, and fry for 20 minutes. Check occasionally to see if the chicken is browning too fast and turn the heat down more if necessary.

Remove the lid and gently turn the pieces once more. Turn the heat up to medium and fry for another minute or two to crisp the skin. Remove from the skillet and lay on several layers of paper towels or clean brown paper sacks to drain. Let cool for a few minutes before serving. This seasoned chicken is best when it's warm, not piping hot. Pass a bottle of good hot sauce on the side.

Serves 8.

Short Ribs and Kitchen Sink Sauce

Short ribs come from the ends of beef ribs and are both bony and fatty. That may be why they ended up in slave kitchens instead of on the master's table, but what a foolish mistake that was. The old saying about "the closer the bone, the sweeter the meat" was probably dreamed up to describe the flavor of these ribs, cooked slowly over coals.

Doris King says that when she fires up her covered Webber grill, neighbors come out of the woodwork. Her juicy ribs are made even more flavorful by the basting she gives them with one custom sauce. Then she slathers them with another before serving. She likes to call this second sauce her "kitchen sink" sauce, and indeed, it is jam-packed with ingredients. She uses a bottle of Open Pit barbecue sauce for the base, but adds so much to it that it is hardly recognizable in the end. If you have a favorite bottled sauce, you may want to use that instead. And you should feel free to experiment with the seasonings. The amounts and ingredients vary when Doris makes the sauce, depending on what is handy in her kitchen.

The recipe here will likely make more than you'll need for this amount of ribs, but you can keep it in the fridge for at least a week, or freeze it for 3 months or so. It's also great on grilled chicken, pork, or burgers and makes a tasty topping for baked potatoes.

Some folks swear by marinating their ribs first, but Doris prefers to put hers on the grill untainted and to paint them with the vinegar baste during the cooking process.

24 meaty beef short ribs
(about 4 pounds)

BASTING SAUCE

1 cup apple cider vinegar
½ cup ketchup
1 tablespoon yellow mustard
1 tablespoon brown sugar
1 garlic clove, minced
½ teaspoon salt
¼ teaspoon turmeric
½ teaspoon paprika
¼ teaspoon freshly ground
    black pepper

Let the ribs come to room temperature for 30 minutes. Meanwhile, light 40 to 50 coals in a covered grill. Prepare the Basting Sauce by blending the vinegar, ketchup, and mustard with the brown sugar, garlic, and spices. A handy way to do this is to put all the ingredients in a wide-mouthed quart jar, put on the lid, and shake until blended. You can put the lid back on and shake again throughout the grilling process to keep the sauce mixed.

When the coals are evenly covered with white ash, place the grill about 5 inches above them and lay the ribs on the grill. Daub them generously with the Basting Sauce. (You can use a pastry brush, but what's really handiest is one of those little rag mops that are used for washing dishes.)

Cover the grill with its lid. Turn the ribs every 20 to 25 minutes, moving them around the grill so they cook evenly, and basting with sauce each time you do. Let them cook, covered, for about 1½ hours, until they are evenly

KITCHEN SINK SAUCE

¼ cup chopped onion

3 cloves of garlic, minced

2 tablespoons olive oil

1 (18-ounce) bottle Open Pit barbecue sauce (or sauce of your choice)

½ cup ketchup

½ cup yellow mustard

¼ cup brown sugar

1 tablespoon soy sauce

½ tablespoon Worcestershire sauce

½ teaspoon Tabasco sauce

½ teaspoon salt

¼ teaspoon turmeric

½ teaspoon paprika

¼ teaspoon freshly ground black pepper

½ teaspoon crushed red pepper

½ cup chopped sweet pickle relish or finely chopped drained sweet pickles

1 lemon

Molasses or pancake syrup (optional)

browned and the meat is tender when pierced with a fork.

(Some short rib aficionados want the ribs to cook longer, until the meat is nearly falling off the bone. Doris sometimes accommodates them by putting the ribs into a preheated 325° F. oven for 20 or so minutes after taking them off the grill. But she prefers her meat "to have a little chew to it. I think it's got a better flavor then.")

While the meat is cooking, prepare the Kitchen Sink Sauce. In a large saucepan, sauté the onion and garlic in the olive oil. When the onion starts to turn transparent, pour in the bottle of Open Pit sauce, then stir in the ketchup, mustard, brown sugar, soy sauce, Worcestershire, Tabasco, and seasonings.

Add the pickle relish. (If you don't have relish, you can chop up drained sweet pickles very fine and add them.)

Cut the lemon in half, remove the seeds, and squeeze the juice into the mixture, then slice the rest of the lemon into very thin pieces and throw them in. Stir everything well as it comes to a boil, then turn down to a low simmer.

Taste and add molasses or pancake syrup if you want a little more sweetness. Adjust the other seasonings to taste also. Add water if the mixture is too thick. You want it to be a sauce that will pour but also stick to the ribs. Continue to simmer, stirring occasionally, while the ribs cook.

When the ribs are ready, remove them from the grill and dip each in the sauce to coat it. Arrange them on a platter and serve with more sauce on the side.

Makes enough for 8.

I never measure or weigh anything. I cook by vibration . . . It don't matter if it's Dakar or Savannah, you can cook exotic food any time you want. Just turn on the imagination, be willing to change your style and let a little soul food in.

—Vertamae Grosvenor, *Vibration Cooking*

Now hopping-john was F. Jasmine's very favorite food. She had always warned them to wave a plate of rice and peas before her nose when she was in her coffin, to make certain there was no mistake; for if a breath of life was left in her, she would sit up and eat, but if she smelled the hopping-john, and did not stir, then they could just nail down the coffin and be certain she was truly dead.

—Carson McCullers, *The Member of the Wedding*

Ocean Hoppin John

"Congri" is the name black-eyed peas were given in New Orleans, echoing the name of Congo Square and reflecting the fact that these tasty legumes were brought to the Americas from Africa as "home food" for slaves. In the South, African Americans soon mixed their peas (actually beans) with the abundant rice to create a sturdy protein dish seasoned with the poor man's pork: ham hocks, jowl meat, or the like.

The dish came to be called hoppin John, although no one seems to be sure precisely why. There are at least a half-dozen speculations on the name, ranging from the etymological (that it is a corruption of *pois à pigeon*, the French for pigeon pea) to the mythical (that it was named after a limping waiter who served it in New Orleans). But while there is little agreement on the origins of its name, there seems to be universal approbation of its virtues.

Traditional hoppin John, made most often now with spicy sausage, can make the mouth of any displaced Southerner water simply at the remembering. Of course, there are many that long for the old-time spicy flavor but would like it in a version that has no meat. This recipe will satisfy them by taking the black-eyed peas back to North Africa for spices that make the sauce for this vegetarian version a saporific delight.

1½ cups dried black-eyed
   peas

2 tablespoons peanut oil
3 cups chopped onion
1 large clove of garlic,
   minced
2 teaspoons cumin seed,
   crushed
2 tablespoons minced fresh
   ginger
½ teaspoon cayenne
   pepper (or less)
4 cups chopped fresh
   tomatoes

2 cups cooked rice
Salt

Rinse the black-eyed peas and pick over them to remove any stones. Soak in water to cover overnight. Drain.

In a large saucepan, bring the peas and 1 quart water to a boil and allow to boil for 5 minutes. Turn the heat down to a lively simmer, cover, and cook for 1½ to 2 hours, until the peas are just tender but not mushy. You may need to add warm water during the cooking process to keep the peas just covered in liquid. Don't add so much, however, that you have a mixture that is very soupy. When the beans have finished cooking, you want them to be in just enough liquid to cover them.

When the peas are ready, heat the peanut oil in a large skillet over medium heat. Add the onion and garlic and sauté for 2 minutes. Sprinkle on the crushed cumin seed and ginger, stir, and continue to sauté until the onions are turning transparent. Add the cayenne and stir. (If you are not a fan of hot foods, you may want to add only ¼ teaspoon cayenne at this point and wait until later to decide if you want to add the rest.)

Add the tomatoes, and when the mixture begins to bubble, stir it into the pot of black-eyed peas. Cook at a low simmer for 30 to 45 minutes, stirring occasionally to keep from sticking.

While the black-eyed peas are simmering in the sauce, prepare the rice according to package directions. (Long-grain white rice is the traditional choice, but the nutty flavor of brown rice adds a nice undertone to this version.)

When the rice is ready, stir it into the pot with the peas. Add salt to taste and the rest of the cayenne, if you wish. Let the flavors mingle at a low simmer for 15 minutes. Serve immediately with the rest of the dishes in this section, or as a main course with a crisp green salad and cornbread.

Serves 4 to 6 as a main course, 10 as a side dish.

In the dining room men were standing around the table, smoking cigars and discussing the emancipation.

They began to smile when they spotted Quicksill laying down his contribution to the slave food that was on the table. Dunbar food: wheat bread, egg pone, hog jaws, roasted shoat, ham sliced cold. He had brought some Beaujolais, which he placed down next to the dishes of meat, fish and the variety of salad with Plantation dressing. Somebody else had brought John Brown à la carte—boiled beef, cabbage, pork and beans.

—Ishmael Reed, *Flight to Canada*

Greens with Pepper Vinegar

Doris King grew up in eastern North Carolina, and when she cuts collard greens in her Madison, Wisconsin, kitchen, the sweet, crisp smell always takes her back there.

"And then when I start cooking them, I remember when I was a child and my mom or dad would be cooking greens and I'd smell that aroma and think, 'Oh boy, when they're done, are we going to have a feast!'"

You could make a feast on nothing more than Doris King's greens and a big pan of cornbread, but she likes to serve them with her ribs, or with fried chicken.

The pepper in the pot is what distinguishes "soul food" greens from the greens cooked by other Southerners, such as Appalachian mountain folk. Doris makes hers even more distinctive with her special pepper vinegar made a couple of days before the greens and served on the side.

African-American cooks preferred collards to the kale or poke sallet that were more common among white Southern mountain folk. Doris also likes a mix of mustard and turnip greens in the spring when the leaves are young and tender. You can prepare any of these greens, or dandelion greens, with this same recipe, although the taste of mustard is so strong that you should mix it with another green for balance. Collards and kale cook longer than any of the other greens.

Doris grows her own collards in her backyard, so can pick them fresh whenever she wants them. Kale and collards are most plentiful in markets in the fall and winter. Early summer is a better time for finding fresh turnip and mustard greens in the market. And it's also a good time to pick fresh, tender dandelion greens right out of your yard.

Look for leaves that are about the size of your hand and don't choose any that are larger than your two hands together. Leaves that are yellowing or have spots shouldn't be used. And with kale or collards, look for a crisp texture. Turnip and mustard greens tend to be a little more limp.

Greens must be washed carefully several times to remove all the grit.

Doris says, "The process of cleaning collards from my garden is pretty involved. First I wash them in salt water. I fill the sink with cold water and add 2 to 3 tablespoons of salt. I take a clean washing rag and I rub the leaves a few times on both sides to get off the spiderwebs and bugs.

"Then I cut those leaves and then I wash the pieces in plain cold water 3 or 4 more times again.

"The mustard and turnip greens are harder to clean. They seem to grab the grit more. I don't cut those, but I break off the stem ends. And I do them in the salt water once and then several more times in clear cold water. You can feel the surface and tell if the grit is gone."

Many folks don't cut collards to cook them but break them into pieces.

"I don't like them that way," Doris says. "I don't think they cook up as nice and tender, so I cut my collards my own special way."

Prepare the vinegar at least 2 days before you're ready to serve.

PEPPER VINEGAR

2 cups white vinegar
8 small fresh hot peppers
   (banana, *jalapeño*,
   habanero, or a mix)
1 teaspoon mustard seed
1 clove of garlic

GREENS

2 ham hocks or 2 smoked
   turkey wings
2 pounds fresh greens
½ tablespoon sugar

Over medium heat, bring the vinegar just to boiling point in a non-aluminum pan. While the vinegar is heating, rinse and dry the peppers and place in a sturdy jar or wide-mouthed bottle with the mustard seed and garlic. Pour the hot vinegar over them, and when mixture has cooled, cover with a non-metal lid. Set aside out of the sunlight for 48 hours.

In a large kettle, bring 6 cups water to a boil with the ham hocks or turkey wings in it. Turn to a lively simmer, cover, and cook for 2 hours.

Clean the greens thoroughly. If you are preparing collards or kale, cut them by laying 3 leaves on top of one another, rolling them up like a newspaper, and cutting pieces about ½

1 clove of garlic
½ teaspoon freshly ground
   black pepper
½ teaspoon crushed red
   pepper
Salt to taste

inch thick from the roll. Other greens may be cooked whole, if small, or torn in 3-inch pieces.

Remove the meat from the pot and place the cleaned greens in the simmering water. Use a wooden spoon to push the greens in under the water. They may have to cook down a little before they can all be submerged.

Cover the greens and leave at a lively simmer for an hour. Meanwhile, cut the meat from the hocks or wings, discarding the fat, skin, and bone. Set aside the meat.

After the greens have cooked for an hour, add the seasonings except for salt. Simmer for another hour, covered, then add the meat. Taste the broth (called "potlikker" in the South) and add salt to taste. Allow to cook, uncovered, for another 15 minutes to an hour, until the greens are very tender.

Serve hot and pass the vinegar so folks can spoon it on their greens to their liking. Serve with Kernel Cornbread (recipe follows), and don't be afraid to crumble your bread into the bottom of the bowl to sop up the potlikker there. That's the way you're supposed to do it.

Makes enough to serve 8 to 10.

Kernel Cornbread

Cracklings were the crisped pieces of hog left over after lard had been rendered. They became a tasty addition to the everyday skillet of cornbread. Cracklings can hardly be come by these days. But if you want to make a special feast edition of cornbread, fresh corn cut into the batter will do just splendidly.

4 ears fresh corn
4 tablespoons butter or
   bacon grease
2 cups white or yellow
   cornmeal
1 teaspoon salt
½ teaspoon baking powder
½ teaspoon baking soda
1 large egg
1½ cups buttermilk

Shuck the corn and remove the silks. (A damp paper towel rubbed around the ear is a good way to get those pesky silks that cling.) Into a shallow bowl, and using a very sharp knife, cut down the cob, removing just the top half of each kernel. Then, using a metal teaspoon, scrape up the cob, extracting the pulp and milk from the corn kernels. Set aside the cut corn and discard the cobs.

Preheat the oven to 450° F. Place the butter or bacon grease in a 9-inch-round cast-iron skillet. Put the skillet in the oven while you mix up the batter.

In a large bowl, mix the cornmeal with the salt, baking powder, and baking soda. Add the egg and buttermilk and mix until just blended. Quickly mix in the cut corn.

Check the skillet in the oven. The butter or grease should be completely melted and bubbling just a bit in the pan, but not turning brown. Remove the skillet from the oven and swirl the grease around in the bottom ever so carefully and gently to coat the bottom and about halfway up the edges of the pan. (Use an oven mitt to protect yourself from a possible nasty burn if you splash the hot grease.)

Pour the melted butter or bacon grease into the batter and mix with a wooden spoon until just blended. Pour the batter into hot skillet and place the skillet back in the preheated oven. Bake for 25 to 30 minutes, until the top is golden brown and the center feels "set" if you touch it with your finger.

Remove and serve immediately. (You can turn the pan upside down on a plate and the cornbread will plop out, but I like to serve mine up right out of the skillet.) You don't need to serve butter, since it's seasoned already.

Enough for 6 to 8.

CORNBREAD

The secret to great cornbread is a crisp golden-brown crust that surrounds a moist and steaming middle. To get that crust, you melt the butter or bacon grease for the batter right in the skillet. That way the crust starts to crisp and form as soon as the batter hits the pan.

You put the skillet in the hot oven to heat the butter or bacon grease so it will heat evenly. If you heat it on a burner on top of the stove, there will be a hot spot in the bottom of your pan that corresponds to the circle of heat from the burner, and your cornbread will stick to that spot.

In the mountain South, where I grew up, cornbread was always made with white cornmeal, but in the deep South, yellow cornmeal was preferred. Most African-American cooks use yellow cornmeal. Either is delicious in Kernel Cornbread.

Sugar in cornbread was heresy in the mountain South, but African-American cooks seem to favor a little sweetness in the bread. My theory is that the fresh corn in Kernel Cornbread obviates any need for extra sweetening.

◇ **Watermelon**

There is no dessert more perfect for ending a Juneteenth celebration than a red, ripe, bursting-with-juice-and-sweetness watermelon.

This fruit, which we think of as quintessentially American, was actually brought to North America from Africa along with the slaves it was intended to feed. It is particularly joyful, then, to toast freedom with a slice.

Once upon a time ripe melons would have been available only in Texas and the deep South in time for Juneteenth. Revellers farther north would have had to wait for local melons to ripen. Nowadays, though, good melons are available everywhere by early summer. Because of their thick rinds, watermelons are one fruit that survives cross-country shipping well. But you must get a melon that was picked ripe in the first place.

There is absolutely nothing you can do to a watermelon to make its flavor any better than the one it's got. The only trick in serving great watermelon is knowing how to pick one.

Look for a good symmetrical shape, well rounded, and not flattened at either end.

The stem end should have a clean break between stem and melon, not a cut stem. The break indicates that the melon ripened fully on the vine, while a cut indicates that it was chopped off before its time.

The underbelly of the melon, which has been nestled to the ground all its life, should have a yellow cast and not appear greenish or whitish. Place your hands on the melon and squeeze. It should feel firm but not hard as a rock.

Lots of folks swear by the thump test—rapping the melon lightly with the knuckles and judging ripeness by the tone. But I've never found anyone who can precisely describe the tone. My husband, Ken, a thumper with a great track record for bringing home drop-dead-dripping-sweet melons, says, "It has a sort of bass-drum tone, a resonance. It has to have good percussive qualities. It's got to bring out the rhythm in you. If it makes you want to dance a little, then it's a good one."

Nothing shows the character of a people more truly than the manner in which it observes its holidays, and the kind of amusements followed by a nation is a fairly true index to its degree of moral development.

—HELEN PHILBROOK PATTEN, *THE YEAR'S FESTIVALS* (1903)

MELON PLUGGING

Back when I was growing up and my dad and Uncle Charlie would take me with them to pick out a watermelon, you got to take a "plug" from the melon before you made your final choice. We'd go to a produce place where the melons were floating in frosty ice water in big aluminum troughs. Daddy and Charlie would eyeball all the possible choices, then pick up several to heft and thump. Finally they'd decide if one looked "pretty good" and ask the produce man to plug it for them.

He'd cradle the melon in a sinewy arm and, with his other hand, pull a jack-knife out of his back pocket, flicking it open casually with his thumb. Then he'd use the knife to cut a triangular cone from the melon's flesh. With the tip of his knife he'd then ease and work the cone out of the melon and proffer it to Daddy and Charlie. They'd examine it carefully, and if it met their criteria, I got the plug to eat on the way home and we got the melon. If it didn't, we'd move on to another melon and another plug.

It's hard to find a place that will let you plug a melon these days. But if you can, or if you are buying a fresh cut half or quarter of melon so you can see the flesh, what you are looking for is uniform intensely red coloring with no white streaks. Seeds that are dark and hard mean the melon has matured, while lots of white ones mean it's still an adolescent and apt to be difficult.

A crisp, juicy appearance is vital, and the smell should be light and sweet.

When one has tasted watermelons, he knows what angels eat. It was not a Southern watermelon that Eve took; we know it because she repented.

—MARK TWAIN

About 27,000 years ago, according to paleontologists, man discovered fire. Later that same day, along about suppertime, it's very likely that he invented barbecue.

—GREG JOHNSON AND VINCE STATEN, *REAL BARBECUE*

Watermelon—it's a good fruit. You eat, you drink, you wash your face.

—ENRICO CARUSO

A PATRIOTIC INDEPENDENCE DAY

Patriot is derived from the ancient Greek word *patriotes*, which meant "fellow countryman." There is a poetry in this definition that comes alive every Fourth of July for Mary Maletis of Portland, Oregon.

Mary's father was born in Greece but came to the United States as a very young, and very poor, man.

"He was able to do well here, though," Mary says. He passed some of that good fortune on to his daughter, and with it he also passed on a sense of responsibility.

"He was always grateful for this wonderful country," Mary says. "And he told us we should always give back what we had been given. He made sure we knew that others might not be so fortunate as we had been, and he wanted us to understand that it was our responsibility to take care of them."

So each year Mary celebrates Independence Day in a way that her father would deem most American, with a party to benefit some of her fellow countrymen.

She invites a hundred or so friends to her house for a buffet and sundae-making party. They gather in the living room, where the walls are crammed floor to ceiling with the original art she loves to collect. Guests spill over into the dining room and den, and tumble out onto the patio that hangs over a little patch of northwest jungle on a hillside just blocks from downtown Portland.

Mary's guests are served good food, given good company, and entertained with good music. All Mary asks in return is that each guest bring a contribution that will go to a local shelter for the homeless.

"I put boxes out on the porch, and people know to put the things they bring in there. The party seems to get bigger each year, and that's great, because the presents and donations get bigger, too. In the early years I used to take the donations in the next day, but now the shelter sends a truck, there's that much stuff."

Mary's friends aren't the sort of folks to bring just a can of beans.

"The quality of clothes people donate is really pretty amazing," she says. "The coats and jackets are good ones, thick and warm. A lot of times we get baby things and lots and lots of diapers.

"Once the brother of a friend of mine was in town and my friend said, 'Mary's having a party. If you bring a canned good, you can go.' So he went by the store and picked up two cases of baked beans. And now some folks don't just bring an item, but they write out a check. That's always useful."

Mary's July Fourth party plan is so popular she repeats it on Boxing Day, the day after Christmas. ("I've noticed everybody is real careful about where they hang their coats for that party," she says with a grin. "You know if you leave your coat, it's mine, and it's gone to the shelter the next day.")

And some of her friends have picked up on the tradition in their own way.

"Since I started doing this, some of my friends have turned one of those major ages—you know, the ones where your idea of a birthday changes. So for their celebrations now, they ask for donations for the poor instead of presents for themselves. At some age you begin to think, 'What more do I need?' But when you give something to someone who does need it, it feels good for you, too."

Mary notes that the July Fourth party is particularly timely, since shelters receive fewer donations in the summer.

Her postcard invitations feature a rippling red, white, and blue flag on the front, and these words on the back:

"On this Day of Independence let us celebrate our freedom and good fortune as Americans. Please continue to bring food, clothing, or a tax-deductible check for Portland's needy families."

The guest list ranges from Senator Mark Hatfield and his wife to the artists whose work fills the walls and every nook and cranny of Mary's home.

"People from all different parts of my life are invited to my July Fourth and Boxing Day parties: artists, church people, friends, business associates. I don't worry who's going to like whom. You can't guess that in advance, anyway.

"When they first get here, people tend to start out in clumps who know each other. You'll look around the room and see the church clump here and the artist clump there. But pretty soon they're all mixed up and everybody is talking to everybody else—a business associate to a lifelong friend of mine or a potter to a politician. And the room will get this certain kind of buzz to it. It's pretty exciting when everything gets mixed up like that. Kind of like the art on my walls," she says with an appreciative grin.

MARY'S BUFFET TABLE USUALLY HAS AN ESPECIALLY FINE PACIFIC NORTHwest item, like smacking fresh Chinook salmon and several tasty dips and salads on the side. She fills out the menu with a cookout spread of burgers and hot dogs.

I was looking for a different kind of spread for the holiday—one that wouldn't keep the cook tied up grillside all day. In keeping with the all-American spirit of Mary's party, the recipes suggested for an Independence Day buffet here are based on the foods and resources of the Americas. Turkey, chili, and chocolate all make star appearances. Corn, tomatoes, potatoes, and summer squash not only are New World delicacies but are exquisitely ripe and abundant in the middle of summer. In honor of Mary's father and the countless other immigrants who have given this country's culture diverse richness, many of the recipes here are variations on themes from other cultures— South American, East Indian, and Italian.

The metaphor of the melting pot is unfortunate and misleading. A more accurate analogy would be a salad bowl, for, though the salad is an entity, the lettuce can still be distinguished from the chicory, the tomatoes from the cabbage.

—CARL N. DEGLER, *OUT OF OUR PAST: THE FORCES THAT SHAPED MODERN AMERICA*

Smoked Turkey Empanadas

Almost every country has its moon-shaped meat or vegetable pie, small enough to fit in the hand but big enough to satisfy the appetite. There are Cornish pasties, Indian samosas, Italian calzones, but my favorite of all is the empanada of the Americas. Although these originated and are ubiquitous in South and Central America, you can also find them in diners and cafés throughout the southwestern United States.

These treats are characterized by an alluring mix of savory meat, sweet dried fruit, and buttery nutmeats. It's a subtle mélange set off dramatically by the fireworks of hot salsa served on the side to be spooned into each bite.

Turkey meat might at first seem a bland substitute for the tangy pork or shredded spicy beef that frequently fills these south-of-the-border pastries. But the turkey we use is the juicy dark meat of the leg, given resonance and richness by sugar-smoking over a charcoal fire.

Raisins traditionally provide the fruity sweetness in empanadas, but dried cranberries seemed so much more appropriate with turkey.

Although smoking your own turkey produces the most flavorful results, you can find smoked turkey, especially legs, in many groceries.

It's best to smoke the turkey the day before the party.

EMPANADA FILLING

1 cup brown sugar
1 tablespoon black tea
   leaves
3 turkey legs,
   approximately 3½ pounds
1 teaspoon cumin seed
½ teaspoon kosher salt
2 teaspoons minced garlic
1 teaspoon fresh lime juice
½ cup dried cranberries
¼ cup pine nuts

Use a grill with a cover. Make sure the bottom vents of the grill are open. Light the coals and wait until all are uniformly covered with white ash. Rake the coals to one side of the grill box.

Place the brown sugar in the center of a 1-foot square of aluminum foil, shiny side up. Sprinkle the tea over the sugar, then loosely gather the edges of the foil to the center, forming a pouch with a small opening at the top.

Lightly grease the grate of the grill. Place the aluminum pouch in the center of the grill box, nestled against the edge of the coals. Place the grate on the grill. Arrange the turkey legs on the half of the grate away from the coals. Place the cover on the grill with the top vents open and positioned over the turkey legs so that the smoke from the burning sugar and tea will be pulled that way.

Roast for 1 hour, turning and moving the turkey legs every 15 minutes so they are evenly roasted.

Remove from the grill and set aside to cool. Discard sugar-tea pouch.

When the turkey legs can be handled, separate the meat from the skin and bones, breaking and shredding the meat with your fingers into small pieces. (Set the skin and bones aside for making stock for chowder: see note at end.)

Toast the cumin seed until browned and fragrant, being careful not to burn. Use a small cast-iron, or other heavy, skillet. Heat until almost smoking, toss in the seed, and then shake constantly for the minute or so it takes to toast.

Grind the seed coarsely and sprinkle over the meat, followed by the salt and garlic. Toss and then sprinkle with the lime juice and toss again. Cover tightly and refrigerate until you are ready to make the empanadas. (Overnight is fine; at least an hour is necessary to let the flavors mingle.)

When you are ready to make the empanadas, cover the cranberries with boiling water (just enough to cover, about ¼ cup or less) and let soak for 15 minutes. Toss the cranberries and liquid with the meat mixture, add the pine nuts, and toss to mix.

DOUGH

4½ cups unbleached all-
    purpose flour
1 teaspoon salt
1 teaspoon baking powder
1 cup vegetable shortening
1½ cups skim milk

Sift together the flour, salt, and baking powder. Using a wooden spoon, mix the shortening and milk until blended. Use a fork to stir it into the flour mixture until just blended. Form into 2 balls, cover with a damp cloth, and let rest for at least 2 hours in the refrigerator. It may be left overnight.

TO MAKE THE EMPANADAS

Preheat the oven to 400° F.

Remove 1 ball of dough from the refrigerator and divide into 12 roughly equal pieces. Roll each out on a floured board to a circle about 4 inches in diameter. Repeat with the second ball of dough.

To fill, place a heaping tablespoon of the meat filling a little bit to one side of the center of the dough disk. Fold the uncovered side over, making a half-moon turnover. Press the edge down lightly with your fingertips, then fold the edge back on itself to make a "hem" about ⅛ inch wide. Use a fork dipped in cold water to press around this edge, securing it. Lightly pierce the top of the dough disk once with the fork.

Lay the empanadas on a baking sheet with at least an inch between them. Bake in the preheated oven for 25 minutes, until golden-brown and crisp.

Remove and let cool to room temperature before serving. Serve with Fresh Chile Salsa (page 194), Cranberry Salsa (page 193), and Cilantro Chutney (page 196) on the side. This recipe makes 24 empanadas, which is enough for 12 when served with Corn and Squash Chowder (page 198) and New World Potato Salad (page 201).

If you want to make more, you can simply double the meat filling recipe, but make the dough in 2 separate batches, instead of doubling it, to ensure the best results. The empanadas can be baked and refrigerated overnight, then reheated when you are ready to serve.

Makes 24; serves 12.

NOTE: The skin and bones from smoked turkey make a rich, tangy broth—an essential ingredient for the Corn and Squash Chowder. To make the broth, place the skin and bones in a large pot and cover with 1½ quarts water. Over high heat, bring to a boil, then turn down and simmer for 30 minutes, covered. Let cool, strain the broth, and discard the skin and bones. You can refrigerate for 2 days. If you don't want to use the broth for chowder immediately, it can be frozen. It's an excellent stock for bean soup.

Cranberry Salsa for Empanadas

What a relish! Tangy up front with a lick of pepper that catches fire at the back of the throat and leaves you burning for more. Empanadas accented in this way give a whole new twist to the tradition of turkey and cranberry sauce.

For this salsa, I highly recommend looking for genuine New Mexico ground red chile. (For mail order suggestions, see pages 17–18.) If you simply can't get New Mexico red, then find a spice store to supply you with fresh cayenne or another ground hot dried pepper. Season sparingly at first, increasing the pepper to taste a little at a time.

Using organic oranges will assure you that there is no pesticide residue or wax on the peel to turn the taste bitter.

2 oranges of a thin-skinned
   and juicy variety
1 cup sugar
3 cups frozen cranberries
Dash of salt
½–1 teaspoon coarsely
   ground New Mexico red
   chile
1 teaspoon dark sesame oil

Using a vegetable brush, wash the oranges in warm water and just a little bit of mild dish detergent. Rinse very well in warm water and towel dry. Zest the peel from the oranges.

Cut the oranges in half and use a reamer to extract the juice. Place the juice in a heavy saucepan, add the sugar, and stir over low heat to dissolve. Add the cranberries and a dash of salt. Turn the heat up to boil while you stir, then boil gently for 6 to 8 minutes, until the mixture starts to thicken. Remove from the heat and add the zest. Sprinkle on the chile and sesame oil, then stir to mix. Remove a teaspoonful and *cool thoroughly*, then taste. Add more chile if you want. Cover and chill until time to serve. Will keep 2 or 3 days, tightly covered, in the refrigerator.

Makes about a quart.

Fresh Chile Salsa for Empanadas

Fresh-made salsa is the classic accompaniment for empanadas. In South America, Mexico, and the southwestern United States, it is made with whatever hot peppers are in season. Lately, as chile fever has swept the country, a lot of interesting peppers—both homegrown and imported—have been showing up in gardens and at fresh produce stands in colder climes. With such plenty readily available at midsummer, there is nothing that can beat creating your own custom blend.

Of course, the heat of chiles varies not only from one palate to another but from one plant to another. In fact, one year a single Espanola green chile plant of mine produced peppers ranging from bland to season-in-hell intensity. Simply knowing your variety or asking the pepper producer how hot the chiles are will not ensure much until you actually taste the pepper. So while this recipe offers guidelines for making a fresh chile salsa, you will want to use your own taste to make the final judgment on how much chile is enough.

Pick peppers that are larger than *jalapeños* for this dish, since you want to roast them before peeling, and the larger they are, the easier they are to handle. (Little peppers are better for pickling whole.) Dark green *poblanos* and long pale green Anaheim or New Mexico peppers are available in many grocery produce departments, as are pale yellow banana peppers. Farmers' markets and local fruit stands are good sources for unusual variety peppers.

After you roast, peel, and remove the seeds, chop each pepper individually and taste a tiny bit from the stem end, which is usually the hottest part. Add part or all, depending on how hot it is and how hot you want your salsa to be. If you're still game, chop another chile, taste, and add it. Whatever chile you don't use can be chopped and frozen in a tightly closed container to be added to soups and stews, or omelets, or used in other recipes.

(Take a swig of milk or beer between tastes to cool down your palate, and even take a bite or two of bread, if necessary. Don't try water or any drink with sugar in it, since this just fans the flames.)

If your chiles turn out to be too mild, add a pinch of sugar to the salsa. You can also turn up the temperature by adding a little bit of ground New Mexico red or another dried red pepper, although it will add a different dimension to the flavor.

Finally, this salsa really must be made with drop-dead ripe tomatoes and a very sweet onion.

8 ounces fresh chile
  peppers
4 large homegrown ripe
  tomatoes
1 medium-sized sweet
  white onion (Vidalia or
  Walla Walla
  recommended)
Kosher salt to taste

Charring the skin of the peppers makes it possible to peel them and also gives them a more resonant flavor. To do this, you want to hold them near, but not in or on, a flame or heating element. You can lay them on a charcoal grill or hold them over the gas flame of a stove, speared on a fork.

Or you can lay them out on a cookie sheet under a broiler or even do them on the pan of a toaster oven, turning the toast control to its highest setting and then turning the chiles over each time it cycles.

However you roast them, you want the skin to blister, but you don't want to burn the flesh of the pepper, so you must turn them frequently. When they are blistered all around, pop them in a brown paper bag, roll up the top to close, and leave them for 10 minutes.

To peel, rub them lightly between the palms of your hand, and in many cases the peel will come right off. If not, you can hold them under cool running water and pull the skin away from the flesh.

(WARNING: You must be very careful not to touch your face, especially your eyes, any time you handle fresh chiles, since the juice from the peppers is highly inflammatory to tissue. When you are finished with the chiles, wash your hands thoroughly with soap and warm water, rinse, and dry well. The heat of the pepper may linger for several hours after washing, though, so continue to be cautious. Some folks wear thin dish-washing gloves to protect themselves.)

To make the salsa: Peel the tomatoes, remove the stem, and cut into ½-inch chunks and put in a bowl along with the juice.

Chop the onion into ½-inch chunks also, and add to the tomatoes.

Remove the stem and as many seeds as you can from a chile, then chop it fine on a cutting board with a very sharp knife. Add the chile and its juice to the salsa, taste, and chop and add more as needed. When the salsa is hot enough, add salt to taste. Let sit for an hour at room temperature for the flavors to mingle, then serve immediately.

Makes about a quart.

Cilantro Chutney for Empanadas

The basis for this fragrant chutney is a recipe from Bharti Kirchner's *Healthy Cuisine of India* (Lowell House, 1992). She promises that the addition of citrus, ginger, and coconut mellows the flavor of the cilantro so that even those who scorn it will admire this sauce. My friend David proved her right by making a total pig of himself when it was passed, all the while declaring how much he hates cilantro.

The chopped fruit gives this usually smooth chutney a little more chunk and makes it an even better companion for the turkey empanadas. If you can get a perfect peach—bursting with ripeness yet still somewhat firm to the touch—use it. Otherwise, a flowery-scented apple, such as a Gala, will do fine. I like to leave the fruit unpeeled for color and texture, but some folks have trouble with the skin of peaches, so you may want to peel before chopping.

½ cup fresh lemon juice

2 tablespoons sugar

2 tablespoons chopped
fresh ginger

1 tablespoon chopped
garlic

2 teaspoons chopped hot
green chile

3 tablespoons sweetened
coconut

¼ teaspoon salt

2 cups coarsely chopped
fresh cilantro

1 medium-sized ripe peach
or Gala apple

Plop the lemon juice, sugar, ginger, garlic, chile, coconut, and salt in a blender. Add 1 cup of the cilantro and blend at medium speed just enough to grind everything together but not enough to liquefy. Add the rest of the cilantro and blend for just a few seconds, then transfer to a bowl.

Cut the peach or apple in quarters, discarding seed or core, then dice in pieces ½ inch square or smaller. Toss with the rest of the chutney to mix well. May be refrigerated for an hour or two before serving.

Makes about a pint.

"The Second Day of July, 1776, will be the most memorable Epocha in the history of America. —I am apt to believe that it will be celebrated, by succeeding Generations, as the great Anniversary Festival. It ought to be commemorated as the Day of Deliverance by solemn Acts of Devotion to God Almighty. It ought to be solemnized with Pomp and Parade, with Shews, Games, Sports, Guns, Bells, Bonfires and Illuminations from one End of this Continent to the other from this time forward forevermore."

So wrote John Adams to his wife, Abigail, on July 3, 1776, following the adoption of the Lee Resolution on July 2. That resolution, introduced to the Con-

tinental Congress by member Richard Henry Lee of Virginia, declared "that these United Colonies are, and of right ought to be, free and independent states."

It was two days later, on July 4, 1776, that the Declaration of Independence was approved in Philadelphia.

It is unnecessary to say that, when done, it was the most remarkable chowder ever cooked, and the quantity eaten would have amazed the world if the secret had been divulged.

—LOUISA MAY ALCOTT, *EIGHT COUSINS*

Corn and Squash Chowder

If you subscribe to the notion that chowders must begin with fish stock, include bacon, and be thickened with either crackers or potatoes, then you're welcome to rename this lovely New World mélange a soup or stew. I like to call it chowder, though, because it has that same tangy flavor, created here by the smoked turkey stock, and it has the thick, satisfying texture of a classic chowder from the thickening of the fresh corn.

This particular chowder makes a dandy contribution to our July Fourth New World picnic, based as it is on two of the Americas' finest contributions to global cuisine, corn and squash. Both should be plentiful and succulent at the beginning of July, and leeks should be readily available as well. The importance of using fresh ingredients in this dish cannot be overstated. If all are ripe and good, these bowls of chowder will be bubbling with flavor.

2 medium-sized leeks

3 tablespoons butter

2 pounds summer squash
  (about 5 medium-sized)

½ tablespoon kosher salt

4 ears fresh corn

1 quart smoked turkey
  broth (page 192)

Freshly ground black
  pepper to taste

¼ cup half-and-half

1 cup slivered fresh basil
  (see instructions)

Clean the leeks well (see the sidebar), saving some of the light green leaves, but discarding the darker tops. Chop into ½-inch dice. You want about 1½ cups chopped leeks. In a large soup pot, melt the butter over medium heat. Add the leeks and sauté until they soften and the whites start to turn transparent, stirring occasionally to prevent scorching.

While the leeks are cooking, scrub the squash well, remove the stem and blossom ends, quarter lengthwise, and chop into 1-inch dice. You want about 5 cups squash. Add this to the leeks, sprinkle on the salt, stir, and cover. Cook over medium heat for about 10 minutes.

While the squash is cooking, shuck the corn and, using a very sharp knife, cut down the cob, removing just the top half of each kernel. Then, using a metal teaspoon, scrape up the cob, extracting the pulp and milk from the corn kernels. If the corn is very juicy, squeeze more liquid from the cobs with your hand.

Add the corn to the squash and leek mixture, stir, and cover. Cook over medium heat for 10 minutes. Then add the turkey broth to the vegetables, bring to a quick boil, and turn down to a simmer. Cover and cook for about 20 minutes.

Remove the cover and grind 4 or 5 turns of fresh black pepper over the soup, stirring. Turn up the heat to a lightly bubbling simmer and let cook and thicken for 5 minutes. Remove from the heat, add the half-and-half, and stir. Let cool for just a few minutes before serving, since the soup is best when very warm but not piping hot.

Using a very sharp knife, cut the fresh basil across the leaf into slivers. Dish up the chowder into bowls and sprinkle a tablespoon or so of basil on top. Pass the black-pepper mill so each can season to taste.

Makes 12 appetizer servings.

NOTE: To double this recipe, double the ingredients, adding an equivalent amount of chicken or vegetable broth for the additional smoked turkey broth. Don't automatically double the salt, but use the amount called for here, then taste and add more as necessary.

SQUEAKY-CLEAN LEEKS

Leeks collect grit like a five-year-old in a sandbox. Even when you've rinsed the outside to perfection, the layers inside will be rippled with fine silt and sand. Old cookbooks sometimes suggest removing the root end and rinsing the whole leek several times upside down, or slicing down into the greens of the leek, making a fan, and rinsing several times.

But the quickest, cleanest method I've found is to chop off the root end and the dark, tough part of the green leaves, then rinse any surface dirt off the leek. Cut the leek in two lengthwise to expose a cross section of the layers. (You'll need to rinse the cutting board and knife at this point, since grit will accumulate on both.)

Hold each leek piece under running cold water, exposing the interior and spreading the layers a little with your thumb if necessary. Usually all of the grit will rinse away and you can shake and pat the leek pieces dry, then chop. If some grit comes to the surface while you're chopping, simply pop the leek pieces into a colander and rinse again.

New World Potato Salad

Potatoes are so crucial to the cuisine of Ireland, Germany, Poland, and Russia that we're tempted to think they must always have been a part of the landscape there. In fact, the potato is a decidedly all-American crop. And the all-American mayonnaise-slathered, pickle-spiked potato salad is such a staple at summer picnics that we're tempted to think of tampering with it as a downright un-American activity. But the rich, roasty taste of this salad, and the light, refreshing way it complements but doesn't overwhelm the other dishes of our buffet, may very well change your mind.

The recipe is written for potatoes roasted in the oven, but you can also roast them over a charcoal grill. In fact, if you want to roast them the day before you serve them—say, right after you've taken the turkey legs off the grill—that would be perfect. They'll take about 20 to 30 minutes and should be started ringed around the edge of the grill. Turn them 4 or 5 times in the course of roasting, and each time move them closer to the center of the grill and the fire. A "done" potato will have a toasty golden crust around it and can be pierced easily by a fork.

2 dozen new potatoes just bigger than golf balls
2 tablespoons olive oil
1 teaspoon kosher salt
2 medium-sized red bell peppers
2 plump scallions
¼ cup balsamic vinegar
1 teaspoon brown sugar

Preheat the oven to 475° F.

Wash the potatoes well, then cut in half. In a bowl, toss with the olive oil and salt until thoroughly coated. Place on cookie sheets with the cut side up and the potatoes not touching one another. Place the cookie sheets on the top shelf of the oven and roast for approximately 20 minutes, or until the potatoes are crisply golden and brown outside but are soft inside when pierced by a fork.

While the potatoes are cooling, slice the peppers in quarters lengthwise, then cut into slivers.

Trim the scallions. Use a sharp knife to split down the length, then slice very thin.

Place the room-temperature potatoes in a bowl and toss with the peppers and onion. Mix the balsamic vinegar with brown sugar and then sprinkle over the potatoes and toss. May be served immediately or covered tightly and chilled for an hour or so.

Serves 12.

Tomato Platter

If potatoes changed the course of northern European history forever, tomatoes changed the course of world cooking forever—and for the better. Tomatoes show up in virtually every cuisine and, from ketchup to marinara, are the basis for the most savory and essential of sauces. But cooking with tomatoes is small pleasure compared to that three-month thrill of eating juice-spurting fresh, exquisitely ripe tomatoes in the summer. There is simply nothing tastier, and nothing could suit a patriotic American food fest finer than a platter filled with thick slabs of fresh-sliced tomatoes.

There is no cooking and very little preparation involved in this "recipe." The secret lies in getting a variety of the ripest, most fragrant, freshly picked tomatoes you can find. The first days of July should be fine for finding fresh homegrowns in all but the most northern climes. Don't look in supermarkets, though, since the tomatoes that survive the mass packing and transportation to the store will most likely be bland and watery. Small groceries that specialize in good produce, farmers' markets, fruit markets that stock local produce, or friends who are gardeners are your best sources.

When picking tomatoes remember that bigger isn't necessarily better, but a good tomato is one that is heavy for its size, whatever that size may be. Look for tomatoes that are fully red or golden yellow, without cracks in the skin, mold, or soft spots. Lift the stem end of the tomato to your nose and breathe deeply. If you get a good strong whiff of tomato perfume, buy it. If you smell nothing, put it back.

Great tomatoes can come in a variety of colors ranging from bright red to purple-tinged to yellow. Using several kinds will make a visually pretty platter and will give your guests a taste treat, since the flavors can range from lip-puckering tart to a buttery, mellow sweetness. Allow 1 tomato per person.

A TOMATO I ONCE KNEW

It talked then it stopped then
it rolled then it choked, it
took a deep breath, then
it walked the rope, after that
it croaked. A tomato I once
knew.

It sang then it
swam, then it laughed,
then it laughed again, then
it left me. A tomato
I once knew.

—Emily Morris, at age ten, from *Some Say Tomato*, edited and published by Mariflo Stevens

◇ Sundaes Will Never Be the Same

Mary Maletis tops off her July Fourth bash with a Do-It-Yourself-Sundae-Making. There's a table full of toppings and plenty of firm good ice cream. Guests can take as much or as little as they want. Aesthetes can savor the subtle complements of one special topping at a time while more exuberant types can pour everything they've ever wanted in one bowl. It's even okay to stir your ice cream and make it into mush. In fact, the more this dessert spree brings out the kid in everyone, the better it is.

Here are some things to know about perfect sundaes:

ABOUT THE ICE CREAM

Homemade ice cream is one of the sublimest joys of summer, and you will find recipes for some scattered throughout this book. But when it comes to homemade, I am a hard-shell fundamentalist, and that's why you won't find a recipe for homemade ice cream in this section. I believe with all my heart that homemade ice cream—especially vanilla ice cream—is meant to be savored pure and unadulterated by any toppings or mix-ins.

This doesn't mean I don't like a fine sundae, however. It simply means that to make a fine sundae you should start with a first-quality commercial ice cream. The operative words here are "first quality." Don't think that superior toppings can make up for an inferior cream. To do the toppings in this chapter justice, you must have ice cream that is as good as they are. Chances are very good you already have a favorite brand of ice cream, and that's what you should go with for this party. But if you don't, here are a few things you should consider when looking for good store-bought cream.

There are three things that distinguish superior ice cream from an inferior one: quality of ingredients, quantity of air, and percentage of fat.

The primary consideration should be given to ingredients. Natural flavorings are a must—that means vanilla, not vanillin; real chocolate and cocoa, not "chocolate flavor"; and actual strawberries, not "fruit flavorings." Too many stabilizers and emulsifiers (commonly used in less expensive ice creams to compensate for a lower fat content) are a no-no.

Air is incorporated into ice cream to make it softer and lighter—without it, your ice cream would be more like ice and less like cream. Government standards permit ice cream makers to as much as double the volume with added air, and inferior ice creams are often made with the maximum allowance to compensate for less fat. They will seem fluffy and somewhat warmer than better ice creams when you eat them. The ingredient listings won't tell you anything about how much air is in your cream, but hefting a half-gallon will. Cartons that feel light as a feather will also be lighter on pleasure.

The fat is responsible for ice cream's seductive, velvety body, and in recent years most premium brands have made their names by using maximum fat. Not everyone is crazy for a super-rich ice cream, however. (In fact, some folks prefer ice milk, which, partly because of its lower fat content, feels colder when you eat it.) Ice creams must contain 10 percent fat to qualify as ice cream, according to federal standards. Premium ice creams may have double that. Ice creams in the mid-range tend to be plenty rich for sundae-making, and they won't be pumped up with the extra air that lower-fat blends rely on.

As for what flavors are best for sundaes, my fundamentalist streak surfaces here as well, since I think vanilla truly provides the best harmony for almost any topping. A really dark, rich chocolate is intriguing with the Orange Blossom Pralines (page 207) mixed in, though, and the Traditional Chocolate Sauce (page 209) recalls fruit cream candies when ladled over a good strawberry and is a mocha delight with coffee.

A gallon of vanilla and a half-gallon each of chocolate, coffee, and strawberry will allow a dozen do-it-yourself sundae-makers to be downright piggy. If you serve one scoop to a bowl for starters, your guests can come back for more and indulge their taste buds with several toppings.

ABOUT WHIPPED CREAM AND CHERRIES

No sundae looks dressed in its sundae best unless topped by a swirly mound of whipped cream and a bright, bright red cherry. While freshly whipped cream simply can't be beaten as a topping for most desserts, those aerosol cans that swirl squiggles on demand are really a lot more fun to wield during this sundae-making. Likewise, a fresh, ripe cherry beats an artificially dyed and preserved maraschino in almost any case except as the appropriate cap to a genuine sundae.

SYRUPS AND MIX-INS

Traditionally, sundaes are topped with a syrup, and nuts, if you wish. But a recent invention has been the mix-in, pieces of candy or cookies which you stir into the ice cream itself—and which can then be topped with syrup, if you're feeling really decadent.

The Orange Blossom Pralines are one mix-in you should definitely have on your table, along with bowls of plain broken walnuts and peanuts. Other favorite mix-ins include M&M's and Reese's Pieces, and Oreo cookies broken into bite sizes. (A handy way to break those Oreos, or any other hard cookie, is this: Place a dozen in a large plastic bag, press to remove the air, and then seal. Lay flat on a surface and lightly roll over with a rolling pin until the pieces are about an inch or less in size. If you don't have a rolling pin, just press down firmly but gently with the heel of your hand.)

One wonderful topping for good vanilla ice cream is pure maple syrup—but make sure it is real maple syrup and not an artificially flavored pancake topping.

Several commercial toppings are fine, but Traditional Chocolate Sauce is better than most any chocolate you will find in a store, keeps its consistency well without heating, and allows you to make the Snappy Peppermint Rendition.

Recipes for these and other homemade toppings follow.

Ice cream isn't an American invention, but the sundae may well be. There are records of fruit ices and cream ices in European history as early as the sixteenth century and recipes in English cookbooks of the eighteenth century. But it was an American woman, Nancy Johnson, who invented the hand-cranked freezer in 1846, and it wasn't long before ice cream was being manufactured commercially and eaten heartily throughout the country.

Ice-cream sodas were the rage in the Gay Nineties, but in the Midwest they were deemed somewhat wicked—at least enough that laws were passed forbidding their consumption on Sundays. To get around such laws, sodas sans fizz were served, and that's how these concoctions of ice cream with toppings got the name "sundae."

Orange Blossom Pralines

Technically speaking, these aren't pralines at all, but there is something so deliciously and decadently Old South in the blended flavors of these orange-candied pecans that the name seems to suit them. And they seem to suit ice cream to a T. They can be sprinkled onto pure vanilla for a very grownup version of that drugstore treat the Dreamsicle. Traditional Chocolate Sauce (recipe follows) is just the addition for those who love the distinctive harmonies of chocolate and orange. And if you choose instead to top the pralines and cream with Ginger Peachy Sauce (page 212), you'll have a Georgia-style treat as fine as any dished up at Tara.

Though it may seem a little formidable at first, caramelizing nuts isn't really that difficult. The trick is to be quick at adding the orange sugar, a bit at a time, and at tossing the nuts by both shaking the skillet they are heating in and moving them with the edge of a metal spatula. If you're timid about possibly burning yourself, wear an oven mitt on the hand you use to shake the skillet.

Minced zest of 1 orange
1 cup sugar
1 teaspoon canola oil
1 cup pecan halves

Mix the minced zest of one orange with sugar. (Be sure you scrub the orange with mild detergent and rinse thoroughly before zesting.) When they are thoroughly blended, put in a place within easy reach of the burner you will be using.

Heat a heavy skillet over high heat until a little bit of water flicked onto its surface beads and skitters. Add the canola oil and twirl the pan to oil its surface.

Add the pecans and gently toss and shake in the skillet so they get well toasted on every side. You can use a metal spatula to turn and move them.

When the pecans are thoroughly hot, sprinkle one-third of the sugar mixture over them as evenly as possible. Shake the skillet gently but constantly with one hand, and toss and turn the pecans with the metal spatula edge. (Try not to get the whole spatula involved, since the melting sugar mixture will stick to it as well as to the nuts. If your spatula edge starts to crust with sugar, scrape it briskly against the hot side of the pan, letting the glaze melt and drop back into the pan.)

The orange sugar will begin to melt and then stick to the pecans. When the first batch of sugar has melted and the nuts are fairly well glazed, sprinkle another one-third of the sugar over them evenly. Continue until all the sugar has been used.

Continue heating and tossing for another minute or so. You want all the sugar to melt and glaze the nuts, but you don't want the sugar to burn. You are done if it starts to turn brown in the bottom of the pan and things start to smell a little too toasty, or if the sugar has all melted and the nuts are all covered.

Remove the nuts from the heat immediately and gently dump out on a cookie sheet or large plate. Use the spatula to nudge apart any nuts that have stuck in large clumps. (Nuts that are stuck to just one or two others can usually be easily separated when cooled.) Allow to cool and put in an airtight container.

The nuts may be used right away, but their flavor seems to get more intense if allowed to sit for 24 hours. They can be kept for 3 to 4 days in the airtight container. In addition to using them as an ice-cream adjunct, you'll find them delicious served with buttery cheese and fruit.

Makes 1 cup.

Traditional Chocolate Sauce and Snappy Peppermint Rendition

We were sampling a variety of homemade chocolate sauces—some too thick, some too thin, some too sweet, some too bitter—when my friend Kathy Attaway said, "My sauce is better than any of these." She was right. It's also easy to whip up from ingredients you have on hand, and it lends itself perfectly to snazzing up with a little kick of peppermint.

2 cups sugar
⅔ cup unsweetened cocoa
1 cup milk (2 percent is
   fine)
½ cup (1 stick) butter
1 teaspoon vanilla extract

¹⁄₁₆ teaspoon peppermint
   extract

This is double the recipe that Kathy usually makes, and you will want to use a heavy saucepan that holds at least 4 quarts so you won't have to worry about its boiling over. If you must use a smaller pan, divide the recipe in half and make 2 batches.

In a heavy saucepan, mix the sugar and cocoa until blended. Place over high heat and immediately add the milk. Stir constantly with a wooden spoon as the mixture comes to a boil. Continue boiling and stirring until the mixture has almost, but not quite, reached the soft-ball stage. (Test by dropping a few drops of the syrup in a cup of cold water. If the syrup disperses immediately, it's not ready yet. If it holds in a loose mass but doesn't stay in a ball when you pat it with your finger, it is ready. On a candy thermometer, the mixture will be just a couple of degrees above 230° F., but not yet to 234° F., which is where the soft-ball stage begins.)

Remove from the heat immediately and add the butter and vanilla. Stir until the butter is melted and incorporated into the syrup. Pour half the mixture (about 1½ cups) into a clean jar or pitcher. That is Traditional Chocolate Sauce.

To make the Snappy Peppermint Rendition, add the peppermint extract to the other half of the syrup and stir. Pour into a clean jar or pitcher.

Both syrups should cool some before serving. A slightly warm, not hot, temperature is best, and they are also tasty when served at room temperature. They can be stored, tightly covered, in the refrigerator, and should be allowed to come to room temperature, or be heated briefly by putting the pitcher or jar in a pan of warm water, over low heat, before serving.

Makes enough to top a dozen sundaes.

Kentucky Bourbon Sauce

When you're talking about all-American spirits, you're talking bourbon. Whiskey is an Old World tradition, of course, but distilling it from corn, that remarkable New World grain, is an American invention. Early distilleries flourished in the Bluegrass region of Kentucky, where the limestone water makes for a superior taste. Ask any Kentuckian, myself included, and they will tell you that the best bourbon still comes from there today. Don't skimp when you're buying the bourbon to go into this sauce, but go for quality. It will make the sauce much more flavorful, and make you much happier when you sip the rest of the contents of the bottle later.

This recipe comes from another exemplary product of Kentucky, Lee Hutchison, who recommends you use premium strawberry preserves.

1 cup brown sugar
1 cup white sugar
Juice of 1 lemon
Juice of 1 orange
1 cup very good strawberry
  preserves
1 cup chopped pecans
¼ cup bourbon

In a heavy saucepan, combine the sugars and 1 cup water and bring to a boil over high heat, stirring constantly with a wooden spoon. Boil briefly until the mixture has almost, but not quite, reached the soft-ball stage. (Test by dropping a few drops of the syrup in a cup of cold water. If the syrup disperses immediately, it's not ready yet. If it holds in a loose mass but doesn't stay in a ball when you pat it with your finger, it is ready. On a candy thermometer, the mixture will be just a couple of degrees above 230° F., but not yet to 234° F., which is where the soft-ball stage begins.)

Remove from the heat immediately. Add the lemon and orange juices and the preserves and stir to blend. Add the pecans and bourbon and stir again. Transfer to a clean jar or pitcher and serve when it reaches room temperature. Will keep for a week, tightly covered, in the refrigerator.

Makes about 3 cups.

Ginger Peachy Sauce

This sauce is outrageously good ladled over vanilla ice cream. And to be truly, madly, deeply decadent, mix in some Orange Blossom Pralines.

6 medium-sized ripe fresh
  peaches
1 tablespoon minced fresh
  ginger
1 cup sugar
⅛ teaspoon salt
2 drops red food coloring
  (optional)

Don't peel the peaches unless the peels are extremely fuzzy. Instead, just rinse and pit them and chop coarsely. You should have about 4 cups. Set 1 cup aside.

When you mince the ginger, be sure first to slice thin rounds against the grain, then chop fine. Otherwise, if you slice it with the grain first, you'll end up with tiny strings of fiber in the sauce.

Put the 1 cup peaches, the minced ginger, and 1 cup water into a blender and process until pureed. Pour into a heavy saucepan, add the sugar and salt and stir over medium-high heat until the mixture comes to a boil. Turn the heat down so that the mixture is boiling very lightly. Continue stirring for 2 minutes, then add the rest of the chopped peaches. Cook and stir for 2 minutes more, then remove from the heat.

The syrup is naturally a pale golden color, but if you want it to look just a little more "peachy" you can add 2 drops of red food coloring, stirring to color evenly. Pour into a clean jar or pitcher. Allow to cool a bit before serving.

This can be kept, tightly covered, in the refrigerator for 24 hours, but should be brought to room temperature when you are ready to serve and is especially nice when heated just a bit. It's also scrumptious poured over waffles or pancakes or mixed with plain yogurt.

Makes about 1 quart.

RISE AND SHINE 1

Most Fourth of July parties start in the afternoon, working their way up to fireworks at nightfall. But Richard Langdon of English and David Weirhake of Bloomington, Indiana, have never been traditionalists.

Back in the 1970s, when both were denizens of Bloomington's thriving counterculture scene, they began a new tradition, a Fourth of July pancake breakfast.

Langdon, a kite-maker, says that although neither he nor Weirhake would call himself patriotic, the party did have a very significant rationale.

"We had a real conscious reason for doing it. It seemed like a great way to meet women in Bloomington."

Indeed, women line up for the pancake breakfast, along with men and children, to the tune of some seventy-five folks each year. Everyone brings a plate, utensils, and their own syrup. Langdon, Weirhake, and usually one other friend mix up batter in 12-quart stockpots.

"David is the traditionalist, while I always make the Mr. Natural Mystery Pancake Batter. One year I just literally emptied the contents of the refrigerator into the pot," Langdon says.

Prizes are awarded for whatever the organizers feel like awarding them for: the person who came the farthest, most interesting syrup, weirdest clothes, most pancakes eaten. The awards range from wide 1940s ties to obscure 1970s albums.

After everyone has pancaked their fill, most of the group moves on to an all-day swim and picnic at another friend's house. The swim party may have been the inspiration for the pancake party in the first place, Langdon says: "I guess we started the Fourth of July picnic because we figured everybody needed a good breakfast to keep up their strength and get them through partying all day."

'Tis not clean Linen only that makes the Feast.

—THOMAS FULLER, *GNOMOLOGIA* (1732)

A CRABBY FOURTH

I met my husband, Ken Jones, in the early 1970s, a time when the concept of patriotism was undergoing dramatic redefinition. We were enthusiastic supporters of peace and protest, so imagine my surprise when the Fourth of July came around and I discovered Ken was downright bullish on celebrating. Or maybe I should say "crabbish."

Our first Fourth began at the home of his brother, Shel, in a suburb outside of their hometown, Baltimore. The Jones boys woke me far too early, marching up and down the hallway of the house singing "The Star-Spangled Banner" at the top of their lungs. Never mind that Ken was singing the entire song in his best Donald Duck voice. It looked like patriotic fervor at its finest to me.

By early afternoon we'd moved on to the boys' parents' house in Dundalk, Maryland, the working-class neighborhood where they'd grown up.

There the annual Fourth of July parade, complete with the Baltimore Colts marching band, was under way. Not only did we go to the parade, we followed the band the whole way, darting down alleys and through boyhood shortcuts to get to a sidewalk somewhere just moments before the band turned a corner. I, who had grown up regarding the Fourth primarily as just a summer day when adults got off work to picnic, thought this might be the finest Independence Day tradition of all. But I had yet to encounter the crabs.

They came after the parade when we returned to the parents' house and a screened-in back porch rife with the heady scent of spices and the salt of the sea. There was a long picnic table covered with thick newspaper layers and, at its end, a huge, damp paper sack oozing steam.

When we were all seated, Ken's mother lifted the sack and dumped the contents onto the newspaper: three dozen crimson, succulent, spice-speckled, and enticing Chesapeake Bay steamed crabs.

I seem to remember there were hamburgers somewhere, and a big bowl of potato salad. But all anyone really had eyes for (and mouths and hands) were the crabs.

We used little wooden hammers to crack the claws gently, a sharp paring knife to split the body, and fingers to coax the meat from the cavities. The concept of finger food took on a whole new dimension as we noisily sucked our fingers clean of the salty sea juice and hot spice. When we were finished and every crustacean in the place had been demolished, Ken's mom simply shoved the shells to the middle of the table, folded the newspapers tightly around them, and stuffed everything back into the original sack and then into the garbage.

We, meanwhile, leaned back in lawn chairs there in the heart of that all-American neighborhood, full of families whose roots were Italian, Irish, Polish, Appalachian, Welsh, German, and so on. That night, though, we all lifted our spice-streaked beer bottles to the cherry bombs bursting in the air and counted ourselves downright lucky to be all-Americans.

Here's what the sage of Baltimore, H. L. Mencken, had to say about the blessings of crab:

"Out of the Bay, Baltimore ate divinely. Any poor man could go down to the banks of the river, armed with no more than a length of stout cord, a home-made net on a pole, and a chunk of cat's meat, and come home a couple of hours later with enough crabs to feed his family."

We hope the cat's meat he refers to was cat food and not an actual cat, but one can never tell with the irascible writer who turned the term "crabby" into a literary art form.

Chesapeake Bay–Style Steamed Crabs

I have had luscious steamed crabs in Maine, delightful Dungeness on the West Coast, and sassy stone crab claws in Florida. In those places they are served with butter or seafood sauce for dipping or whatever manner of gourmet go-with is popular at the time. But if you have Chesapeake Bay blue crabs, there is only one way to cook them: steamed in so much savory Old Bay Seasoning that it sticks to the crabs and your fingers like sand from hog heaven.

Luckily, all crabs seem to thrive from this classic culinary treatment, so you can steam any of the varieties of the crustacean you can get providing that you can get your crabs alive and kicking. But a dead crab—no matter how recently demised—should not be eaten at all, and frozen crab is not to be considered.

Those of us who are landlocked need not despair or start looking into plane tickets for either coast, however. If you've got a hankering for the Chesapeake's finest institution, you have two options.

You can order crabs already steamed from one of Baltimore's classic crab houses or fisheries. They can be sent to you overnight on ice and gently reheated before serving. For more information on that option, see page 220.

Or, if you're lucky enough to have a fishmonger whom you trust and who has good connections, chances are he or she can order live crabs shipped overnight. It will cost a pretty penny and you'll want to steam the crabs and eat them the day they arrive, but you'll think it money and time well spent when you're licking your fingers.

(If you are ordering live blue crabs, be sure to specify that you want jimmies, the males, which are best for steaming. She-crabs usually end up in packing plants, where they are picked for crabmeat. You can tell a male crab by looking at the underside, where you will see an inverted T-shaped piece of shell called the apron. Immature females have a V-shaped apron, and mature ones have a fuller, rounder apron.)

The tricky part of having live crabs shipped in, however, is that some of them just won't make the trip. As a clerk at Faidley's Seafood in Baltimore's Lexington Market put it: "There's no way, hon, to guarantee the life of a crab, no more than there is the life of a person. You could pick one up and it die that moment. Only person who can keep a crab alive is God."

You can help God in the task, however, by promptly pitching any crabs who've died en route. (See "Crab Mortality" on page 220 for instructions on how to tell the quick from the dead in Crabville.) Keep the live ones chilled in the fridge, covered by a damp towel, or on a layer of damp newspapers in an ice-filled cooler, until you're ready to steam them—which should be pretty darn soon after you've gotten them.

To do that, you'll need a big pot with either a rack or a steamer insert. Along the coast, these are called steamer pots. Inland, one of those big old blue enamel canning pots will do just fine. If you can't corral one really big one, 2 medium-sized ones will do—just remember to split the seasonings and liquid equally along with the crabs. Your pot will need a tight-fitting lid. Here's what else you'll need.

½ cup Old Bay Seasoning
  (see page 219)
¼ cup kosher salt
2 cups white vinegar
1 quart water or flat beer
2 dozen alive and kicking
  crabs

Mix the Old Bay Seasoning and salt together. Pour the vinegar and beer into the steamer pan and set over high heat. If the pot has a rack, put it in and make sure the liquid doesn't come up high enough to touch it. Cover and bring to a boil.

While the liquid is coming to a boil, fill a tub or your kitchen sink with cold water and ice cubes. Toss the live crabs in there and let them sit for about 5 minutes. Foreigners may think this trick is to rinse the crabs, but veterans of the crab houses say that it numbs the cranky crustaceans, making it easier to grab them and throw them in the pot. Some folks say it also keeps the claws from falling off and helps the seasoning to stick on.

When the pot is boiling heartily and the crabs are downright chilly, place a layer of crabs on the rack or in the bottom of the steamer insert. Sprinkle the Old Bay Seasoning and salt mixture evenly and generously over the crabs. Lay another layer of crabs on top and season them. Continue until all the crabs are in the pot. Cover tightly and steam for about 25 minutes, until the crabs are bright red and the smell of seasoned crabs steaming makes you almost crazy with hunger. Remove from the steamer and spread out on the table. The crabs will be covered with the seasoning, but don't wash them off! Getting seasoning all over your hands, up to your elbows, and into your mouth is one of the main pleasures of Chesapeake Bay–style crabs.

While folks are waiting for the crabs to cool enough to handle, keep the steamer stoking. Cook corn according to directions for Crabby Corn (page

225). Along with Devilish Spuds (page 226) and a box of saltine crackers, that's all you'll need for a feast.

Serves 4 to 6.

NOTE: How many 2 dozen crabs serve depends on how big the crabs are and where the diners come from. I mean, I know a couple of Dundalk brothers who could do in a pot of small crabs all on their own. But less veteran pickers take longer and seem to be sated sooner, so count on 4 to 6 crabs per person, depending on size.

OLD BAY, THE ONLY WAY

There are lots of seafood seasonings and crab boils on the market, but if you are making Chesapeake Bay–Style Steamed Crabs the Baltimore way, you must have Old Bay Seasoning. This blend of spices includes pimiento, mustard, cassia, bay leaves, mace, cardamom, ginger, paprika, and cloves along with salt and pepper. The problem is that while everyone knows what's in it, nobody seems sure of how much of whatever it takes to make that distinctive Old Bay taste. And the maker, McCormick & Co. in Hunt Valley, Maryland, isn't telling.

McCormick is trying to distribute the spice more widely, however. Once Old Bay Seasoning could be found only on the East Coast, but in recent years the distinctive yellow and navy blue rectangular tins have started showing up all around the country, often in specialty markets but sometimes in chain grocery stores—especially ones that offer fresh seafood.

If you can't find Old Bay Seasoning on your grocer's shelf, you can order it from the source. McCormick & Co.'s number is (800) 632-5847, and the spice can be used in a plethora of other recipes, some of which they'll be glad to send you with an order form.

CRAB MORTALITY

There are those who say you know a dead crab by its complete lack of crabbiness. Live crabs, even ones that are chilled to the point of sluggishness, will have some movement in their legs when picked up or prodded, they aver, and they tell you to throw out any that don't wiggle or twitch.

But the seafood authorities at the Maryland Department of Agriculture fear you may be pitching some live ones if you follow that advice. If your crabs have been traveling on ice for twenty-four hours, some of them may have lapsed into a dormant stage, and even if you prod them, they won't respond, although they are still alive and fine for steaming.

To be sure, the MDA folks suggest you fill a basin with tepid water and about a cupful of salt to create the illusion of the sea. Plop any crabs that haven't responded to your first prods in the salt water for a couple of minutes to get the chill out, then poke again to see who twitches and wiggles. (Use a chopstick or the end of a wooden spoon to do this gentle poking, just in case someone revives and is ornery enough to pinch your finger with a claw.) Any crabs that don't respond to a poke or two after this treatment should be discarded. The others should be promptly removed from the water and chilled again until it's time for steaming.

OVERNIGHT CRABS

I was skeptical about ordering already steamed crabs shipped overnight. How good could they be after a day spent flying and on ice, I asked. Luckily, the answer was: pretty darned good.

Olde Obrycki's Crab House and Seafood Restaurant, 1727 East Pratt Street in Baltimore, was the source I used. They packed freshly steamed crabs in a Styrofoam carton with ice packs and sent it by Federal Express to us overnight.

We reheated the crabs according to the directions they included, and it was almost (though not quite) like being Bayside.

Although we ate our crabs the day they arrived, the folks at Obrycki's said we could keep them in the refrigerator for another twenty-four hours without noticeable loss of quality.

Obrycki's crabs can be shipped on the second of July to arrive on the third and then refrigerated until time to reheat for the Fourth. They advise you call at least a week in advance to place your order for the Fourth, however, because of the big demand. The restaurant ships year round except in December, January, and February, when crabs are too hard to come by.

Obrycki's number is (800) 742-1741. A dozen crabs can range in price from $20 to $48 a dozen, depending on the size of crab.

Other folks willing to ship already steamed crabs include Hales Seafood, 1801 Taylor Avenue, Baltimore, Maryland 21234, (410) 665-4000; Faidley's Seafood, Lexington Market, 200 North Paca Street, Baltimore, Maryland 21201, (410) 727-4898; and Nick's Inner Harbor Seafood, Cross Street Market, Baltimore, Maryland 21230, (410) 685-2020. The guy at Nick's said, "You gotta give me a day in advance, but we'll do anything." That's a good rule of thumb to follow. Call at least the day before you want the crabs shipped (two days before you expect them to arrive). And if you're ordering for the Fourth of July, the more advance notice you can give the shipper, the better.

So now that you've got a couple dozen steamed crabs, how do you eat them? Put on some old clothes for the first step. This is messy work, and there's no point in wasting time trying to keep things tidy.

Cover your table in newspapers, about 3 or 4 sheets thick. Picnic tables outdoors, or on a deck or porch that can also be hosed down, are ideal. Kitchen tables can be cozy. Eating in the dining room—especially one with a carpet—is risky business.

Toss the crabs on the table—in the center, but down the length of the table so everyone sitting around can grab a crab whenever they need one without interrupting their neighbor's progress.

Seize a crab. If you've never met one before, here's a quick primer: The bright red side is up, the whitish part is the underside. The big fat claws are in the front, and at the back are some long, narrower claw-type things, which are called back fins. The little claws around the sides are called the swimming legs. The whole thing may look a little formidable, but inside is a treasure trove of sweet meat.

Here's how you get to that meat. Flip the crab over so you're looking at its underside. That upside-down T shape is the apron, and you should wedge a paring knife or your finger under its stem and pull the whole apron off. Where the wide part of the apron was there is now a kind of slot just right for sticking your thumb in.

Flip the crab back to right side up, stick your thumb in the slot, and pull the top shell right off.

You'll see some stuff there that doesn't look like crab meat. It's the gills, and you want to remove them with your fingers. There will also be some greenish paste called the "devil." Clean that out with your finger, discarding it and wiping your finger clean on the newspaper in a place not directly where you or someone else is dismembering a crab.

There is also some yellow stuff in the middle of the crab. In my husband's family, this was also regarded as part of the devil and discarded. However, it is actually fat, and some people think it is very flavorful. You won't know unless you try. (There's an old wives' tale that says if you eat the devil it will kill you, but according to the Maryland Department of Agriculture's seafood department, there's no truth to that.)

Now grasp the crab in both hands, a claw to each side, and break the body of the crab in half, down the middle. Twist around the "back fins" to break them off the body and you'll find a nice little morsel of meat in each. Eat it. Pull the swimming legs off the body one at a time and suck the little yummy bits of meat out of them. Toss the shells and remnants on the newspaper.

Break off the claws and set aside for the grand climax.

Use a paring knife to cut horizontally through each half of the crab body, exposing the chambers of meat inside. (Old-timers do this by holding the crab half in one hand, the broken or meat side facing out, then deftly cutting into it and work-

ing the knife until the crab half splits. New-timers and mothers who worry about the ten best ways to put out your eye or cut off a finger may think this technique looks terrifying, but it's still the best way we know to get to this part of the crab. If you can come up with a safer one, go for it. Otherwise, proceed cautiously but determinedly.)

When the half is broken open, use your fingers to pick out the morsels of meat and pop them into your mouth. (Some people recommend you use the tip of the paring knife to do your picking, and it's true it may be able to get in some crevices that your fingers won't. But my husband the Baltimorean opines that "the more stuff gets in the way of the hand to the meat is wrong." He insists that fingers work just fine.)

Now it's time to break open the claws. If your crabs have come from Baltimore—steamed or kicking—chances are good you've been sent some light wooden mallets with them. Or if you've got a child who has one of those wooden peg-pounding toys, that mallet will do. Otherwise, you can use the handle of a heavy table knife to do your cracking.

Break the claw at the joint, making two halves. Use the mallet or knife handle to firmly tap (not bludgeon) the shell of one of the halves across the middle. What you're striving for is a nice crack around the middle of the shell that will make it easy to break the shell and pull it apart, exposing a tasty little paw of meat. What you don't want is to hit the shell so hard that it shatters and you waste time picking shards of shell out of the meat before you get to eat it.

Some folks use a paring knife for this operation, driving the point into the shell by tapping the handle of the paring knife with the mallet. Either technique takes some practice to perfect, but you get to eat the mistakes nevertheless.

When you've picked and sucked your crab clean, toss the shells onto the newspaper and grab another one. Lick your fingers as often as you want, and consume quantities of beer or ginger ale. Eat corn and potatoes in between crabs, being sure to get plenty of crab juice and Old Bay Seasoning on them as you do. And revel. It's what the Forefathers would want you to do.

NOT-SO-EASY BIG EASY CRABS

The seasonings are different and the crabs get boiled, not steamed, in New Orleans, but the folks there love their crustaceans with almost as much passion as the people of the Chesapeake Bay.

From The Picayune's Creole Cookbook, *published at the turn of the century, comes this description of "How to Eat a Hard Shelled Crab Cooked in Its Shell":*

> *The shell and claws should be cracked in the kitchen, very gently, before being brought to the table, if the Crabs are boiled and served whole. By a delicate manipulation of the knife and fork remove the "apron" or "tablier," which is the small loose shell running to a point about the middle of the under shell. Then cut the Crab claws off, still using the knife and fork, and finally cut the Crab into parts and those again in two. Proceed to extract the meat from each quarter with a fork and eat with salt and pepper. It is considered quite "comme il faut" to use the fingers, however, in holding the Crabs, extracting the meat with the prongs of the fork.*

Crabby Corn

Fresh corn usually starts to be ripe by July the Fourth, and nothing could be more American than corn eaten on the cob. Steam that corn on the same racks over the same water in the same pot you've just removed the crabs from. Talk about tasty! The kernels get infused with just a hint of the crab scent and a slight kiss of Old Bay Seasoning. Pass with fresh-cut wedges of lime and let your crab-spiced fingers do the rest of the seasoning. You won't miss the butter at all.

1 dozen ears of corn
2 limes

While the crabs are boiling, remove the shucks and silk from the corn. (If you're annoyed by the few wispy threads of silk that cling to the ears, you can rub damp paper towels over the ears and the silks will come right off.) Break the ears in half. When you've removed the crabs from the pot, layer the corn on the rack or in the steamer, cover, and steam for 6 to 10 minutes. The fresher the corn, the less time it takes.

Cut the limes into chunks. Pile the corn into big bowls and pass with the lime chunks and salt and pepper.

Serves 9 to 12 as a side dish.

John Shields, a Baltimore boy and culinary whiz, wrote the book on Chesapeake Bay Crabs, The Chesapeake Bay Crab Cookbook *(Aris Books, 1992). It is crammed with crab lore and recipes, including several tasty ways to use any leftover crab meat from your steamed crab feast. (One of the most popular is to make*

your favorite vegetable soup—with or without meat, but always with tomatoes and slivers of cabbage—and then spike it with crab meat and Old Bay Seasoning.)

Shields notes that beer, beer, and more beer is the traditional quaff with steamed crabs, but abstainers and designated drivers are encouraged to go for icy, icy ginger ale.

And his tip for cleaning up is to sprinkle laundry powder over the shells before folding them up in the newspaper. Shields promises this will help keep the smell in check if you have to keep the crab shells in the garbage overnight.

Devilish Spuds

Potato salad was present at my first Crabby Fourth, and heaven knows, my mother-in-law, Betty Jones, née Canby, a true Irish girl at heart, knew her way around a spud. But although the taste was tantalizing, there was no way I was going to clean my fingers, seasoned with that marvelous mess of crab juice and spices, to pick up a fork and a plate and attack that salad properly.

What a crab feast needs is finger food on the side. But deviled eggs are too slippery and too much for those with cholesterol terror to contemplate. So here's a handy invention, the Devilish Spud: tender new potatoes hollowed out and filled with a savory stuffing to make a wickedly delicious dish.

These are best if chilled for an hour or two before serving. They will keep in the refrigerator overnight, but they lose some of their kick in the process. The flavors in these spuds are potent enough to stand on their own, but are also accented nicely by the spices of the crabs that you will inevitably have on your fingers.

12 new potatoes a little
   larger than golf balls
Rind of 1 lemon
2 teaspoons coarsely
   cracked black pepper
2 teaspoons kosher salt
2 medium-sized red bell
   peppers
2 teaspoons cumin seed
1 large clove of garlic
½ cup mayonnaise
4 oil-packed sun-dried
   tomatoes
3 tablespoons minced
   onion

Wash the new potatoes well but do not peel.

To 2 quarts water in a heavy saucepan with a lid, add the lemon rind, black pepper, and salt. Bring to a boil. Add the potatoes. Cover and turn down to a lively simmer for about 25 minutes. The potatoes should be tender inside but still firm and whole. (I test mine with a cake tester. When the thin wire pierces the potato easily, it's done. If you use a fork, be careful not to break the potato when you test.)

Remove the potatoes from the water and let cool until you can handle them. Cut in half and let them cool again.

While the potatoes are cooking and cooling, roast the red pepper enough to char the skin. You can do this by spearing each pepper on a fork and holding over a burner, turning so it is charred evenly, or by placing the peppers under the broiler element of your stove or toaster oven, turning every few minutes. When the skin is blistered all around, remove the peppers from the heat and place inside a brown paper bag, with the ends folded over to close, for 5 minutes. Remove and rub lightly between the palms of your hands to loosen the skin. If the peppers are too hot to handle, you can hold them under running cold water. The peels should pull off easily. If a little stays on, don't worry about it. Remove the stem and seeds, tear the peppers into strips, and place in a blender.

Toast the cumin seed in a heavy skillet over high heat, shaking the skillet so it doesn't stick, and heating the seed until it just begins to blacken. Add to the blender. Add the garlic and mayonnaise and blend at medium speed until the mixture is pureed but you still see tiny flecks of pepper and cumin.

Remove to a small mixing bowl. Using a paper towel, pat any extra oil off the oil-packed sun-dried tomatoes. Slice into thin slivers down the length of the tomato and then mince. Add to the pepper mayonnaise along with the minced onion and mix.

Using a small spoon or melon scoop, hollow out each half of the potatoes, leaving a rim about ⅛ inch thick all around. Place the potato pulp in a bowl and mash well with a fork. Add the pepper mayonnaise and mix until well blended. Taste, and if the mixture needs salt or pepper, add. Stuff the hollowed potato shells generously with this mixture, making sure to use it all. Place on a plate or serving tray, cover well, and refrigerate for 1 to 2 hours.

Serves 6 to 9 as a side dish.

Star-Spangled Tarts

When John Shields, author of *The Chesapeake Bay Crab Cookbook*, was growing up in Baltimore, all the adults swore that if you ate ice cream after eating crabs you'd get sick: "Yeah! 'Em crabs'll turn to rock, right in your stomach."

I asked my husband, and he said that while he'd never heard this specific piece of wisdom, he was relatively sure that eating ice cream after a crab feast was "wrong."

But what about those of us who can't bear to end a party without a little something sweet? What could be better than these charming twin tarts of bright red cherry and faithful blueberry topped with sparkling stars?

I've named them in honor of "The Star-Spangled Banner," another fine American product from Baltimore. It was dashed off during the War of 1812 by Francis Scott Key as he was detained on a British warship. He watched the "rockets' red glare" and "bombs bursting in air" of the enemy forces through the night, then was so thrilled to see the American flag still flying over Fort McHenry in Baltimore Harbor the next morning that he wrote the verses that were to become the National Anthem. The tune, by the way, was that of a popular drinking ditty of the era.

These tarts will surprise you with the burst of citrus flavor in their cookie-like crust. Because the crust is so short, it may crack or break apart while you are handling it, but don't get frustrated. It's very forgiving to work with, and you can gently press it back together and shape it into the pan, unlike a regular pastry crust.

Instructions for making the dough for one tart is given here. If you want to make both a blueberry and a cherry tart, make the dough twice, don't double the recipe, for the best results.

A small kitchen scale is indispensable in making these tarts, since you need to reserve some of the dough for the cookie topping. The only way to determine really accurately how much is enough for the crust is to weigh it. You will also need a small star-shaped cookie cutter, 2 inches wide from point to point.

**DOUGH FOR
1 (9-INCH) TART**

1 orange
½ cup sugar
1 cup (2 sticks) unsalted
   butter
2 egg yolks
2½ cups sifted all-purpose
   flour

Scrub the orange with a little dishwashing liquid, then rinse thoroughly. Zest the orange. Mix together with the sugar.

Squeeze the orange to extract 1 tablespoonful juice and set aside.

In the bowl of an electric mixer, cream together the orange-sugar mixture and the butter at medium-low setting for about 3 minutes, until smooth. Add the egg yolks one at a time. Add the 1 tablespoonful orange juice. Add the flour and beat until just blended.

Turn off the mixer, scrape the dough off the beaters and the sides of the bowl, then lightly pat it into a ball. Weigh the ball and remove enough dough so that you have a mass that weighs 10 ounces. Lightly form that into a smooth ball with your hands, then pat it into a flattened disk shape 7 to 8 inches wide. (Flour your hands lightly if the dough sticks to them.) Wrap tightly in plastic wrap and refrigerate for at least 1 hour.

Pat the smaller remaining mass of dough into a ball and then a disk also. Wrap and refrigerate. The dough may be left overnight, but if it is in the refrigerator for more than 1 hour, you will need to let it sit at room temperature for 5 minutes or so to make it malleable enough for rolling.

When you are ready to bake the crust, preheat the oven to 350° F. Flour the rolling surface and your rolling pin. Lightly roll the 10-ounce disk of dough to fit into a 9-inch pastry pan, turning it over once or twice and adding more flour underneath to keep it from sticking to the rolling surface. (If the dough cracks when you first start to roll it, let it sit for a minute or two to soften enough to work with.)

Transfer the dough to the pan and lightly press it into the bottom and sides. Trim excess dough from edges of pan (set that dough aside) and use your fingers to crimp the rim.

Cut or fold aluminum foil to fit in the bottom of the pie tin. Lay over the crust and weight down with pie weights or dried beans. Bake in the preheated oven for 10 minutes. Remove and gently lift the aluminum foil and weights out of the crust. Return to the oven and bake 10 minutes more, until the crust is lightly golden.

While the crust is baking that first 10 minutes, roll out the second ball of dough to about ¼-inch thickness. Using the star-shaped cookie cutter, cut 1 dozen stars from the dough and place on a small cookie sheet about ½ inch apart. When you return the crust to the oven for the second 10 minutes of baking, bake the cookies, too. (Press together the leftover scraps of dough from the crust making and cookie cutting and see NOTE for a suggestion on how to use them later.)

Let the crust and cookies cool completely before proceeding.

FILLING FOR
1 (9-INCH) TART

1 cup sugar
3 tablespoons cornstarch
⅛ teaspoon salt
4 cups blueberries or pitted
  cherries

In a heavy saucepan, mix the sugar, cornstarch, and salt. Blend 1 cup water and 1 cup of the fruit in a blender to make a watery puree. Add to the ingredients in the saucepan, turn the heat to medium-high, and stir until the mixture becomes very thick. Add the rest of the fruit and heat and stir for 1 minute. Remove from the heat and pour into the cooled crust. Arrange the star-shaped cookies on top and let come to room temperature before serving. May be tightly covered when cool and kept in refrigerator overnight. Bring to room temperature before serving.

Serves 6 very, very generously.

NOTE: If you want to make the stars stand out even more dramatically, sift a couple of teaspoons powdered sugar over them when they are thoroughly cooled and before you place them on the tart filling.

NOTE: Any excess dough from the cookie cutting and crust shaping may be wrapped up snugly and popped into the freezer, where it will keep for a month. When you're feeling the urge for a little something sweet, let it come to room temperature, then spoon out onto a cookie sheet in balls about an inch in diameter and bake for 10 minutes, or until golden, at 350° F. These may be dusted with powdered sugar when thoroughly cooled. Also, you may want to add a handful of finely chopped walnuts or pecans or of chocolate chips to the dough before baking, for extra flavor.

The pie is an English institution which, planted on American soil, forthwith ran rampant and burst forth into an untold variety of genera and species.

—HARRIET BEECHER STOWE

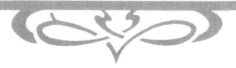

Rosh Hashanah

The Hebrew month of Tishri, in September–October, is when the cycle of High Holy Days known as the Days of Awe takes place. It is marked by the celebration of Rosh Hashanah on the first and second days of the month and ends with the observance of Yom Kippur on the tenth.

The literal translation of Rosh Hashanah is "head of the year." The celebration of Rosh Hashanah is meant not simply to observe the beginning of a new year on the Hebrew calendar but to mark a spiritual beginning as well.

The placement of the holiday as harvest approaches begs observers to consider the year that has passed, what has been sown and is to be reaped from their actions.

Tradition says that God opens three books on Rosh

Hashanah, one each for the righteous, for the wicked, and for those who are caught between. The names of the righteous are inscribed immediately and sealed in the Book of Life, as the wicked are placed in the Book of Death. The rest have the ten days from Rosh Hashanah to Yom Kippur to reflect on who they have been and what they have done.

Yom Kippur, the final day of this period, is the holiest and most solemn of Jewish holidays. Fasting is required from sundown to sundown, and the day is to be spent in penitence and prayer. Worshippers are expected to atone for past sins, and it is a day devoted to acts of thoughtfulness and help for the less fortunate.

Although the time from Rosh Hashanah to Yom Kippur is most solemn, the celebration that marks the new year is not. The Rosh Hashanah meal on the first night of the holiday is a feast to be shared with friends and marked by hope for the coming year with a menu sparked with bites of sweetness. Honey and fresh fruit are ritual parts of this dinner, included to ensure a taste of sweetness for everyone in the future.

EAST-WEST ROSH HASHANAH

When Elaine Corn first met David SooHoo, it seemed as if it might be a text-book study of *When Worlds Collide*.

Corn was from a large Jewish family that extended across New York and New Jersey. She'd spent her adolescence and young womanhood in El Paso, Texas, then cut her teeth as the food editor of the *Louisville Courier-Journal* in Kentucky before moving to Sacramento as the food editor of the *Sacramento Bee*.

David, on the other hand, was born in San Francisco, the son of Chinese immigrants. He didn't speak English until he was six. When he opened Chinois East-West, his own restaurant in Sacramento, he was following a family tradition that had been carried through generations of SooHoo men.

But though their backgrounds were worlds apart, what Elaine and David had in common was powerful: a passion for food. That passion is not simply an interest in the how-to of making things but a lively devotion to the deeper significances of preparing, serving, and eating.

"It's not exaggerating to say that when I met David I needed spirituality in my life, and he gave me that depth. He was someone I could talk to and who talked to me about food as art, as an act of the spirit," Elaine says.

"It was a big part of our courtship to teach one another about our backgrounds through food and celebrations. I went to Chinese New Year with David, to red-egg parties, the lion dance, and the holiday when you eat moon cakes. And he came to my house for Passover and Rosh Hashanah.

"We were learning a lot about each other through these calendar events that we were already accustomed to noting ourselves. Maybe it was a way to show each other who we were. And it was a way that we could talk about what was important."

When they married in 1989 and then had their son, Robert, they incorporated the celebrations that mattered most to each of them into their shared life.

For instance, they celebrate the Chinese New Year the way David's family always did.

"That means," Elaine says, "we go to a restaurant. That's what you do when your husband owns a restaurant. But it's also very much the Chinese thing to do. The meals have so many dishes and it's such a festive, community-oriented thing that most Chinese families here have their big celebration in their favorite restaurant."

But for Rosh Hashanah, the Jewish New Year, the family celebrates at home with an inventive "traditional" meal that showcases both Elaine's and David's culinary backgrounds.

For instance, the classic chicken soup appetizer is made with what Elaine calls "a very traditional Jewish-mother chicken stock," but instead of spiking it with kreplach, David contributes herbed-chicken wontons with tangerine zest. And instead of a roasted hen or brisket, the centerpiece of the dinner is an Oriental hacked chicken.

"We call it our East-West Rosh Hashanah," Elaine says.

The holiday is perhaps her favorite among Jewish celebrations. "Even as a child, I sensed the profound importance of it. The older I get, the more interesting it has become.

"It's not at all a celebration of the New Year like the big bash we do in January. It's actually a very solemn occasion when you look back and assess the year you've just had. And it's solemn in a way that Hanukkah isn't, because it's an inward experience.

"It begins the process of a self-examination which is, of course, resolved on Yom Kippur. If you have the right rabbi and the right service, you can actually grow inside. You might even cry. And in some ways it's scary. You are forced to think, what kind of a person am I?"

But it is also, Elaine says, profoundly joyous. "The holiday is full of the belief that both you and the coming year will be better."

Some of the ritual foods are served to reflect that hope. Apple with honey is meant to prophesy sweetness in the coming year. Elaine also likes to serve simple steamed carrots, sliced thin and flavored with a little sugar and orange juice, their sunny appearance and taste also meant to symbolize hope.

The meal is served on the first night of Rosh Hashanah so the food can remind worshippers to keep hope in their hearts, even as they reflect on the failings of the previous year. David and Elaine usually invite half a dozen friends to the meal, not all of them Jewish.

"I find that anyone can relate to the symbolism of this holiday, no matter what their faith," she says.

"For David and me, almost any religious custom is turned into a food ritual. I guess that is only natural, given our professions. But making foods that really rise to the occasion, really reflect what the holiday is about, is also our way to rise to the occasion. Neither of us is an expert in our backgrounds, in the history of our traditions. We are so many generations removed from the origins of these events. But the food becomes our connection. What we create and share with friends and with one another makes up for what we lack in exactness or purity of spirit."

The passing on of rituals from one generation to another is the subject of a classic Hasidic folktale.

When the Baal Shem Tov, founder and leader of the Hasidim of Eastern Europe, encountered what seemed to be an unsolvable problem, he would go to a certain place in the forest, light a ritual fire, and say a special prayer. This rite would inevitably lead him to a wise solution.

A disciple in the next generation found himself in a quandary, so he went to the same spot in the forest and lit the fire, but he could not remember the special prayer. The fire seemed to be enough, however, since he found his answer.

By the next generation, his son was in need of guidance. He knew where to go in the forest, but did not know how to light the fire, and, of course, didn't know the prayer. Even so, he received the wisdom he needed.

It was many generations later that yet another rabbi found himself in need and reflecting on this ancient ritual.

"Dear God," he said, "we have forgotten the words to the prayer, we don't know how to light the fire, and we cannot remember the place in the forest. All we can do is tell the story of how it was done."

But simply telling the story was enough, and he found the answer that he needed.

A Sweet New Year Applesauce

The most memorable tradition of the Rosh Hashanah meal is the beginning, when slices of apple are dipped into honey as a blessing, a portent for sweetness in the coming year.

The flavor is simple but enticing, a perfect appetizer to the coming feast. The look of the dish did not, however, satisfy Elaine Corn.

"When you cut the apple and fan the slices out, it looks very pretty the minute you do it. But by the time everyone gets seated at the table, the apple slices start to turn brown. And that's not only not very appetizing but not really a good omen for the coming year, when you think about it."

So she devised this delightful homemade applesauce dish, which is now a new Rosh Hashanah tradition at her table. The lightly spiced and pureed fruit is served in individual glass dishes, each with a small pool of honey at the bottom. The ritual is to dip your spoon through the applesauce and into the honey so you get a bit of extra sweetness with each bite.

"It's very pretty and very tasty, and it's also a great treat for kiddies, who love the taste and the look of the wispy golden strings that the honey makes as it comes up. It's such a treat that some years we serve it also as dessert after the meal for a double dose of sweet luck."

2½ pounds apples, any variety

3 tablespoons sugar or honey

2 (2-inch-long) cinnamon sticks

Peel, core, and coarsely slice the apples. Put in a heavy saucepan with ¼ cup water, the 3 tablespoons sugar (or honey), the cinnamon, and cloves and bring to a boil. Cook for 20 minutes, stirring to prevent scorching. When the apple slices are easily pierced with a knife, they are ready to puree.

Remove the cinammon sticks and cloves.

8 whole cloves
Pinch of nutmeg
¼ teaspoon minced fresh
  ginger (optional)
½ cup fresh orange or
  lemon juice
1 tablespoon minced
  orange or lemon zest
1–2 teaspoons vanilla or
  almond extract
½ cup honey

(Elaine says not to worry if you don't get all the cloves—a few blended in will just add another dimension.) In a blender or food processor, puree until very smooth.

Return the puree to the saucepan over low heat and add the nutmeg and the ginger, if you want. Stir in the orange or lemon juice and zest until all is blended and warmed through. Remove from the heat and add 1 teaspoon of the vanilla or almond extract. Taste and add more if desired. Chill until ready to serve.

When you are ready, set out 8 small individual serving bowls. (Glass is most attractive. Custard cups are good, and bowl-shaped wineglasses make a striking presentation.)

Spoon a tablespoonful of honey into the bottom of each bowl. Spoon equal portions of the applesauce over the honey and serve.

If you wish, you may make the individual servings in advance and refrigerate until about 30 minutes before you are ready to serve. Remove from the refrigerator and let warm at room temperature so the honey will be soft.

Serves 8.

No one knew where the pineapple came from. Its scaly skin made it look like some curious fish. But its tail stuck up like an open fan. I touched its rounded belly and it toppled over. I hesitated to touch it again, it sat there so regally. I cleared a space for it in the middle of the table.

But Sasha ruthlessly started to cut it up, and under the knife it groaned like a live fish. The juice was white blood spurting out over my hand. I licked my fingers. They tasted sour and sweet at the same time. Was that how the New Year would taste?

—BELLA CHAGALL, *FIRST ENCOUNTER*

Round Challah

Most often challah is shaped into a braid before baking. For the New Year, though, Elaine explains: "The challah is coiled rather than braided to show that life is a continuous cycle; that it doesn't really have a starting point and a stopping point but is one big circle."

The challah is blessed with the wine and the candles at the beginning of the meal. Everyone tears off a hunk, and that, Elaine says, "opens the door to keep eating challah. You can dip it in the applesauce or drizzle honey on it, and of course you eat it with the fish appetizers. This recipe makes one very big loaf, but I sometimes make two loaves for the Rosh Hashanah dinner so there will be plenty, and some left over for French toast the next day."

You may bake the day before, cooling the bread completely before wrapping well to ensure freshness. But Elaine likes to bake on the day of the dinner: "It's usually coming out of the oven when I start to get supper on the table. I like the house to smell like challah when Rosh Hashanah comes. The house being bread-toasty is the fragrance I associate with the New Year."

6 tablespoons vegetable
  shortening
1½ cups very hot water
2 packages active dry yeast
1 teaspoon plus 2
  tablespoons sugar
½ cup warm water
  (105°–110° F.)
2 teaspoons salt

In a very large bowl, cover the shortening with 1½ cups water that has been heated almost to the boiling point. Allow to cool to room temperature.

In a small bowl, dissolve the yeast and the 1 teaspoon sugar in the ½ cup warm water. Allow it to bubble (about 5 minutes), then add to the melted shortening. Add the 2 tablespoons of sugar and the salt.

Set aside and refrigerate the yolk of 1 egg, then beat the white with the remaining 3 eggs

4 eggs (reserve 1 yolk for
top of bread)
7 cups unbleached all-
purpose flour (about)
Vegetable oil

until well mixed. Add to the rest of the liquid.

Use a wooden spoon or the dough hook of an electric mixer to add the flour, about 2 cups at a time. Stir vigorously until the dough forms a ball and pulls away from the side of the bowl. You will probably use about 6 cups of flour, but this may vary.

Dust the work surface liberally with more flour. Turn out the dough and knead for 5 to 7 minutes, until it is elastic, dusting your hands and the work surface with more flour as needed to keep dough from sticking.

Rinse the large mixing bowl, dry, and oil. Place the ball of dough in the bowl and turn over once to coat the surface with oil. Cover with a damp cloth and let rise in a warm (75°–80° F.) and draft-free place until doubled (1½ to 2 hours).

Punch down the dough gently with your fist to eliminate air bubbles. Turn out onto a very lightly floured surface and roll it out like a fat snake about 2 inches in diameter. Lightly oil a baking sheet (because this bread is round, a pizza pan is perfect.) Shape the snake into a round coil on the oiled baking sheet. (Elaine begins shaping the coil from the outside, tucking the first end under and leaving a little mound in the center.) Lay plastic wrap over the loaf and let rise in a warm place for 45 minutes.

Preheat the oven to 375° F. Mix the reserved egg yolk with 1 tablespoon water. Brush the top of the bread with the yolk, making sure to cover the surface well.

Place in the center of the preheated oven and bake for 45 minutes to 1 hour. The loaf should be golden and sound hollow if you rap it lightly. Remove from the oven and allow to cool 5 minutes before removing from the baking sheet. Most bread must be cooled completely to make even slices, but since you serve this by letting folks pull off chunks as it is passed, you may take it to the table still warm.

Serves 8 generously.

When I was young, I already knew that everything must look good, taste good, mean good things. That way it lasts longer, satisfies your appetite, also satisfies your memory for a long, long time.

—AMY TAN, THE KITCHEN GOD'S WIFE

GEFILTE APPETIZER

Gefilte fish was served right after the ritual apple and honey when Elaine was growing up, and it's still a part of the appetizer course for her Rosh Hashanah celebration.

"Do you make your own?" I asked, knowing Elaine's penchant for creating from scratch. (Her first cookbook, Gooey Desserts, *has from-scratch recipes for "Tunnel of Fudge" and "Better Than Sex" cakes, two ultimate box-mix treats.)*

She hooted.

"Are you crazy? I'm married to a man who thinks Manischewitz gefilte fish out of the jar is the perfect midnight snack."

That doesn't mean Elaine and David don't work a little magic before the fish travels to the dining table, however. The fish from the jar is drained and then arranged on a platter with slices of smoked salmon and mounds of fine caviar.

"With David's eye for the visual, it still can't just be served like that. So he usually cuts some chives and sprinkles them in a kind of crisscross across the foods on the plate. Really, it's very simple, but it's striking," she said.

The platter is passed with more challah, and after guests have had a satisfying taste, it's time for soup.

Chicken Soup with Tangerine-Zest Wontons

For years Chinese waiters have told their Jewish customers that a wonton is simply a kreplach. And Elaine says that she has often told her non-Jewish friends that kreplach are just Jewish wontons, so it was natural that she and David would combine their two cultures in this classic soup. And it makes for a perfect division of labor, with Elaine making a traditional Jewish chicken soup broth (sans dill, which would clash with the Cantonese-style wontons) and David the wontons. Both may be prepared the day before, refrigerated, then brought together just before the meal.

BROTH

1 whole (3–4-pound)
  chicken without liver
3 medium-sized carrots
4 large stalks of celery
1 large onion
A few sprigs of parsley
¼ teaspoon white pepper
Kosher salt to taste

The day before serving, wash the chicken and remove the gizzards, neck, heart, and liver (freeze the liver to use in another recipe) and place in a large pot. Cover 1 inch above the chicken with cold tap water, then slowly bring to a boil over medium heat, uncovered.

Skim the gray scum from the surface, then add the carrots, celery, onion, parsley, and pepper. When the mixture boils again, partially cover and lower the heat. Allow to simmer for 1 hour. Add salt to taste and simmer for another 30 minutes.

Remove the chicken to a colander over a big bowl. When cool enough to handle, remove the meat and return the skin and bones to the pot. (The meat may be refrigerated and used in another recipe.) Add any juices that have drained into the bowl and simmer for another 30 minutes to deepen the flavor.

Strain the broth into a large container, allow to cool, and refrigerate overnight. Fat will rise to the top. Skim the fat off. (For a richer flavor, you may want to leave a tablespoon or so of fat in the broth—or you may skim completely.)

WONTONS

2 cups ground raw chicken
  (about 2 boneless
  breasts—your butcher
  will grind it for you, or use
  a food processor)
1½ tablespoons minced
  tangerine zest
5 dried shiitake
  mushrooms, soaked and
  minced
5 water chestnuts, minced
½ cup minced cilantro
  leaves
1 tablespoon cornstarch
1 tablespoon sesame oil
½ teaspoon salt
⅛ teaspoon white pepper

16 square wonton skins
1 egg

Mix the ground chicken with the remaining ingredients except for the wonton skins and egg. Use your hands to blend the mixture until it is smooth and slightly tacky to the touch.

Dust a cookie sheet with a little cornstarch. Lay the wonton skins out on a flat workplace. Beat the egg. Place a tablespoon of the filling in the center of a wonton skin. Moisten the edges with egg, then fold over to make a triangle. Seal by pressing gently with the fingertips.

Lay each folded wonton on the cookie sheet as you finish. Cover with plastic wrap and refrigerate until ready to serve soup. (May be refrigerated up to 12 hours. If you want, wontons may be frozen on the cookie sheet, then bagged in plastic and kept in the freezer for several weeks.)

When you are ready to serve the soup, bring the chicken broth to a boil. Gently lower the wontons into the broth, turn down to a lively simmer, and cook for 10 minutes. Serve 2 wontons in each bowl of soup.

Serves 8.

SKINNING THE WONTON

Wonton skins are sold ready-made in packages at almost any grocery, and certainly at any Oriental market. You don't need to feel the least bit guilty about not making your own, since the packaged skins not only are easier to handle but also cook up better than homemade, which have a tendency to get too sticky or too soft in the cooking.

Nicole Routhier, author of Cooking under Wraps *(William Morrow, 1993), says that the quality of skin can be gauged by its thickness, with thin being better. How can you tell what's thin-skinned and what's not without opening the package? Look for at least 50 wrappers per pound, Routhier says. Fewer means a thicker, stickier wrapper.*

If you're not using all the skins at once, you may freeze the leftover ones for up to 2 months.

David SooHoo's Red-Cooked Chicken

In the Corn household when Elaine was growing up, the centerpiece of the Rosh Hashanah meal was a well-simmered brisket or a nice chicken. David's version of that nice chicken is a delicate Far Eastern rendition poached in soy sauce and sherry with just a whisper of anise from Chinese Five Spice powder.

David serves it "hacked" with a cleaver, severing the drumsticks, thighs, and wings, then dividing each breast half into 2 or 3 parts. The pieces are then put back together on the serving platter and the "whole" bird garnished with sprigs of cilantro.

Perfectly steamed rice is served in small bowls, and guests use chopsticks to pick up a piece of chicken, then hold it over the rice as they nibble the meat away from the bone. All the juices drip onto the rice, to be augmented by more juice spooned from the serving platter.

1 teaspoon Chinese Five
  Spice powder
2 tablespoons coarsely
  chopped fresh ginger
¼ cup cooking sherry
1 cup soy sauce
⅔ cup brown sugar
3½–4 pound whole broiler-
  fryer
Fresh cilantro sprigs (for
  garnish)

To poach the chicken, you will need a pot large enough to hold the bird and enough poaching liquid to cover. Mix the Five Spice powder, ginger, sherry, soy sauce, 4 cups water, and the brown sugar in the pot and bring to a boil over high heat. As soon as the mixture boils, remove from the heat and let cool to room temperature.

When the liquid is cool, prepare the chicken by rinsing well and patting dry. (Remove the giblets and freeze to use in another recipe.) Immerse the chicken in the soy sauce liquid. If the liquid doesn't completely cover the bird, add water until it does.

Place over high heat and bring to a boil. Immediately reduce the heat so the liquid comes to a low simmer, and cook for 10 minutes. Using tongs, turn the chicken over and simmer for another 10 minutes. Remove from the heat and let the chicken sit in the liquid for 20 more minutes to sponge up the flavor.

Remove the chicken from the pot and use a cleaver to cut into serving pieces. Arrange on a platter and garnish with cilantro sprigs. Serve immediately with individual bowls of steamed rice.

Serves 8.

CHICKEN PICKING

Mass-produced, prepackaged chicken has gotten plenty of bad press lately. Even without the health scares raised by television exposés of the poultry industry, those who value taste and texture have been dissatisfied with supermarket birds for some time. Flavorful fresh birds, preferably from local sources, can often be found in meat markets and small groceries, and kosher chickens meet strict guidelines for slaughter and often have exceptional taste. Birds that are stored unwrapped on ice instead of plastic-clad in a cooler are one sign of a good poultry shop. A butcher who can tell you where the bird came from and how it was raised and shipped is another.

But you don't really have to know the pedigree of a bird to ensure quality, although if you are concerned about such things, it is nice to buy birds that have been raised without growth stimulants or antibiotics.

Freshness is essential, however. First look at the skin. Chickens naturally range from white to yellow, but yellow isn't a sign of better flavor. In fact, bright yellow birds may have gotten that way from dye added to their food. And pristine white birds often have fine texture and taste.

But it's not the color of the skin that matters, it's the quality. It should be taut and moist, and it should not appear transparent, splotchy, or wrinkled. The skin should be unbroken. Any meat you see should also look plump and juicy, and the skin should adhere closely to it, not sag and appear pulled away.

Take a sniff, and if the bird stinks, don't buy it. If your only choice is a prepackaged bird you can't sniff, then check the package to see if the chicken is sitting in blood or other fluids. (If the chicken is shrink-wrapped, chances are good that it will be, since the process doesn't allow the bird to drain fluids the way shipping loose does.) If you do spot blood, pass on the bird, since blood speeds decay.

Rinse the bird inside and out when you get home, then store in the refrigerator, either on a rack over a pan so it can continue to drain or wrapped in a clean dish towel or paper towels to absorb moisture. A fresh whole chicken can keep well in the refrigerator for 2 days, but it's best if you can cook it on the day of purchase. Cut-up chickens should be cooked within 24 hours.

Espresso Honey Cake with Caramelized Walnuts and Fig Sauce

For some Rosh Hashanah celebrations, Elaine simply makes extra applesauce and brings that back at the end of the meal for dessert. Then there are times when she wants something more, and this honey cake with rich fig sauce fills the bill.

You can make the caramelized walnuts in advance, storing for a couple of days in a waxed-paper-lined airtight tin.

CARAMELIZED WALNUTS

1 tablespoon canola oil
¾ cup walnuts
Pinch of salt
2 tablespoons sugar

Line a cookie sheet with waxed paper and set aside.

Have all the ingredients next to the burner where you are working so you can work quickly.

Heat a heavy skillet over high heat until a drop of water flicked in the pan skitters. Add the canola oil and swirl to coat the bottom of the pan. Add the nuts and toss and stir with a metal spatula until they smell toasty. Add a pinch of salt, stirring constantly. Sprinkle the sugar evenly over the nuts, still stirring constantly and very quickly. When the sugar has dissolved and the nuts are shiny, remove the pan from heat and immediately dump the nuts onto the lined cookie sheet. Allow to cool, then break apart any clumps. Use immediately or store in a waxed-paper-lined airtight tin.

CAKE

2 cups espresso or very
   strong brewed coffee
1 cup honey
3 eggs
¾ cup sugar
2 tablespoons vegetable oil
3¼ cups all-purpose flour
2 teaspoons baking powder
1 teaspoon baking soda
½ teaspoon salt
1 teaspoon cinnamon
½ teaspoon powdered
   cloves
2 tablespoons Cognac or
   ½ teaspoon vanilla extract

Preheat the oven to 350° F. and place rack in center. Grease and flour a 9-inch tube pan.

Simmer the coffee until it is reduced to 1 cup and has begun to thicken and darken. Remove from heat and combine with the honey, stirring.

In a large bowl, beat the eggs with the sugar until light-colored, then stir in the oil until completely smooth.

Sift the flour with the baking powder, baking soda, salt, cinnamon, and cloves. Add to the egg mixture in one-third increments, alternating with the coffee mixture and blending well after each addition. Add the Cognac or vanilla and stir in the caramelized walnuts.

Pour into the prepared pan and bake on the center rack for 45 minutes, or until a cake tester or toothpick comes out clean when inserted in the middle.

Cool on a wire rack for 10 minutes in the pan, then invert on a plate to continue cooling. If you are using the next day, wrap well to store overnight.

FIG SAUCE

12 fresh Mission figs or 12
   dried figs (see below)
¼ cup sugar
1 tablespoon cooking
   sherry

Fresh figs are most spectacular for this sauce and are usually in season at Rosh Hashanah. If they are not available, use dried figs that have had 1 cup of boiling water poured over them and been left for 20 minutes to plump up.

If you are using fresh figs and they are especially soft and ripe, you do not need to peel them. Otherwise, peel the figs, then puree in a food processor or blender with the sugar and sherry. Let stand at room temperature until the sugar is fully dissolved. Chill until ready to use.

If you are using dried figs, strain them before you put in the blender or processor, but set the water aside in case you need some to expedite the puree process. Proceed as with fresh figs, adding a little of the reserved fig water if necessary. (I've used as little as a tablespoon or as much as all of the water, depending on how soft the dried figs are.)

Slice the cake and serve each piece with a tablespoon of fig sauce on top. Serves 8 to 12.

THE TAILOR'S ATONEMENT

The Rabbi Levi-Yitzchok of Berditchev, a Hasidic zaddik of the eighteenth century, was called the "poor man's rabbi" and was known to call God to task for neglecting his people.

Once he asked a poor tailor what prayers he'd made on the eve of Yom Kippur, the Day of Atonement. The tailor said he had recounted a list of small sins, such as eating food that was not kosher when there was no other. He had then asked God to compare his small transgressions to those of the Lord: robbing mothers of their children; leaving children without parents; war, pestilence, and famine.

"Your sins are so much greater than mine," the tailor said he told God. "I'll make you a deal. If you forgive me, then I will forgive you."

"Ah," the rabbi cried in frustration, "you let God off too easily. For that you could have asked him to redeem all of the Jewish people."

Nine

Sukkoth

Some of humankind's earliest celebrations were festivals of the harvest. The autumn was marked by community feasts to celebrate the bounty of the fields. They were accompanied by rituals to thank God or the gods for their generosity and to beseech more.

As we have grown to be increasingly less agrarian, the community celebration of the actual harvest has diminished for most of us. September's most universal ritual now is the harried shopping spree for back-to-school clothes and supplies.

An exception to this movement away from family-centered, community-shared harvest celebrations has been the recent revival of the Jewish celebration of Sukkoth. Coming two weeks after Rosh Hashanah and falling usually in late September or early October, this holiday was intended as a way for Jews to recall the forty years spent wandering in the desert after their liberation from Egypt.

Sukkoth is the plural of *sukkah*, which means "booth" or "temporary hut." During the seven-day observance of Sukkoth, the family is supposed to erect a three-sided, roofed shelter in which it dwells. The fragility of the shelter demonstrates one's dependence on God, the frailty of human life, and the plight of the poor.

The Torah also calls the celebration Hag Ha-Asif, which translates as "the festival of Ingathering." The time of year for the holiday was chosen to coincide with the final harvest, and the meals served during the festival are to be created from the gifts of the season.

In colder climates, the holiday may be observed simply by taking meals in the shelter, and this is what many contemporary celebrants choose to do. Families are encouraged to build their shelter together and to decorate it with pictures, especially of the fruits of the harvest, so children become particularly involved with the holiday spirit.

MINNESOTA SUKKOTH

Jackie and Leon Olenick of St. Paul have a portable booth for Sukkoth with three plywood walls and a plywood roof that they lay branches over.

"It's great because the kids can put it up in one hour," Jackie said. But, of course, like their Passover seders (see Chapter 5), the Olenicks' Sukkoth suppers have a way of expanding with friends, so they've added an extension to the portable booth so they can now seat fourteen at the table—and accommodate a few more revelers who want to stand.

"You're supposed to invite people for food every night, and you're supposed to sing, dance, and party. It's a celebration of the blessings of the harvest. We have friends who come every year, and we invite our neighbors over so they shouldn't think we are building something on our house without a permit," Jackie says.

Cramming lots of people into the booth is not a problem, Leon says—especially since the more people there are, the warmer it will be.

"Let me tell you about Sukkoth in Minnesota. You're basically outside with just a roof over your head and a little protection from the wind. And this is Minnesota, so it can very well be snowing—it most certainly will be blowing. So if we're crammed in tight as we can be, that's no problem."

"We have Sukkoth lights," Jackie says. "The kids just love it. They make pictures and little art things to decorate the booth. The hut itself is sort of like a child's playhouse. And there we all are in the little hut, and there are twinkling lights outside and candles glowing inside.

"It's really like a fantasy, like you're living in a child's world for a while. And the best part is, it's a fantasy that goes on for a whole week.

"That's maybe the other reason that it's people's favorite holiday. Because the other celebrations are over after one night, maybe two, and you're left feeling a little deflated. But Sukkoth, the party goes on every night for a whole week: singing and dancing and friends. It's an ongoing celebration of wonderfulness."

Food for the celebration must be simple and very, very hearty, Jackie says. The Olenicks usually serve one-pot suppers, and because they are vegetarians, the soups and stews they make naturally reflect the season. Hearty bread, a simple salad, a good dessert, and hot mugs of apple cider contribute to the coziness. And the Sukkoth booth, for all its fragility and temporariness, becomes a true shelter indeed.

CITY SUKKAH

The sukkah is a natural enough shelter out in the fields where it originated, but erecting one in a city, and leaving it up for the eight-day observance of the holiday, can be dicey.

The story goes that once a pious Jew built his sukkah on the roof of his apart-

ment building in New York. The landlord, an ungenerous man, demanded that it be torn down and, when the Jew refused, hauled him promptly into court.

Now the judge was both wise and just and realized that the man was doing no harm with his sukkah. But the judge also knew that the landlord's demand was backed by city ordinances. So the judge ruled that the man must dismantle his booth.

"And what's more," the judge said with a smile, "you have only eight days to comply with the law, not one day more."

Last-of-the-Garden Soup

That prolific tomato patch which brought you such delight during the summer can fill you with guilt and panic as the first frost approaches. All those fat, lovely green globes that will never have the opportunity to turn red and juicy ripe! What's a conscientious husbandman to do?

Well, of course, you can fry up a bunch of them and revel in their glory. And in the good old days frugal housewives would turn those tomatoes into a tasty Last-of-the-Garden Relish with other final harvest vegetables—but who has the time to slow-cook relish and then can it these days?

One incredibly satisfying way of using those tomatoes, though, is this tangy soup. If you are not vegetarian, you may substitute chicken broth for vegetable broth, and add 2 cups of chopped cooked chicken to the soup, although it is quite sustaining without it.

2 tablespoons olive oil
2 medium-sized onions
1 teaspoon minced fresh
  marjoram leaves
1 teaspoon minced fresh
  rosemary
2 large stalks of celery
2 quarts Chickenless Broth
  (see page 100)
10 medium-sized green
  tomatoes
4 ears of fresh corn or 2
  medium-sized potatoes
Kosher salt to taste
2 cups buttermilk

In a large pot, heat the olive oil over medium heat. Chop the onion coarsely. Add to the oil, sprinkle with the marjoram and rosemary, and sauté. Slice the celery very thin, and when the onions are beginning to turn translucent, add. When the celery has softened, add the vegetable broth and let the mixture slowly come to a low boil.

Chop the tomatoes fine and add to the broth.

If you have fresh corn still available, shuck the corn and remove the silks. (A damp paper towel rubbed around the ear is a good way to get those pesky silks that cling.) Into a shallow bowl, and using a very sharp knife, cut down the cob, removing just the top half of each kernel. Then, using a metal teaspoon, scrape up the cob, extracting the pulp and milk from the corn kernels. Add the cut corn to the broth.

If you don't have fresh corn available, peel the potatoes, dice fine, and add to the broth. Allow the broth to return to the boil, cover, and turn down to a lively simmer for 30 minutes, or until the tomatoes and corn or potatoes are very tender. Add kosher salt to taste, beginning with about 1 teaspoon.

When you are ready to serve, remove from the heat and stir the buttermilk into the soup. Serve immediately.

Serves 8 to 10.

SOUP, MUSICAL SOUP

The music was furnished mostly by the Musical Soup Eaters. They marched with big bowls of soup in front of them and big spoons for eating the soup. They whistled and chuzzled and snozzled the soup and the noise they made could be heard far up at the head of the procession where the Spoon Lickers were marching. So they dipped their soup and looked around and dipped their soup again.

—Carl Sandburg, *Rootabaga Stories:* Part I

Au Gratin Rice

A hearty dish, this baked rice casserole can serve as a main course with salad, or makes a feast when served alongside Last-of-the-Garden Soup (preceding recipe).

The recipe here is adapted from one given to me by my friend Lenore Crenshaw. It is the ultimate celebration food to me because Lenore made the casserole for my husband and me on the day our daughter was born. What joy!

5 cups cooked brown rice
2 tablespoons butter

Have the cooked brown rice ready—I like the short-grain varieties that are almost round and have an especially nutty sweetness.

Preheat the oven to 350° F.

1 cup chopped onion

3 cups sliced mushrooms

1 tablespoon plus 1
  teaspoon tamari soy
  sauce

2 cups grated Gruyère
  cheese

3 cups milk

¼ teaspoon ground mace

¼ cup grated Parmesan
  cheese

Melt the butter in a large skillet over medium heat. Add the onion and sauté until softened. Add the mushrooms and cook for 5 minutes, then remove from the heat and sprinkle 1 tablespoon soy sauce over them.

Liberally butter the inside of a 4-quart baking dish.

In a large bowl, mix the cooked rice with the mushroom-onion mixture. Set aside ½ cup of the Gruyère cheese and mix the rest with the rice. Turn out into the buttered baking pan and smooth down lightly and evenly with a spatula.

Whisk the milk, mace, and 1 teaspoon soy sauce together. Pour over the rice. Mix the Parmesan with the remaining Gruyère and sprinkle over the top of the milk.

Bake in the preheated oven for about 1 hour, until the top is browning and bubbling and the milk has been absorbed into the rice. Serve warm and pass more soy sauce on the side.

Serves 8 to 10.

Also in the fifteenth day of the seventh month, when ye have gathered in the fruit of the land, ye shall keep a feast unto the Lord seven days . . .

And ye shall take you on the first day the boughs of goodly trees, branches of palm trees, and the boughs of thick trees, and willows of the brook; and ye shall rejoice before the Lord your God seven days.

—LEVITICUS 23:39–40

Autumn Greens Salad

Autumn brings a bounty of pungent-flavored tender greens to the garden. Luscious spinach, arugula, radicchio, and endive are all part of our autumn harvest, and their flavors can be accented even more with the cultivated dandelion and sorrel (use sparingly) that show up year round in markets. I like to mix the tarter greens with something like tender Boston lettuce, perhaps a third of it to two parts of the more aggressively flavored greens. You want this salad to have a bracing, cleansing taste. Crisp slivers of pear and turnip give the tongue a seesaw ride between sweet and savory, and the peanut oil in this Oriental dressing gives the whole dish a buttery richness.

    This is very nice as a first course, but also yummy served between courses to clean the palate and give you a chance to eat up the bread in earthy style.

DRESSING

2 tablespoons peanut oil
½ cup apple cider
1 tablespoon tamari soy
   sauce
¼ teaspoon Chinese Five
   Spice powder
1 tablespoon lemon juice
¼ teaspoon sugar
1 tablespoon minced
   pickled ginger
2 cloves garlic

In a small bowl, whisk together the oil, cider, soy sauce, Five Spice powder, lemon juice, and sugar. Add the minced pickled ginger, including a few drops of juice. Cut the garlic cloves in half and add. Whisk once again, cover, and let sit for at least 1 hour.

    When you are ready to serve, rinse the greens, pat dry, and tear into bite-sized pieces into a large salad bowl.

    Quarter the pears and core. Cut each quarter in half and then slice very, very thin. Add to the greens.

    Scrub the turnips well and cut off the ends. Cut in half, cut each half in quarters, and slice very, very thin. Add to the greens and toss.

8 cups assorted salad
   greens, loosely packed
2 crisp Bartlett pears
2 small turnips

Remove the garlic cloves from dressing, whisk, and pour over the greens. Toss the mixture several times so the pears, turnips, and greens are well mixed and thoroughly coated with the dressing. Serve immediately.

Serves 8 to 10.

The branches were fanned out, and soon the booth would be wearing a sort of hat. It stood there in the middle of the yard, as inviting as a cottage in the wood.

The branches were piled so thick no star could shine through. A cool twilight reigned within. Only through a few chinks in the walls could a few rays of light struggle in.

In the middle of the booth a long table was installed, with benches on either side. The floor was just bare earth, and the legs of the table and benches stuck in the damp ground, which clung to our shoes.

We stayed in the booth, pretending we were in the country. We lay on the benches, trying to catch the dancing beams of light, and gazing up at the roof as if it were the sky. We started if a drop of dew fell on us. And to let everyone know that the booth was finished and the holiday about to begin, we sang a song.

Faces appeared in the windows around the yard.

Look, the sukkah's ready.

—BELLA CHAGALL, *FIRST ENCOUNTER*

Irish Soda Bread

These rough, flat pones of wheat bread were once baked in iron pans perched next to the hearth. To get a similar crust and texture, use a baking stone (see page 79). If you don't have a stone, bake the bread on a cast-iron griddle or on a cookie sheet.

The bread tastes a little like a coarse biscuit, or like a rough country cousin to a scone. It's the hearty, wholesome taste that makes it such a winning accompaniment to the harvest soup and salad here. And it's simple to make.

You may want to make several loaves a day in advance. After the breads have cooled, wrap in clean tea towels and store in a cool, dry place. Serve with sweet butter and jam.

4 cups whole wheat flour

2 tablespoons cold butter

1½ teaspoons baking soda

1 teaspoon kosher salt

2 cups buttermilk

3 tablespoons white flour
for kneading

Put the whole wheat flour in a big bowl, then, using a sharp knife, chip little pieces of the cold butter into the flour. Toss with a wooden spoon to coat. Sprinkle the baking soda and salt over the flour and mix lightly with the spoon to incorporate.

Use your fingers to rub the flour and butter lightly together until the butter chunks are blended in.

Pour the buttermilk evenly over the mixture and stir in with the wooden spoon until it is mixed in and the dough is mostly pulling together, although not a solid mass.

Sprinkle the white flour on a board or flat surface for kneading and dust your hands liberally with it. Turn the dough out onto the flour and gently knead to continue the mixing. It will be very crumbly at first, but after just a minute of light kneading, the dough should all hold together. Continue kneading lightly and smoothing the edges with the palm of your hand for another minute or so, until the ball holds together without its edges cracking and has begun to feel a bit elastic.

Transfer to a cold baking stone and, using the heel of the hand in a gentle rocking motion, flatten the dough into a disk that's about 1 inch tall. Use a sharp knife to score air vents in the top, making 8 wedges.

Place in a cold oven and turn it on to 425° F. Bake for 30 minutes. Remove from the oven and transfer the bread to a baking rack to cool. (If it sticks, you may have to use a spatula to ease the bread off the baking stone.)

Serves 8.

Ginger Snappy Autumn Crisp

Before we go one step further, let me tell you that in my twenties I worked at a charming little restaurant in Santa Fe that had apple crisp on its menu. The "crisp" was very popular with the health-conscious crowd who frequented the place, because of its molasses sweetening and wholesome taste. It was also popular with the owners of the restaurant because it used up the ends of the dark, soft, sweet bread that was the house specialty. But it wasn't popular with me. For starters, it was kept in the refrigerator, which made it apple sog in no time. And even in the first hour after it was taken from the oven—absolutely the only time ever to eat it—I found it pedestrian. Better by far to eat an honest slice of grainy bread with thick homemade apple butter.

So I swore I would never, ever make apple crisp myself. And for nearly two decades, I never did. Then one dark and stormy night I found myself with sudden guests for dinner, a couple of apples in the pantry, some oats, some walnuts . . .

Blessedly, I was out of cinnamon (the usual spice) but well supplied with fresh ginger, and not only was the concoction that came out of the oven crisp on top, as it should be, but the filling was snapping crisp with the ginger's bite.

Several versions later, we have settled on this one, which has pears with the apples, as our favorite. A crunchy, just barely ripe Bartlett is perfect, especially paired with a fragrant apple like the Gala. If you can't find a good pear, then use two varieties of apples for a more complex taste.

One warning: lots of folks think you must put ice cream on top of any warm apple pastry. That is a sore mistake with this dish. The heavy cream overpowers the snap of the ginger and completely obscures the subtle flavors of the fruit, oats, and nuts. On the other hand, a big glass of cold milk is just perfect on the side. Or, if the night is cold, a nice, toasty cup of tea.

1 medium-sized crisp pear
2 medium-sized apples
¼ cup minced fresh ginger
¼ cup brown sugar

1 cup oats
1 cup walnut pieces, about
  ¼ inch across
1 cup soft bread crumbs
1 cup brown sugar
½ cup buttermilk
4 tablespoons cold butter

Preheat the oven to 375° F. Butter a 9×9-inch square or 10-inch round cake pan liberally and set aside.

Quarter and core the pear and apples. Cut each quarter in half lengthwise and then slice about ¼ inch thick. Mix with the fresh ginger and brown sugar, then layer into the baking pan.

Mix together the oats, nuts, bread crumbs, and brown sugar. Sprinkle the buttermilk over the mixture and toss until it is thoroughly moistened but still crumbly. Spread evenly over the fruit. Dot with slices of the butter. Place in the preheated oven and bake for 40 minutes, until the top is crunchy brown.

Serve immediately.
  Serves 8 to 10.

Grandma Zel's Chocolate Cake

This recipe comes from Leon Olenick's mother. His wife, Jackie, says that everyone in the family makes the cake for special occasions and no one seems to tire of it. I can understand why. My family thought every crumb was celestial.

The surfeit of sugar in the batter makes icing redundant. It creates a sweet, slightly chewy, brownie-like crust around the tender buttery inside. Make this only with the best ingredients: unsalted sweet cream butter, quality bittersweet chocolate, and excellent, fresh-brewed coffee.

3 eggs

1 cup (2 sticks) unsalted butter

1 cup freshly brewed coffee

3 ounces bittersweet chocolate

2½ cups dark brown sugar

2 cups all-purpose flour

1 teaspoon baking soda

1 teaspoon vanilla extract

Take the eggs out of the refrigerator and let come to room temperature. Put the butter in the large bowl of an electric mixer and let soften. Brew the coffee, measure out a cup, and put it in the freezer to let it chill. Preheat the oven to 350° F. and liberally butter and flour the inside of a tube pan.

When the eggs are at room temperature, the butter is soft, and the coffee is cold, melt the chocolate in the top of a double boiler over steaming water. At the mixer's medium speed, cream the butter, then add the sugar and cream until fluffy. Add the eggs one at a time, mixing to incorporate after each. Add the chocolate and blend well, scraping down the sides of the bowl.

Mix the flour and baking soda, then add ½ cup flour to the butter mixture and mix to blend. Add one-third of the coffee, then another ½ cup flour, and continue until all is mixed in. Be sure to scrape down the sides of the bowl each time you add an ingredient. Add the vanilla, mix to blend, and then turn out the batter into the prepared tube pan.

Use a rubber spatula to slightly smooth the top. Place on the center rack in the preheated oven and bake for 1 hour, or until a cake tester inserted in the middle comes out clean. Remove from the oven and cool in the pan, upright, on a wire rack for 1 hour. Then invert the pan onto a serving plate.

Serves 8 to 10.

Ten

Thanksgiving

Thanksgiving is the one holiday that we think we celebrate uniformly regardless of religious or cultural background. Norman Rockwell visions of the all-American turkey feast are passed around by the media as if they were Jungian archetypes of food and family shared by our collective unconscious. But one doesn't have to travel very far from home to discover that there is, in fact, no truly typical American Thanksgiving menu.

For instance, Shelley Hamel of Madison, Wisconsin, says that for her Thanksgiving means ham, not turkey.

"My best friend and I celebrate together with our families and any wanderlings we can gather up. I always bring a ham, and my husband does boiled onions and a sauce for the ham from his family. The other thing we must have is a heart-of-palm salad I make from some recipe I found years ago in a women's magazine."

But Shelley's variations sound downright prosaic compared to the Thanksgiving ritual of a South Yarmouth, Massachusetts, fellow named Frank who once told me, "This is what I like to do myself for Thanksgiving: throw out the turkey.

"Then I like to plop a nine-pound lobster in the middle of the table and let everyone have a go at it."

The scarlet crustacean stretches nearly two feet from stem to stern. Gorgeously absurd, it inspires even the staidest of diners to join in a giddy, communal assault—and in some ways this informal ritual celebrating abundance and sharing may have more in common with the original Thanksgiving than does the more formalized carving and apportioning of the turkey that has come to be our national rite.

From The Woman's Exchange Cook Book *(1894) comes this suggested bill of fare for a typical Thanksgiving Day:*

Breakfast: Grapes, oatmeal with cream, panned oysters with toast, hot rolls, broiled mutton chops, raw potatoes fried, flannel cakes with maple syrup or honey. Dinner: Turtle, chicken or oyster soup, baked fish if large and fresh, or stewed if canned (cod, halibut, or salmon), mashed potatoes, celery, roast turkey, baked sweet potatoes, lima beans, stewed tomatoes, onions, beets, cranberry sauce, cabbage salad, green pickles; pumpkin pie, mince pie, plum pudding, ice cream, assorted cakes, oranges, grapes, nuts. Supper: Light biscuit, shaved cold turkey, currant jelly, cheese sandwiches, tea cakes, apples, and jelly.

CAJUN THANKSGIVING

Craig Lege is a Louisiana-born keyboard player who has performed on some of the finest stages in the world, in New York, Paris, Montreal, San Francisco, and Montreux, Switzerland. In the off hours, when he's not dishing out zydeco, jazz, or rock and roll, Craig has made it his business to dish up the best cuisine of whatever region he's in. But Lege is convinced that there is "no food, nowhere, any better than the food I grew up eating."

That should come as little surprise to anyone who has visited the southwest Louisiana region that forty-one-year-old Lege calls home. His birthplace, Abbeville, sits right at the heart of Cajun country. When the air is brisk, it carries the salt-musk scent of pearly oysters just pulled from Gulf estuaries; the caramel crisp of sugarcane fields burned for harvest; or the pungent bite of peppery Tabasco sauce being processed just a few miles away on Avery Island.

In Cajun country, food reigns supreme. "It's not like we have celebrations, then food, in Louisiana," Lege says. "It's more like, any food you can eat has a celebration created around it."

Toss a crawfish at a Louisiana calendar and any week it lands on is bound to have a food event dedicated to it.

There are andouille and boudin festivals, étouffée cook-offs, old-fashioned boucheries, and even a Yambilee in Opelousas every fall. And then there are the holidays: Christmas, Mardi Gras, special Lenten meals.

Of all such food celebrations, though, Lege says his all-time favorite is Thanksgiving: "Thanksgiving was better than Christmas because you didn't have all that 'gimme, gimme, take, take' stuff with the presents. Instead you just had the family all sitting around the table, visiting and talking. Everybody's there just because they want to be there with each other—and with that food. Oh my, the food!"

The centerpiece of the Lege family's Thanksgiving table is a pepper-and-onion-studded roast of pork. It is classically served with a highly seasoned rice dressing on the side, as well as potato salad—a warm version with a tangy Creole-style dressing, often as not.

Traditional sweet potatoes do make an appearance on the Cajun Thanksgiving table, but the sugary Louisiana yams are likely to come clad only in their humble russet-colored jackets, for the flavor is sweet enough without dressing them up in a casserole. And corn, too, is often part of the traditional feast, but no namby-pamby sweet corn pudding. Instead, a peppery maquechoux (page 272) will take its place. And instead of (or sometimes along with) a pumpkin pie, a platter full of tasty homemade Acadian fig pies will finish off the meal.

This Cajun reinvention of the Thanksgiving table is very much in keeping with the spirit of the holiday. After all, Thanksgiving began as a celebration of the indigenous abundance of the New World. Wild turkey, American corn, squash, pumpkins, and sweet potatoes represent the bounty the Pilgrims found around them. In Cajun country, plump piggies are more plentiful (and, many would argue, far tastier) than the traditional bird. And rice, peppers, and tomatoes are among the bounteous fruits of the regional earth.

Iris Lege, Craig's mother, is a charming woman, disarmingly modest about her talent in the kitchen. ("I've been knowing her forty years, and all the time, that's her," Craig says of his mother's humble ways.)

"I don't really think of myself as a great cook, certainly not the best one in my family," Iris says as she lays down a plate piled with delicate, half-moon-shaped fig pies that would surely seem to refute her.

"Now, the best cook in the family was Granny, my mother-in-law, who was left-handed, so we always said that everything she made tasted so good because it was made by the left paw. And we would go, 'The left paw is in the kitchen. Are we gonna eat!'

"But I was not all that curious about rice and gravy and such when I was growing up, so when I got married, all I could do was bake cakes."

That soon changed, however. As the children of Iris Broussard and Sol Lege were growing up in Abbeville, they alternated having holidays, including Thanksgiving, at their two grandmothers'. Over those years, Iris was in the kitchen with both her mother and her mother-in-law, helping and watching. When the time finally came for her to take the annual responsibilities of cook and hostess for Thanksgiving at her house, she was able to turn out the traditional family dishes—although no written recipe had ever passed between the women.

"I can show you how to cook the food, and maybe tell you. But I don't think I could write it down. I can't even tell you the name for the cut of pork we use. I just know it's the one that looks like a round steak, but a lot bigger," Iris says.

Like her mother, Iris pokes little holes all through the pork, turning a knife to create pockets that she then fills with savories such as garlic and chopped-up onion and bell peppers. She rubs the outside with pepper, salt, and paprika and plops the whole thing in a cast-iron Dutch oven to cook over very low heat on top of the stove for several hours.

"All that spicy smell fills the house," Iris says with a smile. "It's that spicy, roasty smell that means Thanksgiving to me. And then you use the drippings to flavor the rice dressing, so that flavor is through the whole meal.

"And when I was little, my grandmother would go out to the garden and pick the vegetables the kids liked for the Thanksgiving table. There were always mustard greens cooked in oil and onion. We kids must have had broader tastes than kids do now. My son Bobby says, 'Mama's got the taste of a buzzard. She'll eat anything.'"

Cajun Roast Pork with Eggplant-Rice Dressing

This is a mildly spiced version, but if your family favors pepper, you may want to double the amount here.

The cut of meat Iris Lege couldn't call by name is most often referred to as Boston butt. It's not available in all meat markets, although you should be able to find one at a good butcher shop or from a grocery with an extensive meat department. Some butchers would rather sell you the boneless pork tenderloin, which is more expensive but has the added health advantage of having much less fat. I have made an oven roast similar to this using a 5-pound tenderloin with a single long pocket cut down the length of the top, rubbed with the spices and filled with the onions and green pepper. I roasted it in a 350° F. oven for about 2 to 2½ hours. It sliced easily and the result was tasty, though not nearly so lip-smackingly succulent as the version here. Since it's a holiday, I encourage you to use the more traditional cut, defat the juices, and otherwise go for the gusto in this old-fashioned specialty.

6-pound Boston butt pork
  roast
1 teaspoon salt
1 teaspoon cayenne pepper
1 teaspoon black pepper
1 large onion, chopped fine
1 large green bell pepper,
  chopped fine

Trim the excess visible fat from the roast, although you want some fat on it for flavor. With a small, sharp knife, cut about a dozen little pockets in the meat, turning the knife to widen them. Mix the salt and cayenne and black peppers together, then rub inside each pocket. If there are any natural crevices (along the bone, for instance, or where you've removed the fat), season those as well. Rub any leftover salt and pepper into the outside of the meat. Mix the

1 eggplant, pared and cut in small cubes
4 cups cooked white rice

onion and green pepper together and stuff inside the pockets and any crevices. Push the vegetables in tight and fill as full as you can without anything spilling out. Set aside leftover onions and green pepper to use in the rice dressing. (If you should use all of the onion and green pepper to stuff the roast, chop up about ½ cup more of each to use later in the rice dressing.)

Put the meat in a large cast-iron Dutch oven and cook, covered, over a low flame for 3 hours. The meat should make enough juice of its own to keep it from sticking to the pan, but check it in the first half hour, and if the pot looks too dry, add a couple of tablespoons water to the bottom of the pot.

When the meat is done, remove it from the pan and set aside. Pour off the juices, defat, and reserve. You may wish to deglaze the pan by adding ¼ cup water and scraping the bottom with a wooden spatula to loosen any crust. Add the chopped eggplant and any leftover onion and green pepper to this, and then add a cup of defatted juices from the roast. Cover and simmer over low heat until the vegetables are softened, 10 minutes or less.

Add the cooked white rice and stir lightly to mix together, but be careful not to mush the rice. Simmer uncovered for 10 minutes more, adding more juice and salt, if necessary. The mixture should be moist but not soupy, with the vegetables and rice absorbing the broth, not standing in it. When the dressing is ready, serve hot with the Cajun Roast Pork. Makes enough for 8 with some pork left over for sandwiches or gumbo the next day.

Serves 8.

CHAUDIN

On some Thanksgivings the Cajun pork roast has to concede center-table honors to an equally flavorful, even more exotic main course, chaudin.

"The chaudin is actually the pig's stomach, all cleaned up and stuffed with a homemade sausage—or some people stuff it with rice," Iris Lege explains.

"You use a cow's horn, like a natural funnel, to stuff it. To cook it, you put it in a big iron pot like a pot roast and simmer it low on top of the stove. Then, when it's almost done, you put it in the oven to crisp the skin all around. That's the best part. You slice it like a roast and there's all the good stuffing inside and that kind of crisp, kind of chewy crust of skin around it.

"We used to make them all the time ourselves, but now, around Thanksgiving and Christmas, there's a place where you can buy them ready-made, and that's what we do. It's good, but not like homemade. But we don't raise pigs now and it's hard to find a good clean pig's stomach in the grocery. Sometimes when I can, though, I still like to make a homemade chaudin."

Maquechoux

Perhaps even more than turkey, corn is the most significant part of any Thanksgiving feast—the greatest gift the Indians gave to the Pilgrims. Some say it is the most important culinary gift the New World gave to the rest of this planet.

And there are some who also say that the Cajun staple maquechoux (pronounced "mock shoe" and translated as "smothered corn") is the finest way to present this vegetable. If you are in southwestern Louisiana when the corn is ripe and the tomatoes just bursting from the vine, I strongly recommend you sample this dish in its prime.

But if you want to make it for Thanksgiving, you will be hard pressed in November to find really good fresh corn. Nevertheless, you can make a yummy maquechoux with frozen corn processed with milk in a blender to give it the texture of corn cut from the cob. (Some Cajun cookbooks recommend using a mixture of 1 small can each kernel corn and creamed corn to make a "mock" choux. I find the taste of the canned corn too sweet, although many Cajuns prefer that sweetness to this more tangy version.)

2 tablespoons canola oil
1 cup chopped onion
1 clove of garlic, crushed
1 medium-sized green bell
    pepper, chopped
1 (14½-ounce) can whole
    tomatoes
16 ounces frozen corn
½ cup 2 percent milk
1 teaspoon salt
½ teaspoon sugar
Up to ½ teaspoon cayenne
    pepper (see instructions)
Freshly ground black
    pepper to taste
3 tablespoons half-and-half

In a heavy skillet with a lid, heat the oil over medium heat. Add the onion, garlic, and bell pepper and sauté until the onion is clear and the bell pepper tender.

While the vegetables are sautéing, drain the juice from tomatoes and reserve. Chop the tomatoes coarsely.

Put 1 cup of the frozen corn and the milk in a blender. Process at medium speed for 30 to 60 seconds, until the corn and milk make a thick mush, but with parts of the kernels still evident. Add the blended corn and the rest of the frozen corn to the sautéed vegetables and stir. Then add the tomatoes and the salt, sugar, cayenne, and black pepper. (Half a teaspoon of cayenne makes a peppy maquechoux. You may wish to use less.)

Let it come to a bubbling simmer, then

turn the heat low, cover the skillet, and cook for 45 minutes, stirring frequently. The mixture should be very juicy but not soupy. You can add the reserved juice from the tomatoes or water if it starts to stick while you are cooking. After 45 minutes, add the half-and-half, and let simmer for a few minutes, uncovered, until the mixture is thick and steaming. Serve immediately. (If you want to make ahead, you may freeze the maquechoux before adding the half-and-half, adding it when you reheat.)

Serves 8 as a side dish.

VARIATION: If you want to make this in the summer with fresh ingredients, simply use about 8 ears fresh corn in place of the frozen corn and ½ cup milk. Cut the kernels from the cob, using a sharp knife and taking off just the tops of the kernels. Then take a small kitchen spoon and scrape up the cob again, scraping out the rest of the kernel and the corn's milk. You won't need to put the corn through the blender and you won't need the ½ cup milk called for in the frozen-corn recipe, although you may still want to add the half-and-half.

You can use 3 medium-sized fresh tomatoes, peeled and chopped, instead of canned tomatoes.

VARIATION: To make a scrumptious entree, add 2 dozen medium-sized raw shrimp, peeled and deveined, to the maquechoux just after you add the half-and-half. Simmer until the shrimp are cooked. Served over rice, it makes a hearty main course for 4.

Cajun Potato Salad

There seem to be as many variations of potato salad as of gumbo in Cajun country. Some are dressed with mayonnaise and served cold. This one has a tart Creole-style dressing and is served warm. It's especially tasty with Cajun Roast Pork—and if you think it too much for the already heavy Thanksgiving table, make it fresh the day after to go with leftover pork sandwiches.

6 medium-sized red
  potatoes, unpeeled
2 eggs
2 tablespoons Dijon
  mustard
2½ tablespoons olive oil
2 tablespoons cider vinegar
1 medium-sized onion,
  chopped
1 medium-sized green bell
  pepper, chopped
Salt to taste
Cayenne pepper or Tabasco
  sauce (optional)

Place the potatoes in a large pot with cold water to cover. Place over high heat, cover, and bring to a boil. Turn the heat to medium and simmer for 20 to 25 minutes, until the potatoes are tender when pierced in the middle with a fork, but not mushy. Drain and cool.

While the potatoes are cooking, hard-boil the eggs (about 15 minutes in just barely boiling water for room-temperature eggs). Peel when cool enough to handle. Separate the whites from the yolks, cut the whites into small pieces, and set aside. Mash the yolks fine with a fork.

Place the mustard in a small bowl and, with a small whisk or fork, blend in 2 tablespoons of the olive oil, a few drops at a time. Then blend in the vinegar the same way. Finally add the mashed egg yolks and blend well.

In a non-stick frying pan, sauté the chopped onion and green pepper in the remaining ½ tablespoon olive oil until they just begin to soften. You want them still to have a little crunch but not to taste raw. Dice the unpeeled potatoes. Add the egg-white pieces and lightly toss together with the onions and peppers. Pour the dressing over (use a rubber spatula to make sure you get every last bit) and toss again lightly until the vegetables are coated. Add salt and a sprinkling of cayenne to taste. (You may prefer to omit the cayenne and serve with Tabasco on the side, so everyone can spice to their own taste.) Serve warm.

Serves 8 as a side dish.

DENISE HARDING

Like Craig Lege, Denise Harding has sampled dishes around the world. Born in Virginia to a Louisiana Cajun mother and a career Navy man, Denise had lived in Europe, the Middle East, and California by the time she was in her teens.

"Wherever we lived, that's the kind of food we ate. When we were in Morocco, we lived in the village, not on the base, and my mother would take me into the marketplace to barter for food. I remember the aromatic spice shop—all those strange, enticing fragrances, and then the food we'd have at home would be full of them.

"I wasn't really aware of being Cajun. My mom only spoke in Cajun to yell when she was mad or to call us in to eat. But then we moved back to Louisiana when I was nine.

"The first memory of it I have is going down a dirt road and coming in and seeing this big plantation and all these strange people on the porch and in the yard, all of them speaking French. To me, that was like being in a foreign country."

The plantation where Denise's mother, Margaret Martin Harding, was born and raised was not a fantasy mansion from Gone With the Wind *but a working farm with a big house where Denise's grandparents and many of her aunts, uncles, and cousins still lived.*

"They built a house for my mom and dad right on the property, and another uncle lived in a trailer. Every kid got paired up with a cousin who was your same age, and my cousin Jeanette and I would spend the night together at my grand-parents' house. I remember waking up to the smell of good strong coffee and the sound of Mass in French on the TV. And they'd always have stone-ground yellow grits for breakfast, and Jeanette and I would break soft-cooked eggs in ours and eat them with toast.

"And every dinner hour at noon, my grandmother had all of her eight surviving children and their children come to eat at a big table spread with everything in the kitchen.

"The big difference between holidays and that daily farm feast was that on holidays we ate in the dining room and we had wine. And there would be all the roasts and vegetables and fresh-sliced cantaloupe, potato salad, and rice and gravy."

That rice and gravy, Denise says, is a good example of what captivated her about Cajun cooking. It sounds prosaic, "but what you're doing with that gravy is deglazing the pan and then reducing it to make a really elegant, natural sauce. It is as delicious as anything you'd eat in a fine French restaurant, but my grand-mother made it every day."

Denise, fascinated by her food heritage, became a professional baker, specializing in regional recipes. And she also wrote two cookbooks of her Cajun family recipes.

"Although I came to it late, I've been deeply affected by my Cajun back-ground and by my family. I wanted to give something back to them. Bringing to-gether the recipes for all these wonderful foods they made was my way of honoring my mother and grandmother and the things that they gave me."

Cajun and Creole Cooking *is available by mail order from Denise Colette Harding, 300 Monique Drive, Lafayette, Louisiana 70507. The 44-page book-let—with such recipes as Black-Eyed Peas, Tasso, and Rice; Wild Duck Gumbo; and Creole Honey Cake—costs $5.00 plus $1.00 for postage and handling.*

Sweet Potatoes with Ginger-Sorghum Butter

Most Thanksgiving sweet-potato casseroles turn this distinguished vegetable into a candied-up, tricked-out affair more suitable as dessert than side dish. That's a shame, since a plain hot sweet potato dripping with pure butter has one of the most satisfying flavors found in nature. The only thing I've found better is this version with whispers of sorghum molasses and ginger added to the butter to underscore the potato's natural earthy sweetness.

8 small-to-medium-sized
sweet potatoes or 4 large
ones (all should be of the
same relative size)
1 cup (2 sticks) butter
1½ cups sorghum
molasses
2 tablespoons candied
ginger

Preheat the oven to 425° F. Scrub the potatoes well and remove any strings or blemishes. Dry the potatoes and grease lightly with butter, then pierce the tops with the tines of a fork 2 or 3 times. Place on the oven rack and bake for 45 to 75 minutes, depending on size. They are done when a fork penetrates easily to the center of the potato.

While the potatoes are baking, put the butter in a small mixing bowl and allow it to soften but not melt. Pour the sorghum molasses over the butter. Mince the ginger fine with a small sharp knife, or crush between your fingers and sprinkle over the sorghum and butter. Using a fork, whip the butter, sorghum, and ginger together until well blended. Keep as cool as possible, but don't refrigerate, until ready to serve. If the sorghum and butter separate, just rewhip with a fork right before serving.

When the potatoes are done, serve immediately, with one small-medium potato or half a large one per diner. Pass the sorghum butter for spreading inside.

Serves 8.

NOTE: Any leftover potatoes may be sliced in rings the next day, placed in a shallow, buttered casserole, topped by dollops of the sorghum butter, and re-heated in a 350° F. oven for about 15 minutes, until warmed through. Any leftover Ginger-Sorghum Butter is also heavenly spread on dark wheat toast.

Cajun Fig Pies

These pies are made with a sweet, cookie-like crust rolled out in small rounds, filled with fig preserves, and folded over to make half-moons that can be eaten easily out of hand. Iris Lege rolls her rounds to about 8 inches in diameter with a surprisingly thin crust, but she says you can vary the crust size and amount of filling. I was not so adept at rolling—and especially not at trans-ferring the fragile pies from board to baking sheet—so I chose to make my pies smaller (about 4 inches across) and with a thicker cookie crust. That is the technique described here.

Iris uses homemade fig preserves (recipe follows) to fill her pies, but if figs are not in season, or you don't feel in the mood for canning first and then baking, you can make the pies with a good fig preserve from the grocery. I tried several varieties, including an imported fig jam from a Middle Eastern grocery that looked closest to the Cajun fig preserves with whole figs sus-pended in a translucent jelly. But its flavor wasn't nearly so fresh. The best preserves I found—with a tart, not too sweet flavor and a chunky texture—

are the Kadota Fig Preserve made by Knott's Berry Farm. They're available nationally in 10-ounce jars, but if you can't find them at your grocery, you can mail-order from Knott's at (800) 877-6887.

5 cups all-purpose flour
2 teaspoons baking powder
½ teaspoon salt
¾ cup vegetable shortening
1½ cups sugar
1 egg
1 teaspoon vanilla extract
¾ cup milk
20 ounces fig preserves

Sift together the flour, baking powder, and salt. In a large mixing bowl, cream together the shortening and sugar with an electric beater until fluffy. Add the egg and vanilla and beat until blended. Begin mixing by hand as you alternately add the flour and milk in thirds. You may want to use your fingers to blend the ingredients lightly at the last and then knead the dough 3 or 4 times, patting it together to form a ball. Refrigerate for at least 1 hour.

When you are ready to make the pies, preheat the oven to 350° F. Divide the dough in half, leaving one part in the refrigerator while you work with the other. Pull off a piece of dough a little larger than a golf ball, roll into a sphere, then press between the palms lightly to make into a circle. Roll out on a floured surface or between 2 pieces of waxed paper until the dough circle is about 4 inches in diameter.

Place 1 heaping tablespoon of fig preserves in the center of one half of the dough circle and fold the other half over it to make a half-moon shape. Pinch together the edges where the dough meets to seal. Lift the pie from the board and onto a greased cookie sheet (use a metal spatula if you need to). Pierce the top of the pie 2 or 3 times with a fork to let out steam and keep the pies from bursting in the oven.

Don't crowd the cookie sheet (about 5 pies will fill a standard one).

Bake the pies in the preheated oven for 20 to 25 minutes, until the edges are golden brown. Remove from the baking sheet while warm, and let them cool thoroughly before stacking.

This recipe makes approximately 20 fig pies and can be doubled. Pies may be stored for a day or two in the refrigerator. (Craig Lege swears they are better on the second day.) They will also keep in the freezer—just thaw before eating. Iris wasn't sure how long they could keep frozen, however, noting that "I've never had any around long enough to get freezer burn."

Makes about 20 pies.

Fig Preserves

"When I was growing up, the whole family would get in on the fig harvest in the late summer," Iris Lege's son Craig recalls. "It would be hot and really sticky and some people have allergic reactions to the fig skin, so some of us would be in gloves and long-sleeved shirts and long pants and your head and face wrapped up as best you could. And we would surely sweat, but it was worth it because my granny and aunts and mother would spend the next day or two in a hot kitchen canning fig preserves that were the best in the world."

The fig preserves you find in the store are more like a jam, some with whole figs in them. The Lege family fig preserves have whole figs suspended in a thick, honey-colored jelly. They are used to fill fig pies, but they are also sensational in a plain fig sandwich.

Iris and her husband, Sol Lege, agree that a fig sandwich is a great breakfast dish and, served with a cold glass of milk, is a good snack anytime. They also agree that you use 2 slices of fresh white bread (preferably homemade) to make a real fig sandwich. But Iris likes to pile on the fig preserves "as thick as I can and still hold it."

Sol prefers to spread the fig preserves thin for a more delicate flavor.

"He likes to pretend he's making a fig sandwich," Iris says.

"She has to open her mouth as wide as a truck just to get the sandwich in," Sol says.

I found both ways delectable—and if you can get your hands on a couple of quarts of fresh figs, you may decide for yourself. Here's how Iris makes her fig preserves:

2 quarts unpeeled fresh figs
4 cups sugar

Clean the skins of the figs by covering with hot water and bringing to a boil. Remove the pan from the heat, let stand for 4 minutes, then drain. Some folks peel the figs before preserving, but Iris says the unpeeled figs make for a clearer preserve. She does remove the stems, however, and so should you. (Wear rubber gloves while handling the figs in case your skin is susceptible to their irritation.)

In a large pot, heat the sugar and 1 cup water, stirring until the sugar is dissolved. Turn up the heat and allow to boil for 3 minutes. Add the unpeeled figs and turn the heat down to medium. The mixture should cook, uncovered, at a very gentle boil for 1½ to 2 hours, until the syrup is translucent and beginning to thicken. While it's cooking, don't stir or you may break the figs. Instead, gently shake the pot occasionally to keep the mixture from sticking.

When the preserves are ready and still boiling, pour into hot, sterilized jars, leaving ½ inch space at the top. Wipe the rims of jars with a clean cloth and seal. Process in a hot-water bath for 10 minutes.

Use for fig sandwiches and fig pies. Any syrup left when the figs are gone can be poured over pancakes.

Makes about 1½ quarts.

VEGETARIAN HARVEST

When Niya Standish (no relation to Miles) moved to Portland, Oregon, in 1976, she moved into a large house already occupied by her sister Marcia's family and their mother, Faye. It was the year of the Bicentennial and the family's first Thanksgiving together since they had lived in Chicago a decade before, so they decided to do something significant to celebrate.

"It was Faye's idea," Niya recalls. "We were actually talking about the first Thanksgiving, and Faye said we ought to do a genuinely 'traditional' Thanksgiving."

This did not mean cooking up a turkey with dressing and all the trimmings to Faye and her daughters, who have been vegetarians all their lives.

"What she meant by traditional was that we should try and re-create some of the actual feel of that first Thanksgiving. It was her idea to pack the food things together and go off and cook them over an open fire in the woods."

So they did, heading off to Champoeg State Park, where they created a vegetarian's harvest feast of stuffed squash, nut loaf with mushroom gravy, and mashed potatoes, all seasoned with the scent of woodsmoke.

A rousing tramp through the woods piqued everyone's appetite and underscored the family quality of the event.

"As kids, going to the woods to take a walk was always a special thing for us to do, so it was already something of a family tradition," Niya says.

And to make things even more festive, the whole group, including Marcia's husband and son, dressed up as either Pilgrims or Indians.

"It was the 1970s, of course, still in the midst of hippie days, so it wasn't hard to come up with long dresses or beadwork or feathers for your hair. I'm not sure that anyone who saw us would have realized that we were in costume. But it made us feel like we were together, and it gave us a sense of a really unique family thing we were doing."

Over time the tradition changed slightly. Cooking outside lost its charm in the rainy Oregon climate, so after a year or two the feast became an indoor event, although the menu has stayed much the same. Friends were invited some years, and the family grew as Niya married Will Mustard (no relation to the Colonel) and they had a son, Brett.

But certain elements of the celebration endured, increasing in significance. A group hike is always a part of the day's events, even if it's only a brisk walk in a nearby city park. And if you attend the party, you still have to dress as either an Indian or a Pilgrim.

"Our friends who come know that's part of the deal, and no one ever balks. In fact, I think that's part of the charm for them. And you have to be a little more inventive in coming up with a costume these days. One of my favorites was a year or two ago when Faye wore an old poncho with a hot pink plume from a feather duster in her hair for a headdress. It was quite stunning."

The power of the ritual was brought home to Niya one year when the family endured a particularly rough period. Marcia was not around, following a difficult divorce, and Faye was living in a nursing home after a major stroke. That might have seemed reason enough for abandoning the usual festivities, but Niya, Will, and Brett decided that would be a bad choice.

Instead, they donned their costumes, went for their hike, and prepared the traditional nut loaf dinner. Then they took mashed potatoes with mushroom gravy to Faye, still wearing their Pilgrim and Indian garb.

"She saw right away what we were doing, and she was definitely pleased. I think it was reassuring to her, that sense of the family was still continuing," Niya says.

"And it was important for me, too. I see this holiday as a thread that runs through our family, sewing it together. And it really doesn't matter that we don't do it quite the same from year to year, that the people change or the menu isn't always the same. There's still that core—the putting on of Pilgrim clothes, the hike in the woods. And there's that sense that this is what we do at Thanksgiving, and this is what our family is."

A family is not an abstract cultural ideal; a man, a woman, and children living blissfully in a mortgaged house on a quiet neighborhood street. The family the soul wants is a felt network of relationship, an evocation of a certain kind of interconnection that grounds, roots and nestles. This connectedness doesn't have to be perfect or whole in order to do its business and give its gifts, but it has to be able to stir the imagination and move the emotions in a way that is particular to the family.

—THOMAS MOORE, *SoulMates: Honoring the Mysteries of Love and Relationship*

Niya's Nut Loaf

When Niya and Marcia Standish were growing up in Chicago in the 1950s, America was enjoying a love affair with steak. But in the Standish house, no red meat was served, and very little poultry or fish.

"I'm not sure my mother would even know how to cook a chicken," Niya says.

"But sometimes for Thanksgiving she'd want to do something special, something 'traditional,' so she'd make one of those turkey rolls—you know, the pressed meat. It was just simply awful."

When it came Niya's time to create something special for Thanksgiving, she decided a nut loaf would be a better centerpiece for this late fall feast. She's fine-tuned the original recipe over the years and says that the secret to it is "to chop the nuts very fine. You chop them once, then you chop them twice, and then, on the third round, you get a little tired and you think, 'Oh, maybe I'll stop.' But don't. Just keep chopping one more time."

In addition to chopped walnuts and pecans, the recipe contains almonds ground to a fine meal.

"They give the loaf a kind of stick-to-itness, a meaty texture," Niya explains. "But you want the other nuts to be chunkier so you get little nuggets of flavor."

"Little nuggets of flavor" is an apt way to describe the savory pleasures of this subtle dish. You can snazz it up with additional ingredients, as we do in the variation, but there is something very satisfying in the simplicity of Niya's Nut Loaf in its traditional form as well.

1 cup walnuts

1 cup pecans

1½ cups almonds

1½ cups soft whole wheat
  bread crumbs

¾ cup minced onion

½ cup minced celery

3 tablespoons minced fresh
  parsley

1 tablespoon minced fresh
  dillweed (or more)

1 teaspoon paprika (or
  more)

Kosher salt to taste

Freshly ground black
  pepper to taste

3 eggs, beaten

2 cups skim milk (about)

Preheat the oven to 350° F. and liberally oil the inside of a 9 × 5 × 3-inch loaf pan. (A glass pan will give your loaf a browner crust.)

Using a large, sharp knife and a cutting board, chop through the walnuts 3 times to get pieces about ⅛ inch thick. Do the same with the pecans, but not the almonds.

Mix the chopped nuts together in a large bowl.

In a blender, grind the almonds to a fine meal and add to the other nuts. Grind the bread crumbs fine and add. Mix in the onion, celery, parsley, and 1 tablespoon each dill and paprika. Taste and season with salt and black pepper. (Add more dill or paprika, if you wish, also.)

Mix in the beaten eggs and then add the milk, a little at a time, until the mixture is very moist but not soupy. You want it to be firm but sticky.

Turn out into the oiled loaf pan and smooth the top with a metal spatula. Place in the preheated oven and bake for 25 minutes. Turn the temperature down to 250° F. and bake for 15 more minutes, or until the top is golden and a cake tester inserted in the middle comes out clean.

Remove from the oven and turn upside down on a wire rack for 5 minutes. If the pan doesn't lift off the loaf easily after this time, turn it over and run a knife around the edge of the loaf to loosen it from the sides of pan. When the loaf comes out of the pan, allow to cool on the rack completely before slicing. Serve with Mushroom Gravy (recipe follows).

Serves 8.

VARIATION: For a jazzier version of the loaf, omit the celery and dill from the original recipe. Use cashews instead of walnuts. Before you add the eggs and milk, roast 1 large red bell pepper, peel it, chop the flesh, and mix with the nuts. (To roast the pepper, place it under the broiler until the skin begins to blister and brown. Turn and roast all sides until the skin is blistered and browned all over. Remove from the broiler and, when cool enough to handle, rub lightly between your palms to loosen the skin, which you then peel off.) Then drain a 6-ounce jar of marinated artichokes, chop fine, and add. Add ⅛ cup minced oil-packed sun-dried tomatoes. Taste before adding salt—you may need none or much less than you do in the more conventional loaf. Then proceed as you would for the previous recipe. Leftover slices may be refrigerated and used to make mouth-watering sandwiches the next day.

ᒍ ushroom Gravy

This creamy, musky sauce has a most appropriate late autumn flavor. It's a perfect foil for Niya's Nut Loaf, and also over Savory Paradise Potatoes (recipe follows). And if you should have any left over, simply refrigerate, and reheat the next day with a cup of milk added for homemade mushroom soup.

¼ cup dried porcini mushrooms
¼ cup boiling water
3 tablespoons butter
1 cup chopped onion
1 clove of garlic, minced
4 cups chopped fresh mushrooms (12–15 large ones)
1 tablespoon oil-packed sun-dried tomatoes, drained and minced
¼ cup half-and-half
2 tablespoons flour
2 cups milk
1 tablespoon tamari soy sauce
Kosher salt to taste
Freshly ground black pepper to taste

Place the dried porcini mushrooms in a cup and cover with ¼ cup boiling hot water. Let sit for 30 minutes.

In a large skillet, melt 2 tablespoons of the butter. Add the onion and garlic and sauté until the onion becomes limp and begins to turn transparent. Add the last tablespoon of butter and the 4 cups fresh mushrooms. Stir to coat well with butter, then cover and let simmer over low heat for 5 minutes.

While the fresh mushrooms simmer, put the porcini mushrooms and their liquid, minced sun-dried tomatoes, and half-and-half in the blender cup and process until liquefied.

After the 5 minutes are up, remove the cover of the skillet and sprinkle the flour over the simmered mushrooms, stirring it in until blended. Add the porcini–half-and-half mixture and stir.

Mix the milk and soy sauce, then add to the skillet, stirring as you do. Turn the heat up and continue to stir. The mixture will begin to bubble ever so slightly and to thicken. When it has a thick, creamy consistency, remove from the heat and serve.

This makes enough gravy to make about 8 people happy.

Further advice on dinner parties from The Woman's Exchange Cook Book *(1894):*

Everybody is always out of bread; prevent it if you can.

Two hours is long enough to serve any dinner that Christians ought to eat; three hours and a half is too long.

A spoon should never be turned over in the mouth.

Savory Paradise Potatoes

If I wasn't born a mashed-potato purist, my initiation came not long after. The first solid food I was given was a fingerful of my mother's perfect spuds seasoned only with butter, salt, and milk, and blended to a feathery consistency by a hand masher and then a fork. This is how mashed potatoes should be, I understood then and continue to believe now.

However, the savory spuds they dish up at a local diner, Lynn's Paradise Café, have also won my heart. The kiss of garlic makes them addictive, and the touch of nutmeg or mace (I prefer the latter's slightly more delicate aroma) adds just the right accent for the Thanksgiving table. And while I would never dream of putting gravy on my mother's pristine potatoes, these are assertive enough to be a perfect match for the Mushroom Gravy (preceding recipe).

Whipping them in an electric mixer was against my principles at first, but it quickly makes a good consistency and is a considerable time-and-effort-saver during the last-minute juggling that seems to occur with every holiday feast. So serve these savory spuds whenever you want—just don't call them mashed potatoes.

6 medium-sized potatoes
½ cup (1 stick) butter
½ teaspoon crushed garlic
⅛ teaspoon ground nutmeg
  or mace
½ cup warm milk
¼ teaspoon white pepper
1 teaspoon salt

Peel the potatoes and cut into quarters. Cover with water in a lidded saucepan. Bring to a boil, then turn down the heat, cover, and cook at a simmer for 25 minutes, until the potatoes break apart when pierced by a fork.

Drain and put potatoes in the large bowl of an electric mixer. Cut the butter into chunks and whip with the hot potatoes. Add the rest of the ingredients, using a spatula to scrape down the side of the mixing bowl and make sure everything gets blended together. The potatoes are ready when they are relatively smooth, with a few lumps for character. Serve hot.

Serves 8.

Gala Butternut Pudding

Some squash recipes are too sweet, while others are too "natural." This dish, with just a little added sugar and nuggets of tart juicy apple to give it life, is just right.

You may use any winter squash, but the butternut is easy to handle, and its bright orange flesh makes for a festive casserole. Likewise, another variety of apple would be fine to substitute, as long as it's crisp, with a distinctive taste.

1½–2 pounds butternut
   squash
4 tablespoons butter
½ cup brown sugar
1½ cups soft whole wheat
   bread crumbs
2 eggs, beaten
½ cup milk
2 medium-sized Gala
   apples (about 2 cups
   chopped)

Place the squash in the oven and turn to 350° F. Leave until it is soft to the touch but not mushy—usually 45 minutes to 1 hour. Remove and allow to cool until it can be handled.

Split the squash down the length, discard the seeds, and peel. Place pieces of the flesh in a large bowl and mash with butter and sugar until both are melted and blended with the squash.

Mix in the bread crumbs, then the eggs and milk. Quarter the apples and core, but leave the peel on. Cut each quarter in half lengthwise and then chop in pieces about ¼ inch thick. Add to the squash.

Butter a 2-quart casserole liberally and turn the batter into it. Place in the preheated oven and bake for 40 minutes, until the top is turning golden. Remove and allow to cool for at least 15 minutes before serving. (The apples get quite hot and are still very juicy and therefore apt to burn the mouth if the dish is served immediately out of the oven.)

Serves 8.

RISE AND SHINE 2

Niya Standish's family has another Thanksgiving Day tradition. First thing in the morning they go to the home of their friend Joann Wiser for her biscuit breakfast.

The biscuit bash started more than fifteen years ago because Joann decided "I wanted a tradition that extended outside of our immediate family."

She invited friends of hers and of her husband to their house to eat biscuits and gravy on Thanksgiving morning:

"I'd heard of a man in a little town in the South who put on this big Thanksgiving biscuit breakfast for the community. It seemed a good time for a celebration. Nobody has breakfast plans, since everybody's focused on a big meal later in the day. And I was used to having people over for breakfast. I grew up on a farm in Blythe, California, and in the morning the fertilizer guy and the farmhand and whoever had morning business with my dad would be there in the kitchen with us, having coffee and something to eat."

Joann makes more than a hundred drop biscuits, skillets of sausage and gravy, and a huge salad. Coffee brews perpetually, and friends bring wine and pots of jam. About twenty-five people come each year, including grownups who started coming when they were just kids.

It's a tradition that has weathered changes in Joann's lifestyle. In 1992 she and her husband separated, later to divorce. The initial split came in October.

"My son and I were discussing what to do. People had warned me that the holidays would be the hardest. But we decided we should just take ownership of the tradition, and invite old friends and new people we wanted to include. And it was really wonderful. It was very helpful to me to have that connection, that ongoing link to my past."

Friends get in on the act, and Joann says that is one of the pleasures of the party. One family always arrives early for the first cup of coffee, and the husband insists on washing the dishes. Guests make coffee as it's needed, keep the jam pots full, and have even made biscuits and gravy.

"I like the informality of everybody doing stuff. It gives my friends a feeling of ownership," Joann told me.

"This year I'm going to England for the winter and I won't be here for Thanksgiving. So a friend of mine said the other day, 'You know, I think while you're gone, we should have the biscuits and gravy at my house.' That was such an affirmation for me. It made me realize that this celebration matters to people, that it's really something good."

Maple Spoon Bread

Corn was a part of the original Thanksgiving, but in *The Story of Corn* Betty Fussell tells us that the "parched" corn brought by the Indians to that original feast was in fact popcorn.

While the idea of a big bowl of hot popcorn passed around as a pre–Thanksgiving dinner appetizer has quirky appeal, most of us are looking for something a little more conventional. Unfortunately, conventional can turn out to be as trite as corn pudding or as uninspired as canned or frozen kernels heated and topped with a dollop of butter.

This rendition of southern Spoon Bread with pure New England maple syrup added is a fine one for any Thanksgiving feast. Serve it as you would corn pudding.

3 cups milk
1¼ cups white cornmeal
3 eggs
3 tablespoons butter
1 teaspoon salt
1¾ teaspoons baking
  powder
½ cup maple syrup

Preheat the oven to 400° F.

In a large, heavy saucepan, bring the milk to a boil. Pour the cornmeal slowly into the milk, using a whisk to blend it in without lumping. The mixture will thicken very quickly, and when it does, remove from heat.

Beat the eggs for 2 minutes at high speed in the large bowl of an electric mixer. While the eggs are beating, put butter in a 10-inch cast-iron skillet and place in the preheated oven until the butter is melted.

Add the cornmeal mixture to the beaten eggs a large spoonful at a time, continuing to beat with the mixer now set at medium speed. In between spoonfuls, add the salt and baking powder. Add the maple syrup, and when it is blended in, add the hot butter from the skillet.

Continue to beat for 10 minutes, being sure to scrape down the sides of the mixing bowl frequently so everything is blended together creamily. Turn the mixture out into the skillet and return to the preheated oven for 25 minutes. Serve hot, with butter if you like.

Serves 8.

SOLO THANKSGIVING 1

Much has been written about the solo holiday blues, but there are those who relish the solitude of Thanksgiving without family or friends and revel in the opportunity to celebrate exactly as they wish.

For Kathy Carpenter, the first Thanksgiving after her divorce was actually a heady experience. Kathy lives in Chicago, her parents were in Florida, but it wasn't the distance that made her choose not to leave her own home for theirs.

"I didn't want to go 'home' to my parents because I was an adult and I had a home of my own. I also didn't want to become an orphan attached to someone else's table. But then I didn't want to cook hot dogs and sit around in my pajamas and feel sorry for myself."

So Kathy—who rarely cooks the rest of the time—decided to roast a hen and make a few side dishes according to her mother's recipes. The food filled her apartment with a festive aroma. She set the table with a pretty cloth and a single place setting of her best china, silver, and crystal. She put her favorite music on the sound system and lit candles. She opened a bottle of very good wine and with it feasted on a perfectly elegant meal.

"It was actually kind of exhilarating. Not having to socialize made it seem more like a holiday from the pressures of work. I ate early, and later, when things might have started to drag or seem glum, I created a film festival for myself, going to see several movies, one after another."

She enjoyed the day so much that it's become an annual Thanksgiving ritual. And she says, "It's kind of exciting to realize that holidays don't have to be created by your mommy and daddy."

Pumpkin Brûlée

At the Science Hill Inn in Shelbyville, Kentucky, mother and daughter chef/owners Donna and Ellen Gill specialize in giving traditional regional foods sleek new turns. Their Pumpkin Brûlée is one of the finest desserts I've ever tasted, and an imaginative substitute for the Thanksgiving pumpkin pie. Although it's rich, it feels light. And, as an additional asset, the bulk of preparation takes place the day before the feast, with only the glazing of the brown sugar crust to come just before serving. Save leftover pumpkin for a hearty pumpkin soup.

3 cups heavy cream
⅓ cup granulated sugar
6 egg yolks
4 tablespoons canned
   pumpkin
1 teaspoon cinnamon
½ teaspoon ground nutmeg
Brown sugar

Preheat the oven to 350° F.

Put the cream and sugar in a saucepan and heat over medium-low heat, stirring, until all the sugar is dissolved. With electric mixer at low speed, combine the egg yolks, pumpkin, and spices. Slowly pour into the warm cream and mix well.

Pour into 8 individual (at least 6-ounce) ramekins. Put the ramekins in a large baking pan and fill with water halfway up the side of the ramekins. Bake in the preheated oven for 25 to 30 minutes, until the custard is set. Remove the ramekins from the baking dish and allow to cool to room temperature. Cover with plastic wrap and refrigerate overnight.

Just before serving, cover the top of custard with a thin layer of brown sugar. Pop under the preheated broiler and brown until sugar begins to caramelize.

Serves 8.

SOLO THANKSGIVING 2

Like most college towns, Gambier, Ohio, pretty much closes down when Kenyon College takes a vacation. Not the Kenyon College Bookstore, however. Jack Finfrock, manager of the store and a professor of Chinese language and literature at the college, says that "we decided the store should be open at night and on all holidays because we wanted to be people's second home."

The bookstore has become that, with a lot of students eating breakfast there, then returning later to study and meet with friends. On holidays when most of the students go home, Finfrock says the bookstore is a real haven for foreign students and kids who don't want to or can't go home.

"They come here and get a bite to eat. We've got tables and chairs all around the store. And they can read the magazines and maybe some friends come in, and that's the way a lot of them spend Thanksgiving."

A few years ago, though, the holiday took a surprising and delightful twist when a customer brought in turkey with all the trimmings.

"She lived here in town and was a real regular, a woman in her seventies then. She died a few years ago. She was a very famous breeder of corgis, and I think her family was her dogs. Her husband was gone. She had made Thanksgiving dinner for friends, and there was a lot of food. She said she was afraid whoever was working and hanging out at the store wouldn't get a hot dinner. So she and her friends wrapped everything up in tinfoil so it would stay warm and brought it on over to the store. And everybody got to eat a real Thanksgiving dinner. It was some celebration. It was a total gift."

Eleven

Hanukkah

The evolution of the Jewish holiday Hanukkah is a lesson in how our celebrations change according to the needs of the community.

The origin of Hanukkah was the victory of Judah Maccabee and his followers, who in 165 B.C.E. overthrew the Syrians who had forbidden them to worship as they wished. Subsequently they rededicated the Temple, and it is this religious act, not the military victory, that is emphasized in the celebration.

Hanukkah means "dedication," although the holiday is more commonly referred to as the Feast of Lights. That's because in the rededication of the Temple, the lamps were supposed to burn for eight days, but there was enough consecrated oil only for one. Nevertheless, tradition has it that when the lamps were lit, they burned the full eight days.

Hanukkah is a minor holiday, which means that work is not ceased, as it is on Passover or the High Holy Days. In the past, it was primarily a winter holiday of family and home, with the candle-lighting ritual each night and traditional games played.

But because of its proximity to Christmas (it traditionally occurs in December or at the very end of November), Hanukkah has become a more elaborate celebration, particularly in America. Hanukkah symbols such as the menorah, an eight-branch candelabrum in which ritual candles are lighted each night, are made into decorations and sold along with those for Christmas trees. Hanukkah greeting cards are sold and sent.

The tradition of giving children gold coins, or candies in gold paper, is often supplanted or augmented by a more elaborate exchange of presents. The pervasive commercialization of Christmas has also affected Hanukkah, and some parents and grandparents give their children a gift on each of the eight nights, or a very large present at the end of the holiday, even though originally this was not a part of the celebration.

Contemporary Jews often struggle with how to keep this celebration holy and true to their own traditions while not allowing it to be overshadowed by the Christmas frenzy that permeates American culture at the same time. The evolution of Ken Saltzberg's Hanukkah traces a process we can all recognize of learning to balance assimilation with establishing our own, truly meaningful traditions.

ONE MAN'S LATKEFEST

Ken Saltzberg, forty-six, grew up in Santa Barbara in a fairly typical Jewish family. He still lives in California, but his living situation is not one that the majority of Americans would call typical.

Ken and his wife, Catherine, are members of an intentional community called Monan's Rill, located on several hundred acres in the mountains east of Santa Rosa.

If this brings visions of hippie spiritual cults to mind, wipe them out. The community was not a product of the 1960s counterculture. There was no guru or particular religious or spiritual affiliation that linked the members of the group, although many of their practices are borrowed from the Quakers, including the concept of consensus in decision-making and silence in their meetings.

The members of Monan's Rill share a commitment to using the land responsibly and to being socially active. Ken says the group also "understands that whatever you do affects others, and believes that shared work is often better than individual work."

Ken describes the beliefs of the members as "pretty eclectic." The group has always had a wide age range. The current group of thirty ranges from two to eighty years old.

Ken and Catherine joined the community in 1980, after finishing a Peace Corps assignment in Guatemala, where they had met. They came to Monan's Rill because a Quaker scoutmaster who influenced Ken early in life and had remained a close friend was a member.

"I am not a joiner. I did not want to be a part of a religious organization, but it was very important to us to live as part of a community," Ken says.

At Monan's Rill, every family has an individual home on the property, but there is common green space, shared workdays, and common buildings. There are also shared rituals.

Ken often finds himself in the position of creating these rituals for the community.

One year for New Year's he asked everyone in the community to write down a resolution but not share it with the group. Instead they put the slips of paper in a box. "A year later we took them out and said, 'How did we do?' A lot of people felt very successful and it was a very affirming kind of celebration."

Recently the group wanted to have a retreat in which the members would focus on the use of the land, both in the past and in the future. Ken found himself incorporating some Passover rituals into the ceremonies.

"I was thinking about how to impart to our kids the history of this place, and I thought about the tradition of the four questions at Passover, how the children ask the questions about the meaning of the event.

"So we asked the founders of the community who are still here to choose a spot on the land that they would want to have remembered as theirs. And then, as a group, we took a walk. And at each spot the children, in the traditional Jewish manner, would ask that particular founder the equivalent of the four questions. In the process of the answering we all learned not just why the spot was important but the importance of the person, the community, the land itself. And it had more meaning for the kids than it might have otherwise because they were active participants."

But if creating rituals for the community has come somewhat naturally to Ken, establishing rituals for himself has been a slower process.

Catherine was raised Methodist, and Ken says their three children, all in their teens, "usually call themselves atheist, but if somebody asks questions about Judaism in their school, they can answer."

As for their family's observance of holidays, Ken says, "There is naturally a conflict when you merge holidays. In my wife's family, Christmas was a gift-giving time. In my family, when I was growing up, Hanukkah was changed to be equivalent. But we knew that this wasn't really how we wanted to celebrate the holiday."

Ken and Catherine first looked for shared ground on which to establish their holiday observances.

"What each holiday shares is a celebration of light. So what first evolved for us was a celebration that combined Advent and its candle-lighting with Hanukkah."

The combination celebration was a community ritual for several years, Ken said, because there were other members who were Jewish. But members have come and gone over the years, and Ken is now the only Jew at Monan's Rill.

"It seemed strange to me, having an equally weighted ceremony. So what happened next for the community is we chose instead to have a solstice celebration. We still focus on the light and we draw names for a gift-giving ritual. But for those gifts, we have to think of something special about the particular person and give a gift that represents it. And then we light a candle for that person."

But Ken still felt a strong need to celebrate his own background, to have a Hanukkah that had meaning for him.

"It is not really a religious issue for me. If I could, I would click out all religions, because I see religion dividing and separating people far more than embracing them.

"But I understand the importance of ritual. And I also understand that I am a Jew, and as I grow older, it has become even more important to me to assert who I am.

"I think partly because I have been away from [extended] family and creating a family of my own in this community, I've had to consider what matters and what doesn't, what rituals I want to honor.

"So even though we changed the community celebration, I knew that I still wanted to celebrate Hanukkah. And what made sense for me was to have a big latke party. I liked the idea of a celebration based on the food, because people who break bread together build a sense of community."

Ken invited the members of the community, his extended family, and people from the school where he is a principal and the school where his wife teaches to come to a Hanukkah latke fest at the new Monan's Rill community center.

"The party was on a Sunday, so on the Saturday before, about thirty people—my family plus seven or eight friends—stopped over to help: to peel potatoes and cook and eat some."

There were about a hundred people invited for Sunday, so the frying was a major production.

"We had vessels everywhere. When you're cooking for a hundred, anything that has high sides so it doesn't splatter becomes a frying pan."

On the day of the celebration, the latkes were rewarmed and everyone invited brought a potluck dish.

"We had twenty dreidels and tons of Hershey's Kisses to be used for betting. There was lots of Hanukkah music on CD and we did a little dancing.

We brought the menorah down to the community center, but ended up not lighting it. There had been a lot of rain for a long time prior, and the night of the party turned out to be such a pretty night. So people wanted to go for a walk instead, and that was perfect."

Ken said it also seemed like the perfect Hanukkah celebration for him, at least for the moment.

"In a way I was introducing everyone from my different families to one another, my relatives and the community here and the family of my school. And it was also like I was introducing them to a part of me. It seemed to work."

Potato Latkes

Ken's philosophy is that "it's infinitely easier to say don't eat anything cooked in oil all year long and then on one ding-dang day eat some greasy latkes" than it is to try and come up with a good-tasting, low-fat recipe for latkes.

In addition, he peels the potatoes, uses raw (not sautéed) onions in the batter, and grates both in a food processor—all bones of contention among latke-makers.

"My Jewish mama taught me to save the liquid from the potatoes, let it settle and drain off the top, then mix the starch into the batter. That's the most important trick I know," he says—and a good one it seems to be.

"As far as I'm concerned, there's only one hard and fast rule about latkes: nobody eats ketchup on them ever."

Sour cream is a traditional topper, but Ken says, "Why should we invite tsuris?" (A Yiddish word for heartaches.) Nonfat yogurt is a sensible, though not so savory, substitute, but these crisp and golden latkes are delicious with no condiment.

As for what other dish goes with them, Ken said just about everything seemed to work at the Monan's Rill potluck. I had a friend who always served latkes with plain steamed broccoli, a combination that was just heavenly and also pretty wise. Applesauce is also a traditional accompaniment, and Elaine Corn's recipe for Rosh Hashanah Sweet New Year Applesauce (page 238), but without the extra honey in the bowl, would be perfect.

6 medium-sized potatoes
1 large onion
¼ cup flour
½ teaspoon baking powder
1 teaspoon salt
Freshly ground black
  pepper to taste
1 egg
Vegetable oil

Peel the potatoes and onion. Cut the onion into 4 or 5 chunks and alternate putting the potatoes and onion through a food processor using the grating attachment. Remove the grating attachment and put in the cutting blade. Pulse until the mixture looks like applesauce, but is not too runny.

Put in a colander and push out as much liquid into a bowl as possible. Set aside the liquid and place the potatoes and onions in a large mixing bowl.

Sprinkle the flour, baking powder, salt, and pepper on the potatoes and toss to mix. Break the egg on top and mix in. Drain the potato water from the reserved liquid and add the remaining starch, mixing well.

In a heavy skillet (cast-iron is best), heat ½ inch oil over medium-high heat until very hot but not smoking. (The oil is ready when a fleck of potato tossed into it sizzles and dances.) Use a large serving spoon to drop the potato batter by spoonfuls into the oil. Don't crowd the skillet! Cook a few latkes at a time until well browned on each side.

Remove and drain on paper towels, then transfer to a warm plate until all the latkes are done.

Makes 2½ to 3 dozen.

NOTE: Latkes are really at their absolute most delicious eaten as soon as possible after leaving the skillet. If you can, have several skillets going at once and fry more than one batch at a time, so the process doesn't take too long. Electric skillets and several cooks in the kitchen are a good idea for a latke party.

It was hot in the kitchen, and Chaya's face glowed too. She stood in front of the stove, holding an iron hook, shoving the pots and pans back and forth, heating up one, rubbing another with greased paper, now pouring a spoonful of batter into the bubbling fat, now lifting out a crisply cooked potato pancake. The chubby pancakes, dotted with beads of fat, jumped up and down over the fire like new babies being slapped into life.

We gazed at the cook as if she were a magician.

—BELLA CHAGALL, *FIRST ENCOUNTER*

Twelve

Christmas

Whenever I thought about finding the people to interview and write about in the Christmas chapter, I was haunted by the feeling that somewhere there was the perfect Christmas family having the perfect Christmas celebration, and it was important that I should find them: "I'm dreaming of a right Christmas . . ."

They were people who had simplified their rituals, sure, but they had them, and, in my imagination, those rituals were repeated year after year with purpose. Theirs was a Lake Wobegon Christmas where the men were all active participants, the women were never stressed out, and the children were all above average when it came to sharing presents with brothers, sisters, cousins, and the poor.

I began to believe that I was haunted, not by the ghosts of Christmas Past, Christmas Present, or Christmas Future, but by a tiny Martha Stewart who sat on my shoulder and whispered that everything could be just exactly as it ought to be with enough time, clever thinking, and hoarded egg cartons.

My Christmas miracle is that somewhere along the way I came to my senses. Yes, I found people who loved Christmas passionately, who did certain things each year and felt that the way they celebrated was special. But I discovered that by and large these were people whose celebrations were flexible. The folks who seemed to have the best Christmas memories, the most joyful Christmas rituals, made changes in them on a regular basis.

I began to think about my own tender Christmas memories and realized that instead of all being cut from one identical holiday cloth, they were as different from one another as any year is from the next. Yes, I remember most Christmases as being joyful times marked by the family gathering, a sense of homecoming. But I realized that we had never celebrated in exactly the same way, or even at the same time from year to year. My father often worked the swing shift, so the gathering might be on Christmas Eve one year, Christmas morning or evening the next. And when my husband and I returned to Kentucky with a child of our own, the traditional celebration at my mother's with cousins and kin started moving around the calendar even more, sometimes happening now as much as a week before or after the holiday.

It didn't seem to matter at all when we gathered, however, or whether we ate the traditional turkey or brought in barbecued pork (as we've started to do in recent years), or if there were presents or not. What mattered was the feeling of connection (no matter that it is tenuous, with some of us seeing one another only this once a year) between the people at the gathering and between this one and all the years past.

Of those years past, it was surprisingly the least "typical" or "perfect" Christmases that I remembered with the strongest affection. There was one year when my father was working overtime and lots of late shifts, with hardly time to do anything but sleep restlessly during the day, when he was home. My mother was quite depressed, and since I was in my very early teens, she'd decided that the family dinner would be enough, and we could do without a tree and hoopla that year. But I was determined otherwise and walked up to the tree stand on the corner with two dollars from my allowance and picked out a short and stubby little fir that I dragged laboriously home.

I may have felt like the Little Match Girl for a moment, and this story may sound poignant in the retelling. The fact is, the tree looked ridiculous propped up on a table where it still didn't quite reach six feet and tilted to the side most precariously. And it presided a little absurdly over the dining room, not in the usual place of honor in a corner of the living room. But that sorry little tree soon became a point of hilarity, and every time one of us looked at it, we'd laugh. It wasn't simply that the tree restored some much needed humor to the family at that time; its ridiculous imperfection actually seemed to take the pressure off. And in my memory, at least, that turned out to be one of the best Christmases we'd ever had.

So in the spirit of imperfection and improvisation that marks the very best of holiday cheer, here's Christmas.

A TREE-TRIMMING PARTY

The first two Christmases that Gail and Dick Kaukas were married, they didn't have a Christmas tree. That's because they were living in Africa, where they met as Peace Corps volunteers.

"The first Christmas tree of ours that I remember was when we moved back, in an apartment in Hartford, Connecticut," Gail said. "That was in 1967. We had a party to decorate it, which seemed like a good idea because basically I'm lazy."

Actually, "extremely busy" would be more accurate. In the next few years, the Kaukas family would expand to include daughters Jenny Lee and Robin. The family moved back to Gail's hometown, Louisville, Kentucky, where Dick became a reporter at the *Louisville Times* and, later, the *Courier-Journal*. Gail worked in restaurants and catering, went back to school for a law degree, and eventually took a job with the city's law department.

In the midst of all this activity, in the winter of 1974, the Kaukases moved to their present house, a two-story craftsman bungalow with a cozy, narrow living room and fireplace. It's a wonderful house they have come to love and make distinctively their own, but that first year was not an easy one.

Gail recalls: "We hadn't wanted to leave the house we were living in, but it was a rental and we had to. So we got this house and moved in on December 16. The tree was really important for us that year. It symbolized something about making this our home."

The tree was placed in the front window of the living room, almost blocking the door leading in from the entry hall.

"I recently read somewhere that your tree should be big for your house—that you should have to walk around it, so you're aware of it," Gail says. "That's something I guess we've always done—either instinctively, or just because there really wasn't anywhere else to put it."

Decorating the tree was a family ritual at that time, although Dick says, "The four of us got together to decorate, but mostly it was Gail who did the work."

That worked out until Gail started law school in 1978 and Lee and Robin were thirteen and eleven.

"I realized that I wasn't going to have the time or the focus or the energy to do the tree that year," Gail said. "Of course, we can always find the time and energy for a party, so we decided to invite people over to decorate our Christmas tree."

That impromptu party has become an annual tradition for the Kaukas family and a group of their friends, including my family. No matter how far behind we are in our own holiday agenda, whether our own tree is decorated yet or not, we always try to make room for the Kaukas tree-decorating party.

It seems that most Christmas celebrations are either close-knit family affairs or big social get-togethers without much intimacy, like office parties or open houses hosted by folks you don't see any other time of the year.

But the Kaukas family's tree party is both casual and intimate. And while it's not exclusively for family members, the friends who come by are good ones, and the evening is a celebration of the sustenance that such friendships give—sustenance that is particularly evident as things change for the family over the years.

Both Lee and Robin are now in their twenties and have lives and commitments of their own, although the family Christmas is a ritual they try not to miss.

Still, when Lee was in high school, she began to pursue what looks to be a lifelong love of travel. She spent a year in Spain, followed by several years in Japan during college. And she now makes her home on the East Coast.

"That first year she was gone, I invited lots and lots and lots of people over to decorate the tree," Gail says. "It was real hard not having her here. I wanted to fill up the house. And it really seemed to help. It was hard to be mopey with a house full of funny people. What was really great was she called right in the middle of everything. Somebody asked how we arranged that, but it was just luck that she picked that time to call."

Friends of both Lee and Robin still come to the decorating party, some years when neither of the girls is home.

"Some of those kids become like your family, too, so it's really natural to have them here," Gail says. "One year we had two Japanese exchange students. That was great, trying to see the whole thing through their eyes."

The evening tends to follow a certain order, although no one would likely call it a "ritual" or even suggest it's actually organized.

"I put the lights on the tree before everybody gets here because I still think one person ought to do that," Gail says. For several years there was an electric train that Dick would arrange around the bottom of the tree, but the gradual erosion of the railroad and the acquisition of two cats (Woody and Bernie) and two dogs (Moshi and Arlo) eliminated the train.

"When folks start to come in, at first everybody is doing the tree like crazy," Gail said. "Then it kind of fades off because we put the food out and everybody pays attention to that. Then later a few people head back to the tree, and the anal retentives in the crowd finish up."

The food is always warm and convivial, with a cheese fondue pot standing in as a hearth-like gathering place. Hot cider, red wine, and champagne make the evening festive. Someone may make a stab at caroling, or someone else might pull out a board game, but mostly it's conversation that fuels the evening. Because it's often a weeknight, the party usually winds down around 10 or 11 p.m. And as we drive the blocks back to our house in what is almost always a beautiful and silent night, it seems that the Christmas season has officially begun.

FONDUE STUFF

You can buy a new fondue pot at most any cookware store, but why should you when chances are you can find a used one at any secondhand store for a fraction of the cost?

Then again, you can also make do nicely without a special pot at all. A heavy skillet or a wide chafing dish may be used as a fondue pot. What you are looking for is a pot that can move from stove to warming spot. It should be heavy to retain heat, but wide so that the cheese mixture inside doesn't get too hot and more than one guest can dunk into the fondue at a time.

Long-handled fondue forks provide more maneuverability and make dunking easier, but they aren't absolutely necessary, either. Plain forks will do fine. (Single-pronged skewers, like those used for grilling kebabs, won't grip the bread securely enough. You'll end up with lots of cubes lost and floating in the pot.)

A chafing-dish frame with a candle underneath is a pretty way to keep the fondue warm while serving, and a portable electric burner turned very low will work well. If your party is informal and your kitchen accessible, it can also be fun and convivial to gather everyone around the stove.

Remember that you want to keep the mixture warm but not really hot. If it gets too hot, the cheese may turn stringy and unappetizing. If this happens, try mixing in a little of the warmed beer.

PUT ON YOUR LEDERHOSEN . . .

You can, of course, substitute a variety of cheeses, add seasonings, or make other changes to taste with the following basic fondue recipe, but there are some principles you want to remember. When heated to certain temperatures, the protein in cheese will coagulate and the whole thing will become an unappetizing, stringy mass. Hard, aged cheeses can tolerate higher temperatures and so are better suited for fondues. Also, the addition of alcohol lowers the boiling point so the fondue can be kept toasty without the risk of curdling if it has an alcohol base.

Swiss fondue uses only Gruyère cheese, has ½ teaspoon freshly grated nutmeg instead of Tabasco, and has 2 cups dry white wine and ¼ cup Kirsch, according to that 1947 classic The Dione Lucas Book of French Cooking.

Lucas says Bock beer may be substituted for the wine in season, but only if tested for excellence in the Swiss manner: "Put on your lederhosen, then pour a small puddle of beer on a varnished wooden stool. Sit on the stool for about 30 minutes and then rise slowly. If the stool rises with you, the Bock beer is of excellent quality and should make a nice flavorful fondue."

Christmas Cheese Fondue

"I've always had cheese fondue for the tree party because I thought that everybody scooting in around the pot was kind of festive," Gail says.

The fondue pot, with its warming candle burning merrily underneath, is placed on the buffet table in the dining room, and guests queue up with long-handled forks in hand.

Chunks of French bread with superbly chewy crusts get dipped in the molten cheese and consumed faster than you can say "Yum."

When asked about the bread, Dick Kaukas took a deep breath, then earnestly began to explain: "First you line the oven with ceramic tiles. Ones from Italy are good. And when they are very hot, you must throw water on them to steam—"

He was interrupted by Gail, swatting him with a handy oven mitt.

"We go out and get the bread from a bakery that day so we don't go crazy," she said. "The point of this party is to make things simpler, not more complicated. Every year I start looking through cookbooks and I see these recipes for more elaborate fondues and I think I could do something really different or special. And then I think, why? This is already special. And, more important, it's really, really good."

She is right. So right that it might behoove you to make two batches of this cheese fondue. If you do, make them one after the other. Don't try doubling the recipe, since it is harder to control the meltability of the fondue if you do. One large baguette of good French or Italian bread will make enough cubes to sop up one pot of fondue. And one pot will serve 8 if there are lots of other goodies on the buffet table.

½ pound sharp Wisconsin
   Cheddar cheese
½ pound Gruyère cheese
2 tablespoons flour
½ teaspoon kosher salt
¼ teaspoon freshly grated
   black pepper
1 clove of garlic

Grate the cheese into a large bowl, then toss with the flour, salt, and pepper until mixed.

Split open the garlic clove and rub around the inside of your fondue pot. Pour in 1½ cups of the beer and heat over medium-low heat until the beer is steamy but not near boiling. (Place the remaining ½ cup beer in a saucepan and keep warm on the back of the stove in case it is needed to thin the fondue later.)

Gradually sprinkle the cheese mixture

2 cups beer
Dash of Tabasco sauce
1 loaf crusty bread, cut in
  1-inch cubes

into the warm beer in the fondue pot, a handful at a time. Stir well after each addition, and make sure each batch of cheese is melted and blended into the beer before adding another.

When all the cheese is incorporated, add the Tabasco, stir, and serve immediately.

The fondue will do best if served in its pot over a warming candle or on a portable heating element turned to low. It may be necessary to stir it from time to time while serving. If the mixture begins to thicken, thin it by stirring in a little of the warmed beer.

Serves 8 as a buffet item, 4 as a primary course.

Feliz Fritada

Man does not decorate by fondue alone, nor does woman, so the Kaukas family's buffet table also contains the makings for sandwiches and a hot entree. Sometimes it's soup, but the most fun is when it's one of Dick's fritadas.

That's because Dick's fritadas are not only delicious but entertaining. Although there is plenty to do around the tree in the living room, and even more to entice at the buffet in the dining room, there is always a clump of people who scrunch around the stove island in the Kaukas family kitchen.

The fritada is a perfect production for such theater in the round. The Italian (frittata) or Spanish version of the omelet, it looks dramatic to produce, but is actually more forgiving in execution than its French cousin. While the French omelet requires perfectly set eggs wrapped seamlessly around its filling, the fritada gets everything mixed up together first before jumping in the pan. There the eggs and goodies are cooked over low heat until the bottom and sides are set, then it's flipped out of the pan onto a plate, slid from the plate back into the pan, and browned on the other side.

Although this sounds tricky, it's fairly easy if you follow Dick's tips and loosen the edges of the fritada with a knife before dumping it onto the plate. (Wearing oven mitts prevents burns from flying food or oil.) And even if the fritada breaks in the process, you can just pat it all back together in the pan and pretend that you meant for that to happen. At least, that's what Dick does.

Of course, you can also just slide the whole thing under the broiler long enough to set the eggs on top.

The recipe Dick likes the best was adapted from Penelope Casas's *Foods and Wines of Spain*. It has ¼ pound each of cooked ham and sweet Italian sausage sautéed with the potatoes. For a vegetarian version that still has lots of Christmas color, we've substituted chopped calamata olives for the meat. If you can find good asparagus, you may want to add half a dozen spears cut in thirds to the mix.

2 medium-sized potatoes
1 medium-sized red bell
  pepper
24 calamata olives
½ cup frozen cut green
  beans
½ cup frozen peas
4 tablespoons olive oil
1 small onion, chopped
8 eggs
Salt to taste
Freshly ground black
  pepper to taste

Peel the potatoes, cut in half, and place in a saucepan with cold water to cover. Bring to a boil, cover, and lower the heat to a simmer. Cook about 20 minutes, until the potatoes are tender when pierced with a fork but still hold their shape.

While the potatoes are cooking, roast the red pepper (see Variation on page 287), remove the peel, stem, and seeds, and chop coarsely.

Pit and tear the olives. (Pit olives the same way you peel garlic. Lay a few on a cutting board and lay the flat surface of a large knife over them. Firmly strike the flat surface of the knife with the heel of your hand, lightly smashing the olives underneath. The flesh will separate from the pit and it can be easily removed, and the olives torn into small pieces.)

When the potatoes are ready, remove from the water and set aside to cool for a few minutes before chopping into bite-sized chunks. Add the frozen beans and peas to the hot water and simmer, covered, for 5 minutes, then drain.

Pour 2 tablespoons of the olive oil into a 10-to-12-inch skillet and sauté the onion until it is softened. Add the potatoes and cook for 5 more minutes. Then add the rest of the vegetables and sauté for 5 more minutes.

In a large bowl, beat the eggs until blended. Add the contents of the skillet to the eggs, sprinkle with salt and pepper, and then mix.

Wipe out the skillet with a paper towel. Add 1 tablespoon of the oil and heat again until it is very hot. Pour the egg-and-vegetable mixture into the skillet and turn heat to medium-low. Shake the pan occasionally to keep the fritada from sticking to the bottom. When the eggs are set on the bottom and at the edges (usually about 10 minutes), run a knife around the edges to loosen the fritada, then invert a large plate over the top of the skillet and flip the whole thing over so the fritada turns out on the plate and the skillet is empty. (If pieces of the fritada do stick to the skillet, scrape them out with a spatula and pat them into place on the inverted fritada.)

Add the last tablespoon of oil to the skillet and swirl to coat it evenly. Slide the fritada back into the pan and cook until the other side is just done— a matter of minutes.

Turn out onto a warm serving plate and serve immediately.

Serves 8 as a buffet item or 4 as a main course.

Spicy Sugarplums

While the buffet at the Kaukas party is full of savory items, the dining room table is packed with sweets. Baking cookies and candies is a tradition passed on from Gail's mother, Lee Hutchison, to her daughter and granddaughters. Some years, in the weeks before Christmas, all four of them are crammed into the Kaukas kitchen mixing, rolling, and spooning out a panoply of treats.

Of all the cookies and candies that show up each year, these modest little oatmeal sweets have become my favorite. Perhaps it's their surprising combination of light texture but sturdy chew. Or maybe it's the evocative name. At any rate, visions of sugarplums will dance in your head long after you've nibbled the last.

For Lee's classic recipe, use allspice instead of cardamom and ¾ cup raisins instead of the chopped figs and crystallized ginger. I like to make a batch of each.

1 cup vegetable shortening

1 cup brown sugar, firmly
  packed

1 cup granulated sugar

2 eggs, unbeaten

½ teaspoon salt

½ teaspoon vanilla extract

2 teaspoons cinnamon

¼ teaspoon ground
  cardamom

Preheat oven to 350° F. and lightly grease 2 cookie sheets.

In the large bowl of an electric mixer, cream the shortening and sugars until just blended. Add the eggs, salt, vanilla, spices, and milk. When blended, remove the bowl from the mixer and add the walnuts, figs, and ginger, mixing with a wooden spoon.

Sift together the flour and baking soda and fold into the rest. Add the oats and blend. Spoon out in tablespoon-sized mounds onto the baking sheets, leaving space between the

¾ teaspoon ground nutmeg

1 tablespoon milk

½ cup chopped walnuts

½ cup chopped dried figs

¼ cup chopped crystallized
  ginger

1¼ cups all-purpose flour

1 teaspoon baking soda

3 cups rolled oats

mounds. Press lightly with the back of a fork. Bake for 12 minutes, until lightly browned. Place the sheets on wire racks to cool for 2 minutes before removing the cookies from the sheets with a spatula. Cool completely before packing in airtight containers. (Be sure to eat a few warm ones with milk first, though.)

Makes 4 to 5 dozen.

AN OCCASIONAL CHRISTMAS WITH FRIENDS

For the last few years, Sara Jo Hooper and Trudy Sullivan of Louisville, Kentucky, have celebrated Christmas together. Both are single mothers whose sons, Ian and Paul, were good buddies in high school. Because the boys were in and out of each other's homes so much, the mothers eventually met and, despite a twenty-year difference in their ages, became friends.

One Thanksgiving they packed up a turkey, the boys, and a trunkful of board games and drove off to spend the weekend at a Kentucky state park.

"We both wanted a change in that celebration, to move away from the rituals we'd had when we were married," Sara Jo says. "So it was a marvelous solution to pool our resources, change the place, change the mood entirely. You break a pattern by creating a new one."

Christmas followed rather naturally and casually.

"I don't think it was any big plan, we just decided we should have our Christmas meal together. It was perfect for Ian and Paul—they were going to be spending the day together no matter what we did," Trudy says.

"We don't do presents and there isn't any big pressure about it. We've done it on Christmas Eve and also on late Christmas Day, whatever seems to fit.

"Whenever I've gone to holiday celebrations, I've played a role. First it was the daughter and the cousin, and then when I got married, I was the wife. But my favorite role of all is the mother. And what I appreciate most of all about this celebration is that I can be the mother and that's all."

"It's been a perfect celebration," Sara Jo concurs.

And they may never do it again.

The boys went away to different colleges in 1994, and although the friendship has continued strongly over the miles, the mothers anticipate that the way the boys will want to spend their holidays from now on may change.

"For one thing, they're just going to come back and sleep a lot over Christmas," Trudy says.

And they will probably spend a great deal of time out with friends they've not seen for a while. Christmas break, which used to be a holiday from school chums, a chance to cocoon a little, will now be an opportunity to cram in as many visits as possible with other long-lost friends.

"It could be that it's time to start another tradition, and that would be fine," Sara Jo says.

Neither she nor Trudy is a stranger to change, especially in holiday celebrations.

Trudy grew up in a rural area of middle Tennessee, and her holidays were mountain family feasts with aunts and uncles and cousins all gathered at her grandmother's "homeplace." Her husband's family was also large, "and that was a wonderful time with great families coming together and a lot of talking and food and laughter and joy."

Curiously, though, she relishes the quiet times of Christmas and said that she has often enjoyed the holidays spent on her own, something she traces back to her childhood.

"When I was little, the men would hunt deer together on the day after Christmas. It was a big family ritual, and I guess to make me feel a part of it, they would send me out on Christmas Day to sight the deer. It would be cold, with your breath steaming in front of your face. And I would walk the ridges of those Tennessee hills, looking for the deer. It was a job that made me feel good about myself, and it was something I loved just for that time I had on the ridges alone.

"One of the best Christmas memories I have is a few years ago when it was that lull on Christmas Day. The presents were over and people were gone and Paul had fallen asleep in another room. And I was sitting by a window when it started to snow. Great big flakes coming slowly out of the sky, so peaceful. It was a time of centering for me, a time of reflection. And whenever I think of Christmas, it's that moment.

"I tend to think of the Nativity as a solitude story. I mean, when you consider it, it was the one time they were actually a family. So soon it all blew apart, but for that little moment they were just a family, alone."

Sara Jo also grew up in Tennessee, but remembers that her childhood Christmases sometimes "had a downside. My daddy was a construction worker, and his jobs were seasonal and sometimes not at all. So there were Christmases when there wasn't much to celebrate.

"I think when I married, it became extremely important for me to create a lot of the happiness I'd wanted as a child at Christmas. We really established a lot of rituals. There were stockings and presents, and I felt I needed to have a very special Christmas breakfast, and then right after that it was get into the kitchen and start this fabulous Christmas dinner. We always had a gorgeous Christmas meal that I never, ever, ever enjoyed, I was so worn out."

When the first marriage ended, Sara Jo bought a turn-of-the-century three-story house in Old Louisville and set about filling the rooms with interesting boarders and friends. There were several interns from Actors Theater of Louisville living there the first year, as well as Jewish friends. So they put a huge tree in the hallway and then set up a latke-frying station in the living room where they made potato pancakes for Hanukkah.

"The tree was decorated with little baskets full of snacks and goodies, and the deal was that on Twelfth Night we'd take the tree down and eat all the goodies that were left. We traded gifts, too, mostly silly stuff. And one thing we did that first year was I made a big batch of flour dough and everyone made ornaments for the tree from it.

"We celebrated like that—or some kind of variation on that—for a few years until I married again. But I still have that box of ornaments, and when I take it out every year, that's a really tender moment for me.

"I don't think you have to repeat rituals over and over slavishly for them to have meaning. Sometimes just the memory is enough. And I like the idea of changing the rituals, starting new ones that fit new situations. In fact, I think the common thread for me about all the Christmases I've had is that what we do changes. It's shaped by who is there in our lives at the time, and that's really a wonderful tradition."

Christmas Pimiento Cheese

"There are two things you have to have to eat for Christmas," Trudy Sullivan says.

"One of them is that goofy 'nuts and bolts' snack mix out of cereal and nuts and Worcestershire sauce. My mother always makes that for us and sends it to us in the mail if she isn't going to be here. One year she wrote Paul a letter in October and said, 'I've started the nuts and bolts,' and she sent him the receipt from the grocery so he wouldn't worry."

The other food that Trudy has to have is pimiento-cheese-stuffed celery stalks.

"I don't know why. We always had that when I was a kid. There's something about the way it looks on the relish plate that just starts any Christmas dinner off right."

I agree, and this version of a classic cheese spread, made with roasted fresh peppers and a little minced sun-dried tomato is particularly festive.

2 small red bell peppers or
   4–5 fresh pimiento peppers
1 pound Colby cheese
⅓ cup minced oil-packed
   sun-dried tomatoes
¼ cup mayonnaise
12 average-sized stalks of
   celery

Roast the peppers (see page 287 for instructions) and peel over a medium-sized bowl so you can catch any juice. Mince the flesh of the peppers and add to the bowl.

Grate the cheese and mix it with the peppers.

Remove the tomatoes from oil (you will need about 4 large ones), pat dry with a paper towel, and mince fine. Add to the cheese and mix well. Add the mayonnaise and stir until the mixture is completely moistened and binds together. Use a little more mayonnaise, if necessary.

Trim the ends of the celery and cut the stalks in half. Use a knife to scoop the pimiento cheese down the middle. Serve on a relish plate with black and green olives.

Makes 24.

There never was such a Christmas dinner as they had that day. The fat turkey was a sight to behold, when Hannah sent him up, stuffed, browned and decorated; so was the plum-pudding, which quite melted in one's mouth; likewise the jellies, in which Amy revelled like a fly in the honey pot. Everything turned out well, which was a mercy, Hannah said, "For my mind was that flustered, mum, that it's a merrycle I didn't roast the pudding, and stuff the turkey with raisins, let alone bilin' of it in a cloth."

—LOUISA MAY ALCOTT, *LITTLE WOMEN*

Roast Turkey with Cornbread Dressing

Simplicity and familiarity are the keys to the Christmas dinners that Sara Jo Hooper, Trudy Sullivan, and their sons share. Sara Jo does the bulk of the cooking because she enjoys it. But while the Christmas meals she once cooked years ago were gourmet tours de force, now she opts for plain turkey and dressing and the few familiar side dishes that Ian loves.

The meal has a decidedly Southern country air, with cornbread dressing on the side, cheese grits, and ambrosia all *de rigueur*. This is perfectly fine for Trudy, who says, "The absolutely worst Christmas dinner I ever cooked was one year when I decided I would do it 'right' and I made a classic New England Christmas dinner right out of some magazine. The food all tasted strange to us, and it wasn't Christmas at all."

The turkey is roasted unstuffed, the way Sara Jo and Trudy grew up eating it. The Cornbread Dressing, made in a big pan on the side, is in some ways more important than the bird.

"One year my sister gave us a country ham for Christmas and we went ahead and made dressing anyway, because what's Christmas without the taste of cornbread, onions, and celery?" Sara Jo says.

The size of the bird to be roasted varies from year to year depending on who is going to be at the meal. Roasting time is determined by the weight of the bird. Allow ½ pound for each person to be served and you'll have enough for Christmas dinner and turkey sandwiches the next day.

1 turkey

Olive oil

A generous handful of fresh
   sage leaves (optional)

1–2 tablespoons flour

Salt to taste

Freshly ground black
   pepper to taste

Frozen turkeys must be defrosted either in the refrigerator or totally submerged in cold water, since defrosting at room temperature may allow bacteria to form. Defrosting in the fridge takes about 2 days for an 8-to-10-pound bird, 3 for a larger one. Submerged in cold water, the bird will defrost in 5 to 6 hours.

Starting the bird at a higher temperature is an old roasting tradition. It was once thought that this process seared the outside, sealing in the juices and making for a moister bird. It doesn't, but it does brown the outside, resulting in a richer taste. Therefore, preheat the oven to 450° F. while you're preparing the turkey for roasting.

Remove the neck and giblets from the cavity and rinse. While the bird is in the oven, toss the neck, liver, and gizzard into a medium-sized pot, cover with water, add a dash of salt, and let simmer for an hour or two, adding water when necessary, to make a stock for gravy.

Rinse the turkey inside and out and pat dry with paper towels. Rub inside and out with olive oil and place sage leaves in the cavity if you'd like a subtle hint of its flavor in the meat.

Place the bird, breast side up, on a lightly greased rack in a pan that is about 2 inches deep. Bind the legs together with string or the metal brace that comes on many turkeys, and tuck skin into the neck flap. Don't worry about tucking in the wings. If you leave them untucked, they'll get toasty brown and they are a great addition to the stockpot when you're making turkey broth later.

Place the turkey in the preheated oven and immediately turn the temperature down to 350° F. If the turkey is under 6 pounds, roast for 18 minutes per pound; for a larger one, 15 minutes per pound. Baste the turkey one-third of the way into the roasting time. Two-thirds of the way through, you may want to take the pan out of the oven and, using oven mitts and proceeding carefully, turn the bird over and finish roasting with its backside up. This will brown the bottom and keep the breast moister—but it's not absolutely essential.

The turkey is done when a meat thermometer in the thickest part of the thigh registers 180° F.; or you can check by piercing the thigh with a fork. If the juices run clear and the flesh feels soft, it is done.

Remove from the oven and let the bird sit for 15 to 25 minutes before carving.

While the bird is cooling, strain the giblet broth. Reserve all the juice and browned bits from the roasting pan as well, for making gravy and seasoning the dressing. Put 3 tablespoons of the pan drippings in a heavy saucepan over medium-low heat. (You want some fat in the juices, but more juice overall.) Blend in 1 or 2 tablespoons flour with a wire whisk. Slowly add 2 cups of the giblet broth. Simmer until thickened to a gravy consistency, stirring all the time to keep lumps from forming. Add salt and pepper to taste. Serve the gravy while hot.

(You may add water or more broth to make additional gravy, or you may want to add defatted pan juices—but remember to save at least a cup of drippings and a cup of broth for the Cornbread Dressing. Refrigerate any extra drippings and broth to be used to make gravy with leftovers the next day, or in soup.)

CORNBREAD DRESSING

This recipe calls for 6 cups cornbread, and in my house that means we start freezing leftover pieces of cornbread sometime after Halloween. We eat cornbread often enough that we have plenty when Christmas rolls around. And if it doesn't come out to quite 6 cups full, then I add cracker or soft bread crumbs.

If you're not from a cornbread-eating family, though, you'll need to make a skilletful first. You may want to do this the day before, just so you don't have one more thing to be baked in the oven. Since you're making the cornbread strictly for dressing, it doesn't have to have eggs in it.

2 tablespoons butter
2 cups white cornmeal
1 teaspoon salt
½ teaspoon baking soda
½ teaspoon baking powder
2 cups buttermilk

1 cup chopped celery
1 cup chopped onion
2 eggs
1 cup turkey broth
1 cup roast turkey
  drippings

Turn oven to 450° F. Place the butter in a 9-inch cast-iron skillet, or other heavy pan, and pop into the oven to heat the pan and melt the butter.

While that's heating, mix the cornmeal with the salt, baking soda, baking powder, and buttermilk. When the butter is starting to turn brown and crackling, remove the skillet from the oven. Whirl it gently to coat the bottom and halfway up the sides of the pan with butter, then pour the rest into the batter. Mix to blend, then turn the batter out into the skillet. Bake for 25 minutes, or until the crust is golden brown. Invert the skillet to get it out of the pan. If you are using it the next day, let cool completely, then wrap in plastic.

When you are ready to make the dressing, preheat the oven to 400° F. Crumble the cornbread into a large bowl. Add the celery and onion and mix well. Beat the 2 eggs to blend, then add to the bowl. Add a cup of broth from the turkey giblets and a cup of drippings from the turkey roasting pan and mix well.

Oil an 11 × 7-inch baking pan. Turn the dressing out into the pan and smooth lightly with a spatula. Bake in the preheated oven for 20 to 30 minutes, until the dressing is set but not dry. This makes enough for 6 to 8 servings and can be doubled or tripled. The dressing will keep in the refrigerator and reheats well.

Serves 6 to 8.

ON STUFFING

To stuff or not to stuff, that is the question when it comes to turkey. In the past, the answer has been primarily an aesthetic one. Stuffers say that baking in the bird enhances both the stuffing and the meat with the commingling of flavors. Non-stuffers (and most Southerners, myself included, fall into this category) prefer to bake the dish separately, spooning some of the turkey's pan juices over it to give it a richer flavor. We call the dish dressing and are fond of pointing out that you can make a whole lot more of it if you're not constrained by the size of the bird's cavity.

Recently nutritionists have cautioned that stuffing inside a turkey may harbor bacteria if not cooked thoroughly at a high enough temperature. In On Food and Cooking, however, scientist Harold McGee says roasting a stuffed bird at no less than 325° F. should be sufficient to kill bacteria. The recipe for Roast Turkey here roasts at 350° F. It's for an unstuffed bird, though, to be served with Cornbread Dressing on the side. If you want to stuff your turkey, simply add 5 minutes per pound to the roasting time.

SIMPLE GIFTS 1

Ian Hooper has long liked to wrap his own presents, his mother, Sara Jo, says, so every year they set up a table with wrap, tape, and scissors for him.

One year, when he was still fairly young, they planned to visit relatives up north for the holiday. It was a long drive, so they bought the makings for a picnic lunch to enjoy along the way: ham for sandwiches, cookies, and a tub of Ian's favorite potato salad from a local grocery's deli section.

The night before the trip, Ian was hard at work wrapping presents to be taken with them the next day. When it came time for his mom's, he asked her to leave the room. She did, but was intrigued to hear padding back and forth to the kitchen and the open and shut of the refrigerator door. When Ian told her to come back in, there was a squatty package under the tree and a look of concern on Ian's face.

After some hems and haws and hints around, Ian finally said he was worried about his present for his mom and wondered if he told her what it was, would she pretend she didn't know when she actually had to open it.

She agreed, and Ian divulged that for her, his most favorite person, he had wrapped up his most favorite thing, the potato salad.

Sara Jo assured him he'd been right to ask, that the salad could go bad if not refrigerated. Telling him how pleased she was with his very generous gift, she nevertheless suggested they store it in the refrigerator and open it at the picnic the next day. When she took her package to the refrigerator for safekeeping, she found a note where the potato salad had been: "Mom, pretend like the potato salad is still here."

Garlic Cheese Grits

"No holiday meal happens in my house without garlic cheese grits on the table," Sara Jo Hooper says.

Whether you're cooking up a traditional Southern dinner or not, that's a good precept to follow. Cheese grits have turned out to be the most universally savored dish ever served in my house. Professional food writers, grit despisers, and my daughter's most picky-eater friends have all gobbled up every last bite of this classic casserole and begged for the recipe. The original version, sans garlic, was published in my first book, *Shuck Beans, Stack Cakes and Honest Fried Chicken*. It comes from Emmylou Harris's mother, Eugenia. The extra snap of garlic added here is perfect for a festive meal.

For information on getting good grits, see page 18.

1½ teaspoons salt
1½ cups uncooked coarse-
  ground grits
½ cup (1 stick) butter
4 cups (1 pound) shredded
  sharp Cheddar cheese
3 cloves garlic, minced very
  fine
3 eggs, beaten

Preheat the oven to 350° F. and lightly grease a 2½-quart baking dish.

In a heavy saucepan, bring 6 cups water and the salt to a boil. Pouring in a thin stream, stir in the grits and cook for 10 minutes, stirring constantly.

Remove from the heat and add the butter, 3¾ cups of the cheese, and the garlic. Stir until the butter and cheese are melted.

Slowly add several tablespoons of hot grits to the beaten eggs, stirring constantly as you do. When the eggs are warmed, add to the remaining grits and mix well.

Turn out into the prepared baking dish, sprinkle the top with the remaining ¼ cup cheese, and bake in the preheated oven for 1 hour. Serve warm.

Serves 8.

SIMPLE GIFTS 2

Stumped for Christmas gifts? How about these suggestions from the December 1940 Good Housekeeping:

> *Haven't you a neighbor who would welcome a rubber-coated dish drainer on Christmas morning? Give it with a mat for the drainboard.*

> *For an inexpensive holiday gift, why not choose a set of refrigerator-bowl covers? Easy to pack, they make a good send-away gift.*

—IRENA CHALMERS, *THE GREAT AMERICAN CHRISTMAS ALMANAC*

Ambrosia

"Because I'm Southern, I must have ambrosia for Christmas," Sara Jo says. There could hardly be a better choice for a holiday salad. Unlike many fruit salads, ambrosia is actually finest in the winter when so many varieties of orange flood the market. In fact, it can be so sweet and flavorful that you may want to use it for dessert.

When choosing oranges and tangerines for ambrosia, I gravitate toward thin-skinned, heavy fruit, since it is inevitably juicier and more flavorful than that bred with thick skin for shipping. Try as many varieties of oranges and tangerines or tangelos as you can find in your grocery or fruit market. Blood oranges are stunning for color as well as taste. If you can't get a variety of oranges, substitute fresh pineapple for half the citrus.

Ambrosia is traditionally layered in a footed cut-glass dish so its beautiful appearance can be admired at the table before its delicate flavors are savored. You may use any glass or ceramic dish, however, but not a metal container.

6 medium-small oranges, 1 or 2 each of as many varieties as you can find (minneola, Valencia, satsuma, honey bell, blood oranges)
1 tangelo or 2 tangerines
2 cups shredded unsweetened coconut

Over a bowl to catch the juices, peel the oranges and tangelos or tangerines. Remove all seeds and the white center pith. Cut into bite-sized sections, removing any of the white membrane you can get to easily. (This doesn't mar the flavor, so it isn't necessary to be persnickety about this step, but it does make for a prettier presentation.) Toss the pieces of fruit together lightly with your hands to mix them.

Spread ⅔ cup coconut in the bottom of a glass or ceramic bowl, then cover with a layer of half the citrus. Repeat, then sprinkle the remaining coconut over the top, cover tightly with plastic wrap, and refrigerate until ready to serve. Fresh mint leaves make a beautiful garnish.

This makes more than enough as a side dish for 8, and while it won't keep for long, it is good with leftovers the next day.

Serves 8.

SIMPLE GIFTS 3

"Money was scarce and times was hard, the groceries mighty plain . . ."

So goes one of Norman Blake's most beautiful songs, a ballad about the Depression years in the mountains that actually celebrates the simple beauties sometimes found in hard times. The economic depression has never quite left the lives of many people in the Appalachian Mountains, but folks still cling to the area in part because of the spirit of doing for one another that is part of the mountain ethic.

Each Christmas since 1945 there's been a particularly poignant and exciting reminder of that spirit as the Santa Claus Express makes its annual journey from Pikeville, Kentucky, to Kingsport, Tennessee. On the Saturday morning before Thanksgiving weekend, this train moves slowly through the mountains, slowing down for the groups of children and their parents who gather at various places along the tracks—some of them having spent the night there. Santa Claus rides the train, and from the back he tosses out candy and toys, calls out greetings and endearments to the little ones, and otherwise creates a moment of magic in the mountains.

The toys are provided by businesspeople from the region—some of whom were once children waiting for the Santa train themselves. The train and crew are supplied by CSX railroad.

Cocoa-Yam Spice Cake with Caramel-Buttermilk Icing

With jam cakes practically the Southern national dessert, it was only natural that someone should come up with this variation, a yam cake. It was Camille Glenn, doyenne of Southern food writers and the author of several cookbooks, including the wonderful *Heritage of Southern Cooking*, who introduced me to the idea. This version was extrapolated from her recipe, but with some changes in spices and other ingredients.

Camille tops her cake with a thin, dark chocolate glaze. It's great, but from the minute I heard about a chocolate-yam cake, I couldn't imagine it with anything but Caramel Buttermilk Icing. The good news is, I was right. The combination of flavors is to swoon over. The bad news is that over decades of making this icing—the first I learned in my mother's kitchen—I have yet to produce a foolproof recipe. Sometimes it sets up right and sometimes it just doesn't. But I have given the few hints for success I know, and a few for how to deal with failures. And the best news is that even when your icing runs, it's still delectable.

CAKE

1 or 2 sweet potatoes equal
  to 12–14 ounces
4 eggs
2 cups sugar

Preheat the oven to 450° F. and bake the unpeeled sweet potatoes until very tender when pierced by a fork (about 40 minutes). Remove from the oven and turn the temperature down to 350° F. Allow the potatoes to cool (slicing in half hastens the process), then remove the peel and mash by hand to puree. (A ricer works terrifically, as does a sieve, although it's more

1 cup (2 sticks) plus 3
  tablespoons unsalted
  butter
½ cup plus 1 tablespoon
  unsweetened cocoa
2 cups all-purpose flour
3 teaspoons baking powder
2 teaspoons ground
  cardamom
½ cup milk
2 teaspoons vanilla extract

trouble. Don't use a food processor or blender, however, or the result will be too gummy.)

Measure out ⅔ cup from the mashed sweet potatoes to use in the recipe and either eat the remainder with a little butter on the spot or set aside in the refrigerator to use in another recipe.

Separate the eggs so the whites can come to room temperature while you prepare the rest of the recipe.

Grease 2 (9-inch) cake pans and line with waxed paper.

Set aside ¼ cup of the sugar to be used later, then cream the remaining 1¾ cups with the butter until blended. Add the egg yolks and blend well. Add the sweet potato puree and blend well. Add the cocoa and blend well. Don't overmix, but be sure all ingredients are thoroughly incorporated.

Sift together the flour, baking powder, and cardamom. Blend half with the butter mixture. Blend in the milk. Blend in the rest of the flour. Again, work quickly and don't overbeat, mixing just until the ingredients are thoroughly blended, then set aside.

In a separate bowl, beat the egg whites until they form stiff peaks. Add the ¼ cup sugar and beat again until stiff.

Fold half the egg-white mixture into the rest of the batter, using a large rubber spatula and working swiftly and gently to incorporate thoroughly. Repeat with the rest of the egg white. Spoon the batter equally into the prepared pans and bake on the center rack in the preheated 350° F. oven for 30 to 35 minutes, until a cake tester inserted comes out clean.

Cool on wire racks for 5 minutes before inverting. Allow to cool completely before icing.

When you are ready to ice the cake, place the first layer on a plate or platter that has a lipped edge.

ICING

1 cup white sugar
1½ cups brown sugar
½ teaspoon baking soda
1 tablespoon white corn
  syrup
½ cup (1 stick) butter
1 cup buttermilk
1 teaspoon vanilla extract

Place all the ingredients except the vanilla in a large, heavy saucepan. Over medium-high heat, bring to a rolling boil, stirring constantly. Continue to stir and cook until the mixture reaches the soft-ball stage (234°–240° F. on a candy thermometer). Remove from the heat immediately and do not stir, but let cool for 10 minutes, or until the side of the pan is lukewarm to the touch. (If your pan is made of a heavy metal that retains heat, set the pan in cool water to cool faster.)

Add the vanilla and with a wooden spoon begin to beat the mixture vigorously. (You will need to beat for 10 to 15 minutes, so this is a great time to draft help from strong, eager youngsters.) The mixture will be ready to spread when it begins to lose its gloss and to hold its shape when you lift a spoonful and let it pour back into the mass.

As soon as it is thick enough to spread without running, ice the top of the first layer. Place the second layer on top of the first and ice the sides and top of it.

Serves 8 to 10.

WHAT CAN GO WRONG AND WHAT YOU CAN DO ABOUT IT

The first thing that can go wrong is that you may overcook the mixture past the soft-ball stage. In that case, when you begin to beat, it will harden up quickly and become grainy. You can add warmed milk to the mixture, a tablespoon at a time, to get it to spreading consistency. The result will be hard and grainy in texture, but it will taste quite good.

A more common problem is that you may not cook the mixture or beat the icing quite long enough.

"Surely this is thick enough," you will think as your arm really begins to ache. If you want to test, spread the icing on top of the first layer and wait a minute. If it begins to dribble down the sides, it's not ready and you can beat with renewed vigor, having had a break. When it is ready, no need to re-ice the top of that first layer. Just tell your guests it's supposed to have a thin, soft caramel center.

Sometimes, even when the icing looks just right and the first layer doesn't run, the second layer still will. You will ice the cake to perfection, turn your back, and in two minutes it will be sitting in a golden pool of caramel. This is why you want to put it on a plate with a lip.

If it runs, simply take a table knife and carefully but quickly scoop the runny icing from the pool up the sides of the cake and toward the center. Have a light touch, or you may tear the cake in the process. You may have to repeat this process three or four times over an hour, but the icing will eventually set and stay in its proper place.

If you don't have the patience for this, buy some candied violets, sprinkle them on top of the caramel puddle, and tell your guests that the cake was meant to be served in a "pool of caramelized sauce." Expensive restaurants do it all the time.

And one last question: Is this cake worth the trouble?

Just taste it.

CHRISTMAS JUBILEE

Christmas at Jubilee Partners, a Christian community near the northeastern Georgia town of Comer, is always an international celebration, although its flavor changes yearly.

Jubilee, founded in 1979, has been taking in refugees for more than a decade. The new arrivals live at Jubilee for several months while the partners, the permanent residents of the community, introduce them to their new homeland and its customs. They teach classes in English, money exchange, and business forms, and accompany the refugees to town to familiarize them with the intricacies of American supermarkets, drugstores, and shops. After this initiation, most refugees move on to Atlanta, and Jubilee opens its doors to another group seeking shelter and haven.

Jubilee's guests have come from Cambodia, Laos, Vietnam, and various countries in Central America. The most recent refugees have been arriving from war-torn Bosnia-Herzegovina.

Although the refugees have separate living quarters, each Sunday evening they share a meal at the partners' central kitchen/dining hall. And holidays provide a special chance for the two communities to celebrate together and share a gift of food from each of their cultures.

Thanksgiving and Christmas meals have included Vietnamese spring rolls and empanadas from Central America served with the turkey. One year the partners prepared the whole Christmas dinner, and then the refugees from Bosnia treated them to a New Year's stew served with a traditional meat pastry. Often the partners and guests cook together.

Josie Winterfeld, one of the partners, says, "Preparing food for one another is actually a gift of love. And the meals are a ritual themselves because they bring all of us together. On Sunday nights especially, when we are preparing food with our guests, it becomes an easy way for us to relate to one another, even though we don't speak the same language."

The kitchen at Jubilee was most certainly a meeting ground when I spent a day there with several women from Bosnia-Herzegovina.

I knew nothing of their language, and the translator from the Jubilee community was not there. The only bilingual person in the place was sparkling sixteen-year-old Alma, who had learned most of the English she spoke from the American pop music she'd listened to all her life.

"If you should need me, you just call me, I'll be there," she told me with a grin and a Motown dance move for punctuation.

But despite linguistic barriers, we discovered that we all spoke the same language in the kitchen. Edina, Sadina, Nermina, and Melina at first spoke only to one another, simply nodding politely and smiling at me. But once the heat was on as they began peeling, chopping, and mixing dishes for dinner, I became the gofer while they mimed out the need for utensils: potato masher, eggbeater—there were moments when the kitchen looked like a 1960s sock hop featuring all the new novelty steps.

When Sadina and Nermina had a protracted conversation over how many veal cutlets would be enough, I knew exactly what was being discussed.

And when the four women got into a joking competition over who had the largest behind, I not only jumped right in but won hands down.

What was most amazing, however, was the similarity between many of the foods the women prepared from their country and the cooking of the north Georgia region they were in. A huge pot of stew made from collard greens and potatoes and a platter of savory onion-filled meat patties formed the core of the meal, and looked and tasted much like the food I grew up eating. I took careful notes on the preparation of one dish until I realized that we were making mashed potatoes. And when one of the Jubilee partners whipped up a marinated bean salad for dinner, Edina tasted it, then told me they often had the same thing "back home."

I found several recipes for such bean salads in Yugoslav cookbooks, along with a dish that resembled grits, and a pan bread very similar to classic Southern cornbread. Food may well be the universal language.

And at Jubilee I experienced once again the truth that it's impossible not to love someone who shares their kitchen and their food with you.

"With the Central Americans, we often worshipped together," Josie says.

"But with the Bosnians, we have been careful not to pressure them in any way because of their history with so much religious persecution. So for us, the meals with them have become our way of worshipping together.

"It is very rarely that you can walk past one of their cottages without someone popping out to invite you in for coffee and fresh bread or some baked goody. It's as if we are in the business of hospitality, but they are really the ones who are teaching us."

Christmas dinner at Jubilee is not a big production in terms of food, Josie says.

"We have one decoration day earlier in December where everyone gathers at the meetinghouse and we all sit around making crafts and baking cookies. There are fresh-made doughnuts and apple cider, and then we decorate the tree.

"For Christmas itself, several of the partners go 'home,' although we rotate so we're always sure that some of us are here to share the celebration with the refugees. Usually only two or three of our families stay, so it really is a special, intimate gathering."

Ajvar

I first discovered this all-purpose savory spread in jars at our local specialty food store. Its color was pimiento red, and though there were no directions, I thought I could probably figure out something to do with it. Boy, was I right! It soon took over the utility infielder's position in the refrigerator, capable of going almost anywhere and adding zip to countless recipes. I've used it instead of tomato sauce on pasta. It turns pizza into a very grownup dinner, either by itself or with lots of veggies scattered over it. Dollops on cucumber wedges became summer tea canapés. And, spread thickly on bread with a creamy slice of white cheese, it is the best and quickest sandwich around.

Imagine my delight, then, when I found a recipe for it in a Yugoslav cookbook. Since then I've also unearthed versions in a couple of Mediterranean cookbooks. Virtually all of them call for three or four times more olive oil than I use here, but I can see no reason why.

The homemade spread is chunkier than the kind I bought bottled, not quite so red, and the taste is more immediately intense. I like it enormously and try to keep a jar in the refrigerator at all times. Be sure to keep plastic wrap pressed against the surface of the ajvar to seal it from oxygen and protect its fresh color.

This may be eaten as a salad, but it's best as a spread ladled onto either the Crusty Rye Loaf (page 79) or Irish Soda Bread (page 260).

2 (1-pound) eggplants
1 pound red bell peppers
   (about 4 large ones)
3 cloves of garlic, crushed

Prick each of the eggplants and the red peppers twice with the tines of a fork and place in a preheated 375° F. oven. (I simply lay them on the center rack, but if you are worried about dripping, you can put them on a cookie sheet. If you do, turn the peppers once during the

Juice of ½ lemon
2 tablespoons olive oil
½ teaspoon kosher salt

roasting time and the eggplants 2 or 3 times.)

The peppers should take about 30 minutes until the skins are blistered and loose and browned in some spots, and the flesh is very, very tender. Remove from the oven, using a spatula or tongs, pop into a plastic bag, close it, and let them steam for another 10 minutes. Remove from the bag, and when they are cooled just enough that you can handle them without saying "Ouch," pull off the peel and discard with the stems and seeds. Put the flesh of the peppers into a large bowl. Add the crushed garlic and use a potato masher to mash coarsely.

The eggplants will take 45 minutes to 1 hour to roast, depending on how fat they are. The skins should be browned and the flesh should be very tender, actually mushy to touch. Remove from the oven, cut off the stems, and as soon as you can handle them, pull away the skins.

Add the eggplants to the pepper mash and pour the lemon juice on it immediately. Mash with the potato masher to a coarse chunky puree. Drizzle the olive oil into the mixture while you are mashing. Season with salt. Can be served immediately or put into jars and refrigerated for about 1 week. If you are going to refrigerate it, be sure to lay plastic wrap right on the ajvar, covering the whole surface, before you put on the jar lid.

Serves 8 as a spread.

Kwanzaa

ost of the celebrations in this book are for holidays whose traditions go back centuries. A few are original, created by individuals who wanted a personal annual party. Kwanzaa is neither.

This holiday honoring the culture of black Americans and others of African descent was conceived in 1966 by Maulana (Ron) Karenga, then a professor of black studies at the University of California. *Kwanzaa* is a Swahili word meaning "first harvest," but it is not associated with any particular event in African history. The rites that Karenga established for Kwanzaa are instead drawn from customs in different countries.

Karenga laid out specifics for the holiday, which included laying a table with ritual objects representing elements of African history and community: ears of corn, for the children in the community; the *kinara*, a seven-branched candleholder with tapers that represent seven principles characteristic of the strong black community.

The primary ceremony is the nightly illumination of one of the seven candles (red, green, black, and sometimes gold are the colors used) and a discussion of the principle that the candle represents. Other rituals may be created by the family or the community to demonstrate the seven principles which are: *umoja*, unity; *kujichagulia*, self-determination; *ujima*, collective work and responsibility; *ujamma*, cooperative economics; *nia*, purpose; *kuumba*, creativity; and *imani*, faith.

On the next to the last night of this seven-day celebration, there is a feast with foods of the African diaspora, ranging from the traditional dishes of African countries through the cuisines of the Caribbean, South America, and the American South. Music, dance, storytelling, and other demonstrations of culture are encouraged.

The holiday usually takes place beginning the day after Christmas and ending on January 1, a time that has been traditionally family- and neighborhood-oriented. It is not a religious holiday and is not meant to replace one. Some celebrants incorporate Kwanzaa elements into their Christmas rituals or vice versa, segueing the two holidays together.

Kwanzaa began small, with Karenga's concept, but now, only three decades (one generation) later, it is celebrated by more than 5 million Americans. That such a holiday would take hold in such a short time demonstrates not only the need black Americans have to rejoice in their culture but the need of all humans to remember where they came from, to acknowledge who they are and dream together of who they may become.

Eric Copage, who has written a most beautiful book called *Kwanzaa: An African American Celebration of Culture and Cooking* (William Morrow and Company, 1991), says, "There is a jazzy quality to everything black people do, a spirit of improvisation and self-creation. It is part of the African aesthetic. And it is very much a part of Kwanzaa."

A FAMILY KWANZAA

When Adriene Cruz was growing up in New York City, her family celebrated Christmas.

"As a child, I enjoyed it immensely. We had a big tree we would decorate and then there were all the presents underneath. What could be more exciting for a kid?"

But as she got older, the excitement waned and was eventually replaced with a feeling of empty duty.

"Somewhere about the time I was twenty years old, Christmas didn't make sense anymore. I wasn't celebrating for any particularly spiritual reasons.

"And then one year I had this list and was running around like mad shopping and feeling really pressured to do this gift thing and not having enough money. And suddenly I just stopped and asked myself: What are you doing? Why are you behaving like this? And why is this list getting longer? And why is the pleasure getting so much less?

"And I didn't have any good answers for those questions. So I just put that list away and stopped cold turkey. I didn't do presents. I didn't even send Christmas cards.

"People thought I was strange. But after a while it just became one of those things people accept about you. You know, friends would say, 'Oh well, Adriene just doesn't do Christmas.' And I have to tell you, I never missed it."

Neither did her husband, Larry Dunham, whom Adriene describes as "not a big holiday kind of guy."

But when they were expecting their first child about ten years ago, the issue of holidays came up.

"Tradition is very important," Cruz says. "We need to pass on values to our children, and one way of doing that is in how we celebrate."

Cruz knew she didn't want "to do the Christmas thing. That frenzy of buying gifts and wondering what you're going to get wasn't what I wanted them to value.

"Kwanzaa seemed to make a lot more sense, since the seven principles it honors are all things that we wanted our children to honor and respect. And observing the holiday seemed to be a fine way to pass on those values to our children, a way for it to be a natural part of our lives, but also a celebration."

Cruz and Dunham had moved to Portland, Oregon, in the early 1980s, and there they had begun to observe Kwanzaa at the Black Educational Center.

When their daughter Tasnim was born, they decided to bring the holiday home. Now Tasnim, nine, and Ola, six, look forward to the weeklong celebration, which brings their grandmother, Beryl "Mubbie" Cruz, to Portland from New York.

Adriene says the family celebration is relaxed. She is a fabric artist with an eye for color and an appreciation of unusual objects, so their house is already "decorated" with things that invoke their African heritage.

"We do set up a space. Technically, it's not an altar, but since I have an altar fetish I call it that. But it's a table that the kinara sits on, and then we put around it some of the African artifacts and things I've made that we like.

"We also put fruit out on the table. The kind depends on the color. I'm a color freak, so whatever looks bright and interesting at the market and then looks good arranged together is what we get. Also, we put out the ears of corn which represent the children of the house and of the community. This is one of the most important things, symbolically, because for us the holiday is really about how you raise your children."

At some point on each day, the family gathers at the kinara to light the appropriate candle and to discuss the principle of the day. Some families do this before the evening meal each day, but in the Cruz/Dunham household it's sometimes difficult to align everyone's schedule.

"If we're going to be spread out all day and the only time is in the morning, that's when we do it. And what we do is to talk about the principle, what it means, and how we can incorporate it into our daily life.

"For example, kuumba is creativity, so on the day when it is the focus, we might discuss how creativity works in daily problem solving. Like, if you have something to do and you don't have the materials to do it, then you come up with something creative as a substitute. A good example of that would be making a gift if you don't have the money to buy one."

Gifts are a very small part of the family's Kwanzaa celebration and are homemade. Adriene says that Tasnim and Ola do get Christmas presents from relatives, but they don't yet seem to want any of the big trappings of that holiday.

"My children are pretty different," she says. "They don't ask for a lot of stuff, so the presents aren't that big a deal. As for the tree thing, they have a lot of respect for the planet, so chopping down a tree to bring in the house doesn't make sense to them.

"Of course, I knock on wood and know that the day may come. Some of my friends and I joke and say when they get older they'll have those big trees that fill the living room and all these decorations and the biggest presents money can buy. But so far we really haven't had to deal with that too much. Kwanzaa has been full enough of ritual, and beauty, and family that I don't think they believe they're missing out on anything by not having Christmas."

If presents are a small part of the festival, food is a great one. During the week, Adriene often serves dishes with roots in Africa, or in Jamaica, where her family is from.

The sixth night of the celebration is marked by a community feast, often a potluck held at the Black Educational Center. Then the family may have a get-together with friends on the final day, which is also a celebration of the New Year.

There's one ritual that Adriene loved from Christmas that has been carried over into the Kwanzaa celebration, however: light.

"Oh, I love those lights. If I had my way, people would have colored lights all around the house all the time. And I just couldn't let that one part of Christmas go. My birthday is in December, and we put the lights up then and they stay up through Kwanzaa.

"And I guess that's become a part of our tradition now. And I kind of like knowing that when Kwanzaa is on the horizon and my birthday comes around, even if I'm not there, my children can put the lights up and say, 'Hey, Mother loved the lights. Remember?'"

A tasty soup attracts chairs.

—AFRICAN PROVERB

Curry Cruz's Yam Soup

Adriene Cruz's good friends call her Curry.

"I just love it." She laughs. "I buy these big old cans of curry powder at the Indian market, and anything I cook that I can sprinkle it in, I do."

For Kwanzaa, she especially likes to make this curry-spiked vegetable stew featuring yams and kale because it reminds her of her father, who liked it, too.

It also makes the house smell fantastic.

"When you start with the oil and onion and garlic and then all the spices, yummmm. Second to eating it, I love the way it makes the house smell. I can smell it just talking about it, and just talking about it makes me want to cook up a pot."

As for ingredients, "Curry" Cruz insists that the soup contain yams. (She means the deep-orange-fleshed sweet potatoes that are marketed by the name "yam," not the African vegetable of the same name but very different taste, which is not easily found in the United States.)

"I put the yams in early because I like the way they break down into the broth and I like the sweetness."

She says the dish must also have kale. It's customary in many African cuisines to have fresh greens cooked into any stew, and black Americans continued this tradition in the South with collard, turnip, and kale greens, and the like.

The corn, peas, and beans are more or less optional.

"This is really a soup of grabbing whatever is at hand," Adriene explains. "If I don't have corn, I don't worry. And if I've got something else in the fridge that looks like it might be tasty, I might throw it in."

The curry she uses is a premixed spice blend, but in the recipe here you mix the spices yourself. This allows fresh ginger, a refreshing addition. And it gives the cook more control over the flavors. Feel free to add more or less of each spice according to your taste. And you may want to increase the quantity of spice overall, since the flavor that you get with the proportions listed here is very subtle. But I suggest you try it like this first, since the subtle spice is a perfect undercurrent to the medley of unique vegetable tastes.

Any leftover soup can be frozen.

1 large onion, chopped

4 cloves of garlic, minced

¼ cup olive oil

1 medium-sized red bell pepper, chopped

2 tablespoons minced fresh ginger

12 whole cloves, ground

1 teaspoon cumin seed, ground

½ teaspoon mustard seed, ground

1 teaspoon ground cardamom

½ teaspoon turmeric

In a large soup kettle, sauté the onion and garlic in the olive oil over medium heat. When the onions begin to soften, add the chopped bell pepper and fresh ginger. Mix the ground cloves, cumin, mustard seed, cardamom, turmeric, and cinnamon together, then sprinkle over the sautéed vegetables and stir. Add the soy sauce and the juice from the canned tomatoes. Let come to a boil, turn the heat down, cover, and simmer gently while you prepare the sweet potato.

Peel the sweet potato, cut out any blemishes, and cut into 1-inch cubes. Add to the pot along with 1 cup water. Bring to a boil, turn the heat down, cover, and simmer for 20 minutes. Watch carefully and stir occasionally to keep from sticking.

½ teaspoon ground
  cinnamon
¼ cup tamari soy sauce
1 (24-ounce) can whole
  tomatoes
1 large or 2 small orange
  sweet potatoes (1 pound)
½ pound broccoli
1 large or 2 medium-sized
  white potatoes (½ pound)
2 quarts boiling water
1 cup frozen corn
1 cup frozen cut green
  beans
1 cup frozen green peas
½ pound fresh kale
Kosher salt to taste

Chop the broccoli stem and florets into bite-sized pieces. Wash the white potatoes well and, leaving the peel on, chop into 1-inch pieces. Add the broccoli and potatoes to the pot with the 2 quarts boiling water, cover, and cook for 20 minutes.

Chop the tomatoes into small pieces. Add to the pot along with the frozen corn, beans, and peas. Cover and cook for another 20 minutes.

Wash the kale, remove the stem ends, and tear the leaves into small pieces. Before adding to the pot, taste the broth and add salt as you wish. Add the kale and use a wooden spoon to push and stir it down into the soup. Cover and simmer for 20 to 30 minutes, until the kale is cooked. Serve immediately.

Serves 12.

Corn Dodgers

Although corn is an American original, it made its way to Africa by the 1500s and was soon rivaling native grains on either coast. Fire-roasted cornbreads became a natural part of the slave diet in the South because they were familiar, the meal was plentiful, and the cooking was quick. But they stayed in the diet because absolutely nothing else tastes so fine dunked in the potlikker of savory slow-cooked greens or stews. These corn dodgers are easy to bake up for a party and will make your mouth water dunked into the juices of Palaver (page 358) or Chicken Yassa (page 354).

2 cups yellow cornmeal
1 teaspoon salt
1 tablespoon melted butter
2 cups boiling water
   (about)

Preheat the oven to 450° F. and have ready an ungreased cookie sheet.

Blend the cornmeal and salt. With a wooden spoon, mix in the butter and enough boiling water to make a dough that is completely moist, but firm enough to hold its shape. Drop heaping spoonfuls of the batter onto the cookie sheet and use the fingertips to pat each lightly into mounds. Bake for 20 to 25 minutes, until golden-crisp on the outside. Serve straight from the oven.

Serves 6 to 8.

Cumin Salmon Cakes with Pepper Aioli

Sure, Adriene Cruz lives in the Pacific Northwest now, but when she makes salmon cakes for Kwanzaa, what she wants are the patties made of canned salmon that are synonymous with the northern soul food of the American black diaspora.

Adriene laughs as she says, "You know, I got out here and went to a grocery and said, 'Gee, you mean a salmon is a real fish and it doesn't come in a can? You're not gonna tell me a tuna is a fish, too, are you?'

"And I've grown to love them both, especially the fresh salmon we can get around here. But canned salmon really has a different taste and is good in its own right in certain dishes. I've made salmon patties out of both canned and fresh, and the old-fashioned kind are the ones that taste best."

While most fresh foods are nutritionally superior to canned, canned salmon packs an extra boost of calcium from the tiny bones that are a part of the meat.

This version of salmon cakes is jazzed up with spices in the cake itself, and with the garlic and cumin in the pretty pepper aioli that is served with it. You can make the patties palm-sized to serve as a main dish, or shape them into circlets the size of silver dollars for an appetizer.

Roasted red peppers are festive, and yellow ones make the aioli look like a rich mustard. If you're making an appetizer plate, you may want to double the salmon recipe and make two batches of the aioli, one with red peppers, the other with yellow, for a colorful presentation.

SALMON CAKES

1 (14-ounce) can salmon
½ cup chopped onion
½ teaspoon cumin seed
½ teaspoon paprika
⅛ teaspoon turmeric
1 tablespoon Dijon mustard
½ cup cracker or matzo
  meal
1 egg
Canola oil for frying

PEPPER AIOLI

2 large yellow or red bell
  peppers
2–3 large cloves of garlic
½ teaspoon cumin seed
¼ cup mayonnaise

Place the salmon, including the juices, in a bowl and toss together with the onion.

The cumin for both the salmon cakes and the aioli is toasted and then ground, so you may want to do one full teaspoon now, setting aside half to use in the aioli later. In a small skillet over high heat, toast the cumin for 1 minute, until it is dark brown and toasty. (Toss or stir continuously to keep the cumin from burning.) Grind coarsely. Sprinkle ½ teaspoon over the salmon and reserve ½ teaspoon.

Sprinkle on the paprika and turmeric and mix. Then blend in the Dijon mustard and cracker or matzo meal. Beat the egg to blend white and yolk, then add to the salmon and mix.

Flour your hands lightly to prevent sticking, and shape patties that are the size of your palm, if you are serving as a main course. If you are making appetizers, make the patties small, about the circumference of a silver dollar. Lay the patties on a plate, using waxed paper or plastic wrap to separate if you have to make more than one layer. Cover and refrigerate while you make the aioli.

To make the aioli, roast the peppers and peel. (See page 287 for instructions on roasting peppers.) Place the flesh of the peppers in a blender. Add the toasted cumin and the garlic, which has been crushed and peeled. Add the mayonnaise and blend to a smooth puree.

To finish the salmon patties, heat a skillet over high heat and add enough canola oil to oil the bottom liberally. Place several patties in the skillet, but don't crowd too closely. Fry for a few minutes, until crisp and brown. Turn over and fry on the other side until crisp and brown also. (Add more oil if you need it, and turn down the heat if the skillet starts to smoke.) Place on a warmed serving plate. Serve immediately, with aioli in dollops on the top of each patty or passed in a serving dish on the side.

Makes enough for 6 to 8.

Chicken Yassa

Some years ago, when friend and cookbook author Jessica Harris was in town, she inspired me to teach a unit on the cooking of Africans and African Americans to thirty middle-school students. Jessica set the tone with a vibrant lecture tracing the food connections back and forth between the continents, a history she has covered well and deliciously in her classic, *Iron Pots and Wooden Spoons* (Ballantine Books, 1989), from which this recipe was adapted.

Then the students spent a week digging further into the subject, writing reports, illustrating maps, and making art objects for demonstration. It was much more than a lesson in food. We also covered geography; the history of exploration, trading, and slavery; the differences in cultures of the myriad countries of Africa; and the often overlooked but very significant contributions of blacks to this country's cuisine.

The culmination of the lesson was the preparation of an African feast to be served to parents and fellow students.

We peeled and boiled sweet potatoes, steamed rice, and stirred up skillets of cornbread. It was yummy, but, without doubt, the most memorable experience was the preparation of chicken yassa, the signature dish of Senegal.

Smothered in the savory harmony of a lemon, onion, and chile pepper sauce, this chicken is lip-smackingly memorable. It is also quite simple to prepare for friends in the proportions listed below. But for our feast, we had to serve 120. That meant juicing a huge carton of lemons and peeling and slicing dozens of pungent onions.

We worked at the counters of an old home economics classroom that was soon awash in onion vapors. Big, strapping guys and perpetually blasé young women who hardly ever showed expression were soon dropping huge tears and laughing uproariously at themselves and the situation. Best of all, several kids who'd never excelled in a classroom before turned out to be clever and adept in the kitchen. And the visceral counterpoints of hands-on, nose-tweaking, tear-provoking tasks made the lesson one that may never be forgotten.

You will never forget the fresh bite of this simple chicken dish, either. Its juices are far too good to waste, and it is traditionally served with rice to soak them up. But it also pairs up perfectly with the light nuttiness of couscous.

3 lemons

3 large onions

1–2 fresh *serrano* or *jalapeño* peppers

1 teaspoon salt

½ teaspoon freshly ground black pepper

3½-pound broiler-fryer, cut into pieces

2–4 tablespoons olive oil

Several hours before you are ready to serve, prepare the marinade. Extract the juice from the lemons. Add 1 teaspoonful grated zest from the lemons.

Cut the onions in half and slice about ½ inch thick. Discard the seeds and stem of the chile pepper(s) and chop very fine. (Use 2 peppers for a hot dish, 1 if you like things a bit milder.) Mix the pepper with the lemon juice, adding the salt and black pepper.

Rinse the chicken well, pat dry with paper towels, and place the pieces in a large, non-metal container. Cover with the onions and marinade. (If you have to layer the chicken, make sure to pour marinade and scatter onions over each layer, so all the chicken pieces soak up the flavor.) Cover well and refrigerate for at least 3 hours or overnight.

To prepare the chicken, heat a Dutch oven or other wide, heavy pan with a lid over medium-high heat. Add olive oil to coat the bottom of the pan. Remove the chicken pieces from the marinade, shaking off any onions that cling. Brown the chicken lightly in the oil, turning once. (Don't crowd the pan, but brown in batches, if necessary.) Set the browned chicken aside.

Add a little more oil to the pan. Remove the onions from marinade and sauté in the hot oil until softened. Add the remaining marinade and ½ cup water to the onions in the pan and bring to a boil. Return the chicken to the pan, cover, turn the heat down, and simmer until the chicken is very tender, about 35 minutes.

Serve hot with rice or couscous, spooning the onions and pan juice over each serving.

Serves 6 to 8.

AFRO-POP STOP

If you satisfy your taste buds with Senegal's classic Chicken Yassa, you should also do as well for your ears by serving them the music of Youssou N'Dour. With a voice that can pierce like a shaft of light or ripple like water, and a pop sensibility that has made him the brightest star in World Beat circles, Senegal's N'Dour first moved into Western pop circles in collaboration with Peter Gabriel. He has several albums of his own, however, all marked by his signature mesmerizing blend of traditional African rhythms and melodies with contemporary instruments and arrangements.

Other shivery sounds can be found on the discs of Nigerian guitar master King Sunny Adé, who makes music that is like an aural sauna. The music of Fela Kuti, also from Nigeria, has sharper edges and deeper funk. It also carries a powerful political message. And a singular recording for Rounder Records by American blues man Johnny Copeland called "Bringin' It All Back Home" reveals the connecting threads between African music and the blues.

Cardamom–Sweet Potato Bites

The flowery musk of cardamom cozies up perfectly with the sugar of deep-orange-fleshed sweet potatoes. These are a breeze to make and taste best served at room temperature. You could spear them with toothpicks and serve as an appetizer, or mound into a big bowl and pass along with the Chicken Yassa (preceding recipe).

If you want to up the flavor ante one more notch, mix a tablespoon of honey with a cup of plain yogurt, add a tablespoon of lime juice, and dip the spicy bites into it before popping in your mouth.

2 pounds deep-orange-
    fleshed sweet potatoes
2 tablespoons peanut oil
1 tablespoon ground
    cardamom (about)

Preheat the oven to 425° F. Peel the sweet potatoes and cut in 1-inch cubes. Put in a bowl, drizzle the peanut oil over them, and toss until all the cubes are well coated. Sprinkle the cardamom over the potatoes, tossing as you do so they are fairly evenly coated with the spice.

Spread out on cookie sheets, leaving some space between the pieces. Roast on the top shelf of the preheated oven for 15 minutes. The outsides will be brown-golden and the inside very soft. Remove and allow to come to room temperature before serving.

Serves 6 to 8 as a side dish.

YAMS 1

Sing a song of Dixie, cotton bursting in the sun, shade of Chinaberry trees, per-simmons after frost has fallen. Hounds treeing possums October nights. O, sweet potatoes, hot, with butter in their yellow hearts.

—Langston Hughes, "Home," in *The Ways of White Folks*

Palaver

The name has many variations (*palava* and *palawa*, for instance), as do the in-gredients. In Sierra Leone, it is made with tripe, while a friend recalls that the dish she had in Ghana had yam leaves and palm oil. But spinach seems to be the more common green, and all variations are liberally spiced.

I did not have to travel far to find my favorite, served at the Café Kili-manjaro only a mile or so from my home. While most palavers are used as a sauce for chicken, say, or a vegetable, the café serves its version as the perfect side dish. Snapping with fresh ginger followed by the hum of cloves, it's actu-ally good enough to be dinner all on its own, with a pan of cornbread on the side, of course. This may be the great-great-great-grandmother of Southern slow-cooked greens, but though it looks similar in the pan, it will sashay across your palate with its own distinctive style.

3 pounds fresh spinach
¼ cup peanut oil
1 large onion
8 cloves
1 teaspoon minced fresh
  ginger
½ cup plain tomato sauce
⅛ teaspoon ground
  cardamom
⅛ teaspoon cayenne
  pepper
Kosher salt to taste

Rinse the spinach several times to remove all the grit. When clean, remove the stems and tear into 3-inch pieces. Set aside.

In a non-aluminum saucepan, heat the peanut oil over medium heat. Cut the onion in half, then quarter each half. Separate the layers of onion. Add to the oil in the pot. Crush the cloves and sprinkle over the onion, stirring occasionally, until the onion begins to soften.

Add the minced fresh ginger and stir. Add the tomato sauce, 1 cup water, and the cardamom. Cook at a bubbly simmer for 4 minutes to marry the flavors. Add the cayenne, stir, and then add the spinach. Stir the spinach down into the liquid, a handful at a time, then cover the pot. Simmer for 30 minutes, until the spinach is tender. Add salt to taste and serve warm.

Serves 6 to 8 as a side dish.

In English, palaver means a conference or discussion, or a long parley between natives and colonials. Its root is the Portuguese palavra, *which is also the likely root for the same word in Ghana. There it means trouble or a difficult situation that will require a great deal of discussion to sort out. There is speculation that the sauce of the same name is so called because it is often used to bring together disparate ingredients, such as fish and beef, that might not otherwise harmonize without its intervention.*

Sweet Potato-Fig Pie

Like its pumpkin cousin, sweet potato pie has been a classic for so long that most attempts to fancy it up seem sacrilege. Or so I thought until I tasted Scott Peacock's pie, on which this one is based. Scott is the owner/chef at the Horseradish Grill in Atlanta and an outstanding purveyor of new Southern cooking. Scott works closely with Edna Lewis, doyenne of African-American cookbook writers. The food he creates is often original and always remarkable. What makes it so is the respect and affection he has for the real food, the real classics, of the South.

His pie is an excellent example. Instead of gussying it up, he takes a simplifying approach. The sweet potato filling is traditionally a custard enriched and thickened by eggs and cream. But Scott, recognizing that the potato itself is the star here, whips it up simply with butter, sugar, and a little spice. Then he pairs it with a thin layer of his mother's fig jam, an inspiration that seems made in heaven's kitchen.

The character of this pie varies depending on the flavor of the potatoes used and on the fig spread. You can use a commercial fig jam (see page 279) or a homemade variety (page 281). Or you can quickly whip up a fig spread with the recipe for Fig Sauce that accompanies the Espresso Honey Cake in Chapter 8 (page 249). If you choose to do that, half the recipe will be more than enough.

CRUST
FOR 9-INCH PIE

1¼ cups soft winter wheat
flour (see page 146)

In a large mixing bowl, blend together the flour, salt, and sugar. Cut the butter into ¼-inch pieces and scatter through the flour mix. Use 2 knives to cut the butter into the flour until the mixture resembles coarse meal. Sprinkle 3 tablespoons of the ice water over

½ teaspoon salt
1 tablespoon sugar
½ cup (1 stick) chilled
   unsalted butter
3–4 tablespoons ice water

the flour and quickly work it into the flour mixture. (A large rubber spatula is a good tool for this process.) Add another tablespoon of ice water, if needed.

When the dough holds together, pat into a smooth ball and then flatten into a disk about an inch thick. Wrap in waxed paper and refrigerate for 30 minutes.

Preheat the oven to 350° F. and cut a circle of aluminum foil to fit the bottom of a 9-inch pie pan. (Do not put it in the pan.)

Roll out the chilled dough on a lightly floured surface until it's about an inch wider around than the top of the pie pan, and about ¼ inch thick. Transfer to the pie pan, fold the edge under itself, and crimp. Prick the dough lightly all over with the tines of a fork. Lay the aluminum foil over the bottom of the crust and lay pie weights or dried beans on the foil to keep the crust from puffing up.

Bake for 20 minutes in the preheated oven. Remove, and when cool enough to touch, remove the beans and foil from the crust. Return the crust to the oven and bake 15 to 20 minutes more, until the crust is a dark gold.

FILLING

1½ pounds sweet potatoes
½ cup (1 stick) unsalted
   butter
½ cup brown sugar
½ teaspoon ground
   cardamom (optional)
½ cup fig jam

1 pint heavy cream, chilled
¼ cup brown sugar
1 teaspoon vanilla extract

Preheat the oven to 425° F. Scrub the sweet potatoes well, pierce twice with a fork, and bake in the preheated oven until you can insert a fork easily into the center. (The time may vary from 30 minutes to 1 hour, depending on how large the potatoes are.) When cool enough to handle, remove the skins and cut out any dark spots.

Put the warm potatoes in a large mixer bowl along with the butter. Blend at medium speed, adding the brown sugar and cardamom while blending. When the butter is melted, all the ingredients are blended, and the mixture is starting to fluff a bit, it's ready.

Spread the fig jam evenly over the bottom of the pie crust. Spread the potato mixture over that. Serve at room temperature.

When you are ready to serve, whip together the chilled cream, brown sugar, and vanilla until the cream begins to form peaks. Serve each slice of pie with a dollop of cream on the side.

Serves 8.

YAMS 2

Then far down at the corner I saw an old man warming his hands against the sides of an odd-looking wagon, from which a stove pipe reeled off a thin spiral of smoke that drifted the odor of baking yams slowly to me, bringing a stab of swift nostalgia. I stopped as though struck by a shot, deeply inhaling, remembering, my mind surging back, back. At home we'd bake them in the hot coals of the fireplace, had carried them cold to school for lunch; munched them secretly, squeezing the sweet pulp from the soft peel as we hid from the teacher behind the largest book, the World's Geography. Yes, and we'd loved them candied, or baked in a cobbler, deep-fat fried in a pocket of dough, or roasted with pork and glazed with the well-browned fat; had chewed them raw—yams and years ago. More yams than years ago, though the time seemed endlessly expanded, stretched thin as the spiraling smoke beyond all recall.

—RALPH ELLISON, *THE INVISIBLE MAN*

Ginger Beer

Adriene Cruz's great-great-grandmother from Jamaica made ginger beer, and the tradition has been passed down through generations. This potion is tart and has a hot bite that grabs you in the very back of the throat. For novices, the first taste threatens to be the last; but after a moment or two, the effect is so refreshing that you come back for more.

The recipe here is strong, but some like it that way simply poured over ice. Others will want to add sugar to taste. I prefer to mix the ginger beer with something sweet and soothing. Half and half with apple cider is superb, pineapple juice tastes tropical, or a carbonated lemon-lime drink turns this into a very grownup soft drink. It's also zippy with rum.

4 ounces fresh ginger,
   sliced thin
2 lemons
½ cup honey

In a non-aluminum pan, bring 2 quarts water to a boil and toss in the ginger. Cover the pot and turn down to a low simmer for 20 minutes.

Scrub the lemons well. Halve, extract the juice, and discard the seeds. When the ginger water is ready, remove from the heat, add the lemon juice and the rinds, cover, and steep for 30 minutes.

Strain into a pitcher, pressing gently on the ginger and lemon rinds to extract all the liquid. Add the honey to the warm liquid and stir to dissolve. Chill. Serve over ice as is, with a little more sugar added, or mixed with water, cider, juice, soda, and/or rum.

Serves 8 to 10.

Permissions

Index

eggplant
    —bell pepper spread, 340–41
    grilled, with pomegranate-walnut
        sauce, 65–66
    in grilled marinated vegetables,
        158–59
    -rice dressing, for roast pork,
        270–71
    stuffed, 102–4
eggs, Easter, 74, 77
Eight Cousins (Alcott), 198
Ellison, Ralph, 362
Emancipation Proclamation, 167–69
empanadas
    cilantro chutney for, 196–97
    cranberry salsa for, 193
    fresh chile salsa for, 194–96
    smoked turkey, 189–92
Ephron, Nora, 53
espresso honey cake, 248–50
Esquire magazine, 116
Esquivel, Laura, 49

F

Faidley's Seafood, 221
Fairfield Four, 168
Faster, Cecy, 35, 38, 40
Faster, Karen, 32–38, 41, 42
Fernandez, Leo, 8–10, 19, 22
Fernandez, Mary, 8
Fernandez, Salvador, 8
Ferris, Beth, 132
fig
    pie, 279–81
    preserves, 279–80, 281–82

sauce, 249–50
    —sweet potato pie, 360–62
Finfrock, Jack, 297
First Encounter (Chagall), 94–95,
        239, 259, 306
fish
    gefilte, 117–18
    gefilte, appetizer, 242
    sauce (Asian), 156, 161
    See also specific fish
Fisher, M.F.K., 51
Flight to Canada (Reed), 178
Flounder, The (Grass), 29
fondue, 312
    cheese, 313–15
Foods and Wines of Spain (Casas),
        316
fool, fruit, 110
fritada, 315–17
Fritschner, Sarah, 53–54
fruit
    fool, 110
    salad, 162–63
    See also specific fruits
Fuller, Thomas, 214
Furlong, Molly, 54
Fussell, Betty, 13, 293

G

Galli, Franco, 79
garlic cheese grits, 329–30
gefilte fish, 117–18
    appetizer, 242
Geography of the Imagination, The
        (Davenport), 90